EMPLOYER-SUPPORTED CHILD CARE

EMPLOYER-SUPPORTED CHILD CARE

Investing in Human Resources

SANDRA L. BURUD
PAMELA R. ASCHBACHER
JACQUELYN McCROSKEY
National Employer Supported Child Care Project

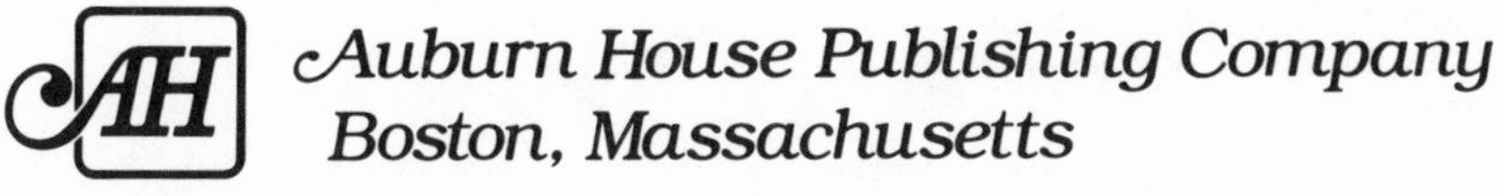

Preparation of this book was made possible by a grant from the Administration for Children, Youth, and Families, Office of Human Development Services, United States Department of Health and Human Services.

Library of Congress Cataloging in Publication Data

Burud, Sandra L.
Employer supported child care.
"National Employer Supported Child Care Project."
Bibliography: p.
Includes index.
1. Employer-supported day care—United States.
I. Aschbacher, Pamela. II. McCroskey, Jacquelyn.
III. title.
HF5549.5.D39B87 1984 658.3′12 83-22365
ISBN 0-86569-119-3 (hardbound)
ISBN 0-86569-122-3 (paperbound)

Printed in the United States of America

FOREWORD

Changing family and career patterns in America mean increasing numbers of mothers in the workforce. More children need care at younger ages than ever before. This transformation in the nation's work and family life affects employers, parents, children, and the community as a whole. Employers need a workforce which is motivated, reliable, and productive. Parents need care for their children which is affordable, accessible, and responsive to their unique family circumstances. Children need the security of sound, age-appropriate care arrangements. The community needs a child care system which works to the benefit of all.

This Administration is committed to enhanced development of the private sector and is aware of the challenges faced by American families in their child-rearing and work-related roles. The National Employer Supported Child Care Project was initiated in response to growing interest among employers concerning how child care might benefit both them and their employees. Based on the actual experiences of 415 firms with child care programs, this project was designed to help employers explore whether child care might make sense for their companies and, if so, what options might be most appropriate.

We are grateful to all who helped to develop this book as a resource for employers: Sandra L. Burud, the Principal Investigator for Child Care Information Service; Patricia Divine-Hawkins, the Project Director for ACYF; Raymond C. Collins, Director of the ACYF Office of Program Development; and members of the National Advisory Panel. This panel, composed of representatives from major corporations, business associations, employee unions, and employer-supported child care programs, worked closely with an able project staff to help insure that these materials will be useful to employers.

The National Employer Supported Child Care Project represents one of several child care initiatives to assist employers in developing child care programs. During the spring of 1983, in cooperation with the Administration for Children, Youth and Families, the President's Advisory Council on Private Sector

Initiatives launched a series of forums for Chief Executive Officers to describe the benefits of child care for employers and to outline possible ways for businesses to be involved. This initiative is continuing in 1984. In addition, a number of research and development projects are underway to document more fully the costs and benefits of employer supported child care as well as to refine various program options.

January 1984

LUCY C. BIGGS
Acting Commissioner
Administration for Children, Youth and Families

PREFACE

This manual is designed to guide employers from the initial stages of investigating child care to the actual establishment of programs. It was created in response to the rapidly expanding interest of employers in the child care needs of their employees. Managers clearly want information about the options and advantages of child care and about the related decision-making process. Many different types and levels of company support for child care are discussed, from direct services such as work-site child care centers, to indirect assistance such as directories to help employees find child care in their community.

The major source of information for the book was the study of employer-supported child care programs conducted by the National Employer Supported Child Care Project in 1982. Written and telephone surveys were used to gather information from the 415 active employer-supported programs in operation as of June 1982. Major employer-supported child care programs throughout the country were visited and company representatives were interviewed. Additional meetings that helped to direct the scope and direction of the book were held with business people, researchers, policymakers, employer-supported child care professionals, governmental officials, and employers. Guidance also came from the Project Advisory Committee, which was comprised of high-level corporate representatives as well as union, child care professionals, and government representatives.

Information from the study appears throughout the book. Some of it is presented quantitatively, some is used to illustrate program development approaches, and some has been drawn upon in developing the how-to materials. Once designed, the how-to materials were field-tested in numerous business settings to ensure maximum practicality. The needs assessment materials, for example, were field-tested by a bank, a telephone company, a post office, two hospitals, and a city organization.

The book is organized into five major topic areas: (1) overview, (2) benefits to companies, (3) determining needs and decision making, (4) implementing program options, and (5) conclusion.

Part One gives an overview of employer-supported child care, discussing the labor force changes that have increased child care need and the level of current child care activity among employers. There are also brief reviews of benefits, options, and the decision-making process.

Part Two reports data on the benefits experienced by employers with child care programs, such as improved recruitment and retention of workers. It also shows how a company can predict the potential value of child care.

Part Three presents practical guidelines and a systematic model for deciding whether and how to become involved in child care. Several strategies for collecting information are described, including the use of focus group discussions, written surveys, and child care referral records. Sample materials are provided for each phase of the decision-making process.

Part Four describes the many different ways in which companies can support child care, ranging from minimal to maximum involvement. Each option is discussed separately. Factors relevant to selecting an option are considered and detailed information is given on how to set up each type. Variations in program sponsorship are also examined—for example, the situation in which unions rather than companies sponsor programs.

Part Five contains a brief summary, discusses the impact of employer-supported child care on the larger society, and presents creative systems for planning and delivering child care supports.

General information for the preliminary investigation of employer involvement in child care is included, as well as detailed information for assessing child care feasibility and implementation. Where possible, sample materials show how to expedite the process and enable companies to utilize the experience of others. The appendices contain additional technical information and sample materials from the National Employer Supported Child Care Project Study, such as a description of the employer-supported programs in operation in 1982.

THE AUTHORS

ACKNOWLEDGMENTS

The authors would like to express their appreciation to the many people who so generously shared their knowledge with us during the course of this study. First and foremost we would like to thank Kay Clarke, Research Assistant, and Lynn E. Roth, Project Editor, who were essential members of the Project team and carried out their tasks with extreme conscientiousness and good humor. We benefitted greatly from the knowledge and skills of our advisory committee members: Frances Berry, Program Manager, Licensure of Regulation, the Council of State Governments; Alice Duncan, Child Care Program Director, Intermedics Inc.; Larry Dzieza, Staff Associate, National Governor's Association; Wayne Enslow, District Engineer, and Paula Carter, Staff Supervisor, Personnel Department, AT&T Long Lines; Berwyn Fragner, Vice President, Human Relations, and Betsy Houser, Personnel/Employee Relations Manager, TRW Inc.; Elinor Glenn, National Executive Board, Coalition of Labor Union Women and Child Care Task Force, United Way Region 5, United Way, Los Angeles; Malcolm Grover, Chairman, Los Angeles Chapter, Service Corps of Retired Executives, Small Business Administration; Donald Hasbargen, Consultant, Hewitt Associates; William Magee, Vice President and Controller, and L. D. Norris, Manager Employee Relations Policies and Procedures, Atlantic Richfield Company; David Millington, Director Administrative Services, Tosco Corporation; Ruth O'Berem, Assistant Vice President and Manager Employee Services, and Kathy Castillo, Personnel Officer, First Interstate Bank of California; Muriel Tuteur, Co-Chair, National Child Care Task Force, Coalition of Labor Union Women. Special thanks go to David Millington and Tosco Corporation for contributing printing and word processing services. Our ACYF Project Officer, Patricia Divine-Hawkins, helped guide and direct us throughout the two years of the project. Raymond C. Collins, Director of the Office of Program Development, ACYF, also gave assistance.

The people in the companies participating in the study were extremely informative, helpful, and gracious about sharing their experiences. In five additional companies that served as field test sites for our how-to materials, the following were forthcoming with assistance: Ruth O'Berem at First Interstate Bank, Sally Simms at St. Luke Hospital, Paula Carter at AT&T Long Lines, employees at the Pasadena Branch of the United States Post Office, and Pasadena city employees. We also thank Pat Ward and Bonnie Negen at Steelcase, Inc. and Harrison Johnson at TRW for allowing us to include in this book materials which they developed.

Many other people generously shared their thoughts and experiences with us during the course of the project, and their ideas contributed to the final shape of this book. A list of the people with whom we met is included in Appendix F.

The manuscript was reviewed by the following, whom we also thank for their contribution of time and talent: Ellen Galinsky, Luis Gomez, Nan Hatch, Judy Kaufman, James Levine, Joe Maciariello, Kathy Malaske, Nadine Mathis, Ethel McConaghy, George Milkovich, Anne Mitchell, Gwen Morgan, Katherine Senn Perry, Fran Rodgers, June Sale, Patti Siegel, Will Tease, Karen Woodford, Mary Young, as well as members of the Advisory Committee.

The Child Care Information Service in Pasadena, California was the sponsoring agency for the Project, and we could not have completed this book without the encouragement and help of the Director, Kathy Malaske, and all of the CCIS staff. Special thanks go to Gwen Fowler, the project Secretary, to The Branch Office, our word processing service, and to Dr. Michael Girard and Dr. William Wallace, who did the data analysis.

The authors were assisted by outside authors on several sections of the book. Ellen Gannett from the School-Age Child Care Project, Wellesley College Center for Research on Women, wrote Chapter 14 on School-Age Child Care. Noa Mohlabane from the Child Care Information Service in Pasadena co-authored Chapter 15, on care for sick children, with Jacquelyn McCroskey. Kathleeen Murray, from the Child Care Law Center, wrote the sections on liability and co-authored Chapter 4, on tax considerations, with Anne Mitchell from Bank Street College. Marci Whitebook co-authored the section on child care center staff with Sandra Burud. With these exceptions, the three authors wrote this book as follows: Sandra Burud wrote Parts One, Two, and the Conclusion; Jacquelyn McCroskey wrote Part Four in cooperation with Sandra Burud; and Pamela Aschbacher wrote Part Three.

THE AUTHORS

CONTENTS

APPENDICES

Part One

WHAT IS THE OVERALL PICTURE?

Chapter 1

OVERVIEW: THE RELEVANCE AND POSSIBILITIES OF EMPLOYER-SUPPORTED CHILD CARE

Why Are Employers Interested in Child Care?

Today's work force is experiencing the consequences of a generation of social change. One of the most important aspects of the new work situation is the need of more employees than ever before for child care while they work. This situation has developed with the rapid rise in the number of dual-career families, single parents, working parents with young children, and the sheer numbers of young children. A few statistics will underscore the point:

- The dual-career family has become the dominant mode, with 60% of all American families now in this category.[1]
- The number of single-parent families has doubled in the past decade to over 6.6 million and is continuing to rise.[2]
- The number of working parents with young children has increased steadily. In 1970, 37.6% of all children in two parent families had mothers in the labor force. By 1980 the figure had grown to 51.7%.[3] Including both single and two parent families, there are now 22 million children in families where all parents work.[4]
- By the mid-1980s and continuing into the 1990s, there will be about 4 million babies born per year—almost as many annual births as during the height of the baby boom in the late 1950s.[5] By 1990, there will be over 23.3 million children under age 6, a 23% increase from 1980.[6]

Probably the most significant factor stimulating this change in employees' child care needs is the dramatic increase in the number of women entering the labor force.

- During the 1970s, the proportion of children with mothers in the labor force increased from 38.8% (in 1970) to 52.8% (in 1980). For children under age 6, the increase was from 28.5% to 43.0%; for school age children, from 43.2% to 57.0%.[7]
- The participation rate of mothers with children under age 3 has more than doubled since 1959, rising from 17.3% to 41% in 1980.[8]
- It is projected that by 1990, 10.4 million preschool children and 19.6 million school-age children 5–13 will have mothers in the labor force.[9]
- As of March 1983 half of all women are in the paid labor force, 80% of whom will become pregnant sometime during their working years.[10]

Families no longer fit the traditional mold of a father breadwinner and mother homemaker. In fact, the traditional family only amounts to 11% of the population.[11]

Several trends indicate that women will continue to comprise a significant portion of the permanent labor force: more and more higher education for women; smaller, more closely spaced families born after the woman has entered the labor force; and the tendency for women to return to work within a year after childbirth rather than stay out of the work force for several years as in the past. In addition, national attitude surveys indicate that women have joined men in viewing work as central to their identities and would continue to work even if they could live comfortably without the earned income.[12] The reality of economic life, however, is that women—like men—work primarily for economic reasons. U.S. Department of Labor statistics show that nearly two-thirds of the women in the labor force are single, widowed, separated, divorced, or married to men earning less than $10,000 a year.[13]

The need for child care is not, however, exclusively the concern of working women. Employers have already begun to note that, as men's and women's roles evolve, men are assuming more responsibility for the care of their children. Evidence of this change includes increased numbers of men taking paternity leaves and increased numbers of single-parent families headed by fathers.[14]

Unfortunately the need for quality, dependable, affordable care far exceeds the supply. Of the millions of children under age

13 in families where both parents work, approximately 46% have no adult supervision at all for a significant part of the day.[15] Centers serve a relatively small proportion, estimated in 1978 at 10% to 15% of all preschool children of working mothers.[16] Family day care homes are the most widely used form of care, followed by care provided in the child's home by a relative or non-relative.[17] As more women enter the paid labor force, however, the supply of this care is decreasing because fewer relatives, neighbors and traditional family day care providers are available. This trend has particularly acute consequences for parents with infants and toddlers, because they have traditionally relied on in-home care.

At the same time, there has developed an increasing need for care of school-age children of working parents. In 1981 there were an estimated 16 million children between 5 and 13 whose mothers worked.[18] The problem of insufficient care supply is exacerbated by the difficulty of finding suitable arrangements, which are often unadvertised and constantly changing; the relatively high cost of care; and the complicated logistics of transportation and scheduling difficulties.

Parents form such a large part of the work force today that the child care dilemma can no longer be ignored. The growing interest of employers in child care is therefore not surprising.

How Many Employers Support Child Care?

The number of companies that provide child care has increased dramatically. A growth of 395% was noted between 1978 and 1982 in the number of companies with programs. In 1978, 105 company child care centers were identified;[19] by 1982 the number had risen to over 415 and included other forms of employer supported child care services in addition to company centers. These alternatives included child care reimbursement, information and referral services, family day care homes, educational programs for parents, and corporate contributions to community child care programs. Approximately half of the total programs in 1982 were comprised of these forms of services. The types of companies providing child care also changed during this period. In 1978, 71% of the programs were found in hospitals and only 9% in industry; the rest (20%) were in government agencies or unions. By 1982 the number of industries with child care (197) surpassed the number of health care organizations (195). Each group represented 47% of the total, with the remaining 6% made up by public agencies and

Table 1-1 Programs in Operation

	1978[14]	1982	
Government agencies*	14	17	(13 centers, 4 other)
Hospitals†	75	195	(152 centers, 43 other)
Industries	9	197	(42 centers, 155 other)
Labor unions	7	6	(4 centers, 2 other)
Total	105	415	(211 centers, 204 other)

NOTE: Although the figures for 1978 are for child care centers only, they represent very nearly all the employer-supported programs at that time. The 1982 study includes centers and other forms of employer-supported child care as well. Not all existing employer-supported education programs for parents are included in these figures; only a sample was included in the study.
*Public agencies are included under this category in the 1982 study.
†Health care organizations other than hospitals are also included under this category in the 1982 study.

unions. The number of industries supporting child care had risen from 9 in 1978 to 197 in 1982, an increase of over 200 percent. Although the number of companies with child care is still small in absolute terms, a growth trend is clear.*

Many new conditions are paving the way for an even greater expansion in the level of employer involvement in child care in the near future. Awareness of the need for child care is growing rapidly among companies. Employees are also becoming aware of this new concept, and they can be expected to exert more pressure on their employers for such services. More flexible alternatives now available to employers reduce complexity and make it easier to adapt programs to suit a wide range of situations. Finally, the growing number of demonstrated models means that many communities have witnessed the success of such endeavors first hand. It is no wonder that predictions of expected future expansion are echoed throughout the businesss community. In a recent Harris Poll 67% of corporate human resource executives reported that they expect to be providing child care services within the next five years. A report for the Carnegie Foundation predicts an expansion in both the number and variety of employer-supported child care programs over the next three to five years. The U.S. Chamber of Commerce predicts, in fact, that child care will be among the fastest growing benefits in the coming years.

---

*At the time this book goes to press, it is estimated that there are over 600 employer-supported child care programs—roughly a 50% increase since our survey was conducted in 1982.

What Have Companies Gained From Child Care?

Since the labor pool is increasingly comprised of working parents, the availability of good child care services directly impacts employers. The potential effects of unmet child care needs cover a broad range, from lost productivity as employees call home to check on children left without supervision and absenteeism caused by unreliable care or the need to care for sick children, to the loss of female employees who cannot return to work as soon as desired after childbirth for lack of infant care. Over the past decade more and more companies have found that helping employees obtain the child care they need benefits the employer as well as the employee. They have noted positive influences on working parents who are either present, past, or future child care users as well as on other employees. These positive influences are reported in the following areas of management concern:

- Turnover.
- Absenteeism.
- Recruitment.
- Public Relations.
- Morale.
- Taxes.
- Scheduling.
- Equal Employment Opportunity.
- Quality of Work Force.
- Quality of Products or Services.

The costs of child care can be partly, and in some cases entirely, offset by gains in these areas. The management value of child care depends on whether the most appropriate type of program is selected, whether it fills the specific needs of employees, and whether it closes the gap in the community between supply and demand of care. Chapter 2 discusses the benefits that companies receive from child care in more detail, citing statistical data and the case studies of four companies with child care programs.

How Do Employers Support Child Care?

The term "employer-supported child care" describes a broad range of programs including those that help employees learn about, locate, and pay for care as well as those that provide direct care for children. These programs may have been established to serve employees only or they may serve both employee and community families. Some employers cover all or most of the program's cost, while others give relatively small amounts of money and services to supplement incomes derived primarily from parent fees and public or private funding arrangements.

Some employers provide care in a child care center on or near the work site. In the past, such employer-supported centers received so much publicity that, for a while, "employer-supported child care" became almost synonymous with "on-site child care centers." Today, however, a much greater diversity of options is available to employers. These options fall into four basic categories. The first, which requires the least company involvement, is *flexible personnel policies* which often reduce the employee's need for child care—for example, flextime, job sharing, part-time work, work at home, and flexible leave policies that make it possible for families to work around their child care needs more adequately. The second category is *information* given to parents through information and referral services or parent education programs. The third is *financial assistance,* including child care reimbursement systems and corporate contributions to community child care programs. The fourth category, which has the highest level of involvement, is the provision of *direct child care services,* such as those in child care centers and family day care homes. Two additional types of child care that can fall within more than one of these four basic categories are programs for ill children and programs for school-age children, both of which address unique child care needs. The following describes the major program types within the four categories.

Flexible Personnel Policies

Flexible personnel policies include flexible scheduling, flexible leave, and flexible work location. Scheduling options such as flextime, job sharing, and part-time work can reduce the amount of child care needed, although they do not eliminate it entirely. They can also make it easier for spouses to coordinate their child care responsibilities. Extended maternity and paternity leaves and family leave time allow workers to meet their family responsibilities without a reduction of salary level or loss of seniority. Work at home, now more feasible with the computer revolution, can also reduce the need for outside child care for some parents, although it has a somewhat limited application. These policies reflect a growing trend among employers to establish business policies that reduce the stresses of balancing work and family roles.

Child Care Information and Referral Programs

Employees need information on where to find child care and related resources in the community. This service can be provided by in-house staff or under contract with an outside agency whose staff comes to the work site or is available by telephone. Some companies choose to distribute written directories of child care homes and centers. In some communities, several businesses and agencies have combined efforts and computerized their systems for child care referrals. Where child care information and referral is already available at no cost to parents, companies have contracted with the referral agencies for supplemental services. Child care information and referral is one of the least expensive of the employer-supported services. Although it does not solve the problems of inadequate supply or high cost of care, it can make programs more accessible to employees. A good first step for companies, this option can help them document their need for further involvement by identifying gaps in services and refining the identification of employee child care needs.

Educational Programs for Parents

Some employers sponsor educational seminars or meetings designed to give parents a forum for discussing parenting issues and for learning of new information and resources. These seminars can be offered by in-house staff or by using community resources. This option incurs minimal expense while still demonstrating the company's support of work and family issues, and it can be used as a first step toward ascertaining the need for other child care services.

Child Care Reimbursement Programs

Company reimbursement programs help employees pay for child care by reimbursing them or their child care providers directly for part or all of the cost of child care. The company may restrict the programs that parents can use. Some, for example, limit the subsidy to licensed care; others allow reimbursement for all types of care, including that provided by relatives. For this approach to be effective, there must be an adequate supply of convenient, affordable, quality care for children of all ages. Several advantages of this form of employer support are minimal administrative involvement and low costs, flexibility, and responsiveness to changing utilization rates, while at the same time leaving the selection of care to the employee.

Flexible spending accounts are a variation on reimbursements whereby the employee elects to have a portion of salary set aside for child care expenses. This amount becomes nontaxable income.

Support of Community Child Care Services

Some employers provide support in the form of money or services to existing child care programs in their communities. In return for this support employees often receive preferential admission, free or low-cost child care, or simply a place in the program. This type of arrangement allows companies to maintain a greater distance from the administration of the program and permits maximum use of existing resources. Where these programs do not already match the needs of employees, contributions are sometimes used to help make adjustments in the programs, such as expanding hours, adding new age groups, improving program quality, or adding transportation services for school-age children. The start-up time of this option can be minimal, and the start-up cost is usually much less than that of a company-operated program; it is also more adaptable to changes in utilization. The ongoing contribution can vary in type and amount (for example, in-kind service donations as well as a financial contributions), according to the resources a company has available and changing employee needs.

Child Care Centers

Company child care centers can be organized in a number of ways and adapted to the desired degree of company involvement. Some companies set up their center as a department or subsidiary of the company; some have an outside firm run the program. Sometimes non-profit organizations are established to administer the center, with a board of directors consisting of parent and company representatives. The amount of company subsidy varies from a small contribution toward either the start-up or operating costs, to large contributions for both. Programs are located either at the work site or elsewhere. Some programs admit only employees' children, while others admit community children as well. Programs also vary in size, but successful ones range from 30 children up to 300. Company centers are one of the more expensive options for employers, but they seem to have the greatest potential for solving a wide variety of child care needs if properly designed, including attention to cost, convenience, and quality of care. They also help to create more child care supply.

Highly visible, they may afford companies maximum benefits in terms of recruitment, retention, and public image.

Family Day Care Homes

In this option, companies support providers who care for children in their homes. Most states which license or register such homes permit the care of up to six children in a home with one caregiver. Companies have brought caregivers together in networks or helped to establish new sources and referred parents to them. This form of employer-supported child care is quicker and less expensive to initiate because there is no need for a facility. Capacity can be adjusted more easily in this model, because homes can be added or subtracted as the need for care changes. The day care home is a more flexible approach for families with children of different ages. Company support may take the form of financial or in-kind service donations which lower the cost of care to parents and which make possible support services such as backup caregivers for times when a caregiver is ill or unavailable. The homes can be located wherever convenient to parents, usually in their home neighborhood so that school-age children have easy access to their schools. Family day care homes can also be attached (as satellites) to either company or community child care centers.

Care for Sick Children

Sick children pose a particular child care problem, as most formal child care facilities make no provisions for them. Employers experience the drain caused by this dilemma through worker absenteeism and parental anxiety. Solutions include using special family day care homes alone or as satellites to child care centers for the care of sick children, special sick-care components on the grounds of the child care centers, and care for the child in his own home. Other solutions involve preventative measures; for example, health care personnel on the staff of child care programs can reduce the incidence of illness and contagion. Programs for the care of ill children, although the newest of employer-supported programs and among the more expensive per capita, can have a substantial impact on worker absenteeism.

Care for School-Age Children

School-age children also present special child care demands.

These children need supervision from kindergarten age until adolescence (generally through age eleven) before and after school, during vacations, and in the summer. They need to be transported twice during the work day between school and their child care arrangement. Employers can use many of the previously mentioned forms of child care to meet these needs, such as child care centers, family day care homes, reimbursement systems, and support of community child care programs. In addition, some employers have developed cooperative arrangements with city schools in order to provide care for school-age children at a school site.

Often, a combination of options accomodates school-age children best. For example, a company might offer reimbursement for school-age child care close to home in addition to use of the company center for infants and preschoolers. This type of arrangement allows the child to be close to school or home and reduces the need for transportation. Another way employers have helped with transportation is by donating the use of company vans or by making donations to help child care programs acquire their own.

Determining the Need and Selecting the Right Program

In order to decide whether to become involved in child care and, if so, what type of program is appropriate, a company should take the following well defined steps.

1. *Determine Needs.* Working parents need care that is dependable, affordable, congruent with their work schedules, conveniently located, suitable to their children's age, and compatible with their child-rearing philosophy. Since many arrangements do not provide care when the child is sick or when the employee has to travel overnight, working parents may also need special arrangements for such occasional circumstances.

The supply of child care to match these parent needs varies tremendously from community to community. Most existing services are geared to the preschool child, while there is usually a dearth of care for infants, toddlers, and school-age children. The small amount of care that does exist for children under two is often very expensive, and care for school-age children is frequently complicated for working parents by transportation problems. Another common difficulty is finding child care arrangements that match work hours, particularly when parents work odd shifts or have to commute long distances.

It is the gap between supply and demand that affects a company's employees and, in turn, the company itself in such areas as recruitment and productivity. The gap for a given company can be defined by comparing the array of local services with employees' needs and preferences. To fill the gap in services experienced by their workforce, companies can create more child care spaces, lower the cost to parents, and/or make child care easier and more convenient to find and to use. They can accomplish such objectives on their own or work with others in the private or public sectors.

Careful consideration of the many facets of supply and demand will help a company decide when and how to become involved. For example, it may be unnecessary to establish an entirely new program when the existing supply is sufficient but inadequately utilized because of minor problems that could be corrected. Sometimes a referral service may be all that is needed to help the parents locate the kind of care they want. In another situation, a company may want to provide some financial assistance so that low-income employees can take advantage of care that is available but simply too expensive. This might be accomplished in a number of ways, such as reimbursing employees through a voucher plan or donating in-kind services to existing centers or family day care homes so that their operating costs and fees to parents are reduced.

Where logistics is the primary concern, the most cost-effective program for a company to establish may involve an arrangement with existing community child care programs to adapt their hours, schedules, age range, number of children served, and so forth to meet employees' needs. Sometimes, however, community programs cannot be adequately adapted, and the creation of new care space in centers or family day care homes is necessary to meet the need.

The effect of a child care service on the company is likely to be greater when the service addresses the full range of factors defining the gap between supply and demand. Thus, a program that not only provides needed new care spaces but also charges a fee low enough for low-to-middle income families to afford enables more employees to use the service and results in a wider positive effect on employee work behaviors.

Part Three of this book assesses the need for a child care program in a company. Three methods for assessing need are given and sample materials provided for each.

2. *Consider Alternatives.* Ways in which employers can support child care include:

Flexible Personnel Policies:	• Flextime • Job sharing • Part-time work • Work at home • Flexible leave
Informational Programs:	• Information and referral programs • Educational programs for parents
Financial Assistance:	• Child care reimbursement systems • Corporation contributions to community child care programs
Direct Services:	• Company child care centers • Family day care home systems

Additionally programs to care for ill children and programs for school-age children are possible services that fall under several of the above alternatives. Detailed information about all programs is given in Part Three. The programs can be given as an employee service, a benefit, or a corporate contribution. Each form has its own tax and other implications.

The choices to be made in child care involvement depend not only on child care supply and demand but also on the company's rationale for considering child care in the first place. Companies establish child care services for many reasons. Each company has its own unique pattern of motivation, which may include a general concern for employees and their families, a desire to be in the forefront of the employee benefits field, or the desire to achieve corporate goals such as reduced turnover, improved morale, and better community relations. Clarification of a company's goals helps determine what information is needed for decision making and also facilitates selecting and tailoring the company's child care involvement to achieve desired objectives. For example, if better community relations is a goal, the company may want to investigate how existing employer-supported programs have helped their supporting companies achieve it. Companies contemplating child care may also want to examine carefully the variations in program design that could contribute to accomplishing their goals. For example, to maintain good community relations, a company may want to operate its program in partnership with other businesses or agencies, and it might consider providing a program that serves other children in the community as well as employee children.

3. *Estimate Costs and Benefits.* The company's rationale for considering child care can be as important in the selection of a program as the nature of the child care supply and demand. The benefits it can receive from filling unmet care needs influences both ultimate involvement and selection of the most appropriate type of program.

The value of such expected benefits as reduced turnover, absenteeism, enhanced recruitment, productivity, and morale should be considered at this phase of the process, for they can considerably alter the net cost of each type of program. Data on these effects and formulas for projecting their value for a particular company are discussed in Chapters 2 and 3. Projected costs specific to the particular type of proposed program can be found in the discussion in the chapters about each individual option. It is critical to evaluate both costs and benefits together, for the most cost-effective program may not be the least expensive.

4. *Identify Resources.* Resources that the company can potentially contribute to child care include the following:

Money
Space
Technical expertise
In-kind services such as maintenance, accounting, and printing
Products

Non-financial resources can make a significant contribution and also accomplish important goals such as lowering the cost of the services to employees and improving their quality.

The type of resources used also affects the level of administrative approval required. Sometimes a company branch office can give one type of resource at the local level, whereas another type of resource would require corporate approval. For example, a branch manager could often give maintenance services to a local child care center without prior corporate approval (and receive in exchange, perhaps, preferred admission for employees). A financial arrangement such as child care reimbursement, on the other hand, may affect company-wide policy and therefore need corporate approval.

Other potential sources of funding include government child care programs such as the Child Care Food Program, Social Services Block Grant, and state and local contributions. Collaborative efforts with other companies, private foundations, and community organizations can broaden the program's funding base.

5. *Select Program.* Once needs and resources have been identified and alternatives considered, the company can decide whether to implement a child care program and to finalize its design. Companies may decide to use a phased-in approach with less ambitious types of services (such as information and referral) initiated first, to be followed by more direct services as the need is documented.

A service may be selected which combines more than one of the types of programs, such as a company center for children under 5 and a group of satellite family day care homes to accomodate special needs such as the care of school-age children and mildly ill children.

In summary, this chapter has given an overview of employer-supported child care—its advantages, possibilities, justification, prevalence, and procedures. Each of these aspects is discussed in more detail in the rest of the book.

Because of the sweeping demographic changes occurring in the work force, the need for child care is more acute than ever. Employers are finding it more advantageous to help with solutions, and they are discovering in child care a new management tool. Once they have identified a need for child care among their employees, they are assessing their possible roles and available resources to select a program. Employer-supported child care is a new concept that addresses the needs of three diverse groups: the corporation, the family, and the society, and it can bring benefits to each.

Endnotes

1. "Is Corporate Child Care the Next Big Benefit?" *Houston* (December 1981).
2. Child Care Coordinating Council of San Mateo County, Inc., *Parents in the Workforce* (Burlingame, Calif., 1982).
3. Children's Defense Fund, *Employed Parents and Their Children: A Data Book* (Washington, D.C.: Children's Defense Fund, 1982), p. 59.
4. Allyson Sherman Grossman, "Working Mothers and Their Children," *Monthly Labor Review* 104 (May 1981), Table 3, cited in Chidren's Defense Fund, *Employed Parents and Their Children: A Data Book* (Washington, D.C.: Children's Defense Fund, 1982), p. 7.
5. U.S. Department of Commerce, Bureau of the Census, *Current Population Reports*, Series P–20, No. 704, p. 25, "Projections of the Population of the United States: 1977 to 2050" (July, 1977), Table 8, cited in Children's Defense Fund, *Employed Parents and Their Children: A Data Book*, (Washington, D.C.: Children's Defense Fund, 1982), p. 3.

6. Children's Defense Fund, *Employed Parents and Their Children: A Data Book* (Washington, D.C.: Children's Defense Fund, 1982), p. 49.
7. U.S. Department of Labor, Women's Bureau, *Most Women Work Because of Economic Need* (March 1978).
8. J. Levine, *Who Will Raise the Children?* (New York: Bantam Books, 1976).
9. S. L. Hofferth, "Day Care in the Next Decade: 1980–1990," *Journal of Marriage and the Family*, 41 (August, 1979), p. 649–658.
10. U.S. Department of Commerce, Bureau of the Census, *Current Population Reports*, Series P-20, No. 358 "Fertility of American Women: June 1979" (December 1980), Table 6, cited in Children's Defense Fund, *Employed Parents and Their Children: A Data Book* (Washington, D.C.: Children's Defense Fund, 1982), p. 3.
11. D. Friedman, *Encouraging Employer Support to Working Parents: Community Strategies for Change*, (New York: The Carnegie Corporation, 1983), p. 12.
12. S. B. Kamerman and A. J. Kahn, *Child Care Family Benefits, and Working Parents. A Study in Comparative Policy* (New York: Columbia University Press, 1981), p. 25.
13. U. S. Department of Labor, Women's Bureau, *Most Women Work Because of Economic Need* (March 1978).
14. J. Levine, *Who Will Raise the Children?* (New York: Bantam Books, 1976).
15. Children's Defense Fund, *Employed Parents and Their Children: A Data Book* (Washington, D.C.: Children's Defense Fund, 1982), p. 8.
16. S. L. Hofferth, "Day Care in the Next Decade: 1980–1990," *Journal of Marriage and the Family*, 41 (August 1979), p. 652.
17. S. Fosberg, *Family Day Care in the United States: Summary of Findings*, Final Report of National Day Care Home Study, U.S. Department of Health and Human Services (OHDS 80–30282, 1982), p. 2.
18. R. K. Baden, A. Genser, J. A. Levine, and M. Seltzer, *School-Age Child Care: An Action Manual* (Boston: Auburn House Publishing Company, Inc., 1982), pp. 2–3.
19. K. Perry, "Survey and Analysis of Employer Supported Day Care in the United States," doctoral dissertation at University of Wisconsin in Milwaukee, Wisconsin (1980).
20. *Ibid.*

Part Two

WHAT DO COMPANIES GAIN FROM CHILD CARE?

Chapter 2

INDENTIFYING THE BENEFITS OF CHILD CARE TO COMPANIES

> *The program has.been successful in all regards. It has helped our recruiting, cut down on turnover, shortened maternity leaves, and has generated a tremendous amount of free publicity for the company. Those employees who have no need for the center seem as enthusiastic about it as those who use it, and it has enhanced our image in the area as a progressive, employee-centered company.*
>
> Larry G. Honeywell, Senior Vice President Official Airline Guides, Oakbrook, Illinois

Companies overwhelmingly report that child care advances management aims and has tangible corporate payoffs. In this chapter we shall review data on the benefits of employer-supported child care from the survey conducted by the National Employer Supported Child Care Project in 1982. Four hundred and fifteen companies with child care were studied throughout the country—virtually all of the known employer supported programs in operation at the time. The companies included 197 in industry, 195 health care organizations, 17 public agencies, and 6 labor unions. Their programs included child care centers, reimbursement systems, information and referral services, family day care networks, educational programs for parents, and contributions to community child care programs.

The following information about the effects of child care on the company came primarily from human resource managers of these companies. Although not every employer had all of the various types of requested data, the information does present a composite indication of the strength of child care as a management tool.

Four of the companies from the study were selected as case studies. They all had well-established child care programs and had kept the most substantive records about their program's impact on the company. Excerpts from these cases are reported in this data summary, and each case is discussed at greater length later in the chapter. All of the case study programs were child care centers, inasmuch as companies with other types of programs generally were too new or did not have adequate records about the effects of their programs.

The following summarizes the major findings of the study. Further relevant background and descriptive data are given in Appendix A.

Data Summary

Turnover in Companies

- 65%* reported that child care had a positive effect on turnover.
- 15% considered child care more effective than three-fourths of the other turnover control methods they use.
- 62% considered child care more effective than half of the other turnover control methods they use.
- 18 had records that allowed them to compare the turnover rates of child care program users with the rates of other employees. Among these companies, employees who used child care had turnover rates 25 percentage points lower than the overall work force.

Case #1: Approximately $25,000 to $29,000 was saved in turnover in one year from the child care program's impact on turnover.

Case #2: Over $2 million was saved on turnover in one year from the child care program's impact on turnover.

---

*NOTE: These percentages are based on the employers who responded to each question. Many companies did not respond at all because their programs were too new or because of a lack of data. On average, 175 did respond to questions such as this. Of those that did respond, the percentage given reported that child care had a positive effect. The balance essentially reported that either it had no effect or its effect was unknown. Appendix A reports the raw data, including the number of nonrespondents.

Case #3: $50,000 was saved on turnover in one year from the child care program's impact on turnover.

Case #4: $160,000 was saved on turnover in one year from the child care program's impact on turnover.

> *Child care was initiated to retain a small number of key employees . . . all of these people are still with the company. In addition the center has benefited other employees; turnover and absenteeism are very low for these employees.*
> Eleanore Wohlfarth, Personnel Director, Union Fidelity Life Insurance Company, Trevose, Pennsylvania.

> *As a databased publishing firm with a predominantly female work force, we looked to day care to attract and retain skilled technical, sales, and managerial workers. It has certainly accomplished that goal. An added bonus has been the peace of mind and security it has given parents, contributing toward positive feelings about the company.*
> Susan Doctors, Manager Personnel Development, Official Airline Guides, Inc., Oakbrook, Illinois.

> *Providing day care has had a positive impact on maintaining hard-working staff who would otherwise find work wages minus child care costs less than worthwhile.*
> Charles Dickeman, General Manager, Playboy Resort, Lake Geneva, Wisconsin.

Recruitment by Companies

- 85% reported that child care had a positive effect on recruitment.
- 32% considered child care more effective than three-fourths of the other recruitment incentives they use.
- 73% considered child care more effective than half of the other recruitment incentives they use.
- 10 estimated the value of child care as a recruitment tool. Among these companies $16,400 was the annual estimated savings in recruitment per company from child care's impact on two job categories targeted for recruitment.

Case #1: 95% of job applicants applied to work at the company because of the child care program.

Case #2: 20% of the previous recruitment effort was needed after the child care program was established.

Case #3: $30,000 was the estimated annual savings in recruitment due to child care.

Child care provides a valuable service for employees and helps the company attract and keep a good work force.
Hubert T. Sullivan, Director Industrial Relations, OPP & Micholas Mills, Inc., Opp, Alabama

An invaluable tool in employee recruitment and retention.
James Phillips, Director Human Resource Development, Consolidated Hospitals, Tacoma, Washington

Morale in Companies

- 90% reported that child care had a positive impact on morale.
- 83% reported that child care had a positive impact on worker satisfaction.
- 73% reported that child care had a positive impact on worker committment.
- 63% reported that child care had a positive impact on worker motivation.

The child care program has had a great positive influence on morale, just the fact that it was made available.
George Mones, Director Human Resources, St. Dominic-Jackson Memorial Hospital, Jackson, Mississippi

Because of our child care referral services, employees feel we care enough about their personal lives to make an effort and expenditure to help them. That's got to be of positive benefit in employee attitudes and their ability to come to work and have peace of mind. All the comments from employees about the child care service are wonderful.
Jack Spaulding, Vice President Human Resources, Steelcase, Inc., Grand Rapids, Michigan

Public Image of Companies

- 85% reported that child care had a positive effect on public relations.
- 39% said child care was more effective than three-fourths of the other public image enhancement techniques they use.
- 69% considered child care more effective than half of the other public image enhancement techniques they use.
- 9 companies estimated the value of their child care program in terms of the publicity it received. Among these companies $13,000 was the estimated average annual value per company of publicity received from the child care program.

Case #1: The company has been featured in *Industry Week, Business Week, U.S. News and World Report, North Carolina Magazine,* and on television programs because of its child care program.

Case #2: The company's child care program appears an average 63 times annually in journals and newspapers and on radio and television, including for example the *Wall Street Journal, Business Week,* and the *Washington Post.*

Case #3: $30,000 is the estimated annual value of public relations from the child care program.

We have always been known as a community-minded company. This (child care) just fits in with our role. The response has been outstanding both in and out of the company.
Alec J. W. McBarnet, Jr., Benefits Administrator, Maui Land & Pineapple Co., Inc., Kahului, Hawaii

We've become known as a company that cares about its employees and their children.
Bob Szalanski, V. P., Operations and Alan Goodman, Controller, Neuville-Mobil Sox, Hildebrand, North Carolina

Child care helps *"the community see us as a caring organization."*
Diane Wendt, Employee Relations, Boise Valley Sunset Home, Boise, Idaho

Child care is one of those small pockets of excellence by which corporations and their people are judged.
Amory Houghton, Chairman of the Board of Corning Glass, Corning, New York

Productivity in Companies

- 49% reported that child care had a positive impact on productivity.
- 12% rated child care in the top 20% of all the employee benefits they offered in terms of its impact on productivity.
- 41% rated child care in the top 40% of all their employee benefits in terms of its impact on productivity.

Case #1: 15%–25% fewer production workers were needed. Child care's capacity as an increased production incentive was estimated to be worth between $6,000 and $10,000 annually in 1981.

Child care people work harder and do better because they want to progress and keep their jobs.
Craig Bushey, Manager, Burger King, Hartford, Connecticut

Absenteeism in Companies

- 53% reported that child care had a positive effect on absenteeism.
- 18% considered child care more effective than three-fourths of the other absentee control methods they use.
- 56% considered child care more effective than half the other absentee control methods they use.

Case #2: 15,000 manhours were saved in one year in the production department by the child care program's impact on absenteeism.

Case #4: $90,000 was the estimated annual savings in fiscal 1980–81 by child care's impact on absenteeism. The absentee rate of child care users dropped from an estimated 6% during the year prior to the program opening to 1% during the year after it opened, while the rate of other employees remained the same (4%) before and after the program opened.

Companies also reported that their child care programs have enhanced the following areas in addition to the major areas listed above:

- Tardiness: 39% reported that child care had a positive effect.
- Scheduling flexibility: 50% reported that child care had a positive effect.
- Equal employment opportunity: 40% reported that child care had a positive effect.
- Quality of products or services: 37% reported that child care had a positive effect.
- Quality of workforce: 42% reported that child care had a positive effect.

The charts that follow provide data about these benefits. A large number of companies reported on the areas that child care impacted. A smaller group had statistical information about the size and the value of that impact.

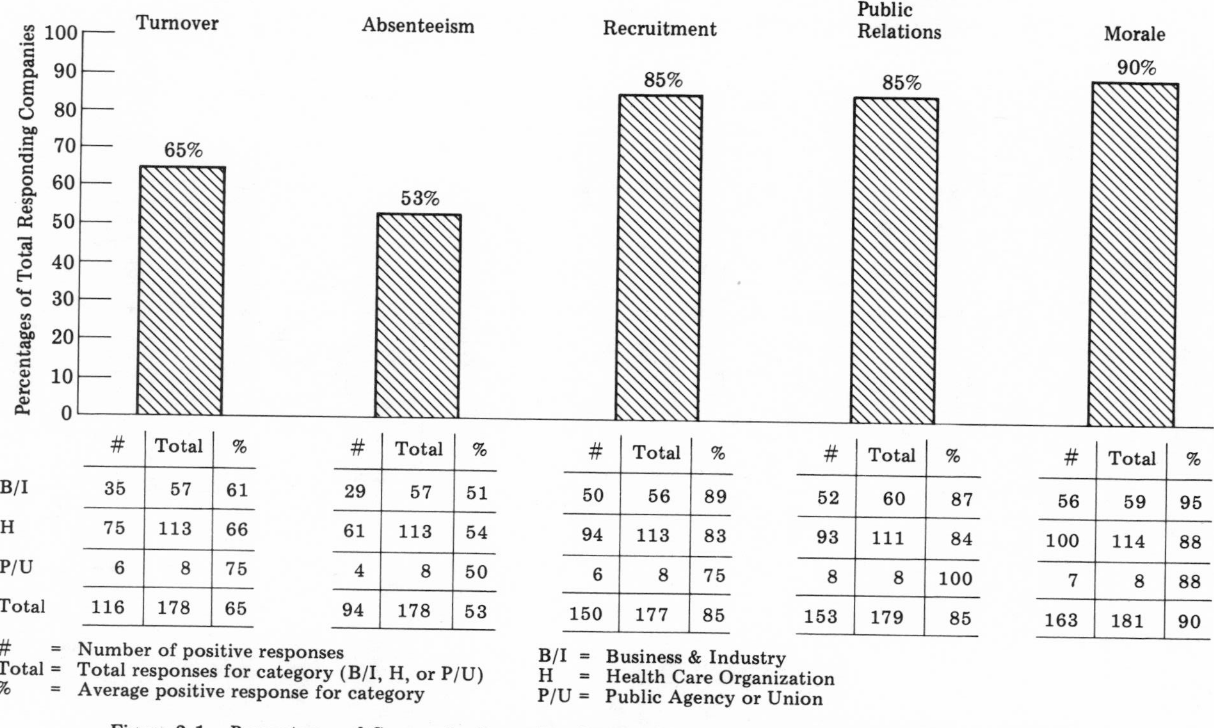

	Turnover #	Turnover Total	Turnover %	Absenteeism #	Absenteeism Total	Absenteeism %	Recruitment #	Recruitment Total	Recruitment %	Public Relations #	Public Relations Total	Public Relations %	Morale #	Morale Total	Morale %
B/I	35	57	61	29	57	51	50	56	89	52	60	87	56	59	95
H	75	113	66	61	113	54	94	113	83	93	111	84	100	114	88
P/U	6	8	75	4	8	50	6	8	75	8	8	100	7	8	88
Total	116	178	65	94	178	53	150	177	85	153	179	85	163	181	90

# = Number of positive responses
Total = Total responses for category (B/I, H, or P/U)
% = Average positive response for category

B/I = Business & Industry
H = Health Care Organization
P/U = Public Agency or Union

Figure 2-1 Percentages of Companies Reporting Positive Effects of Child Care. (The balance of responses indicated that there was no effect or an unknown effect. There were virtually no negative responses.)

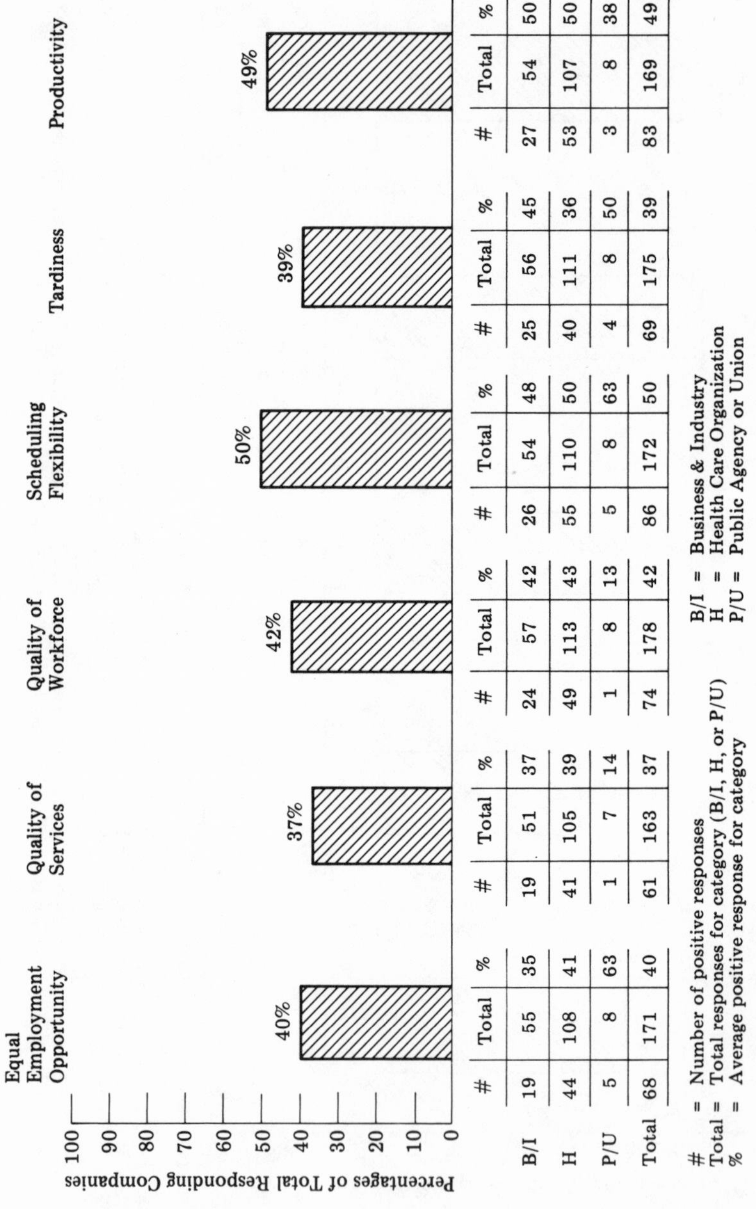

	Equal Employment Opportunity			Quality of Services			Quality of Workforce			Scheduling Flexibility			Tardiness			Productivity		
	#	Total	%	#	Total	%	#	Total	%	#	Total	%	#	Total	%	#	Total	%
B/I	19	55	35	19	51	37	24	57	42	26	54	48	25	56	45	27	54	50
H	44	108	41	41	105	39	49	113	43	55	110	50	40	111	36	53	107	50
P/U	5	8	63	1	7	14	1	8	13	5	8	63	4	8	50	3	8	38
Total	68	171	40	61	163	37	74	178	42	86	172	50	69	175	39	83	169	49

\# = Number of positive responses
Total = Total responses for category (B/I, H, or P/U)
% = Average positive response for category

B/I = Business & Industry
H = Health Care Organization
P/U = Public Agency or Union

Figure 2-2 Percentages of Companies Reporting the Effects of Child Care. (The balance of responses indicated that there was no effect or an unknown effect. There were virtually no negative responses.)

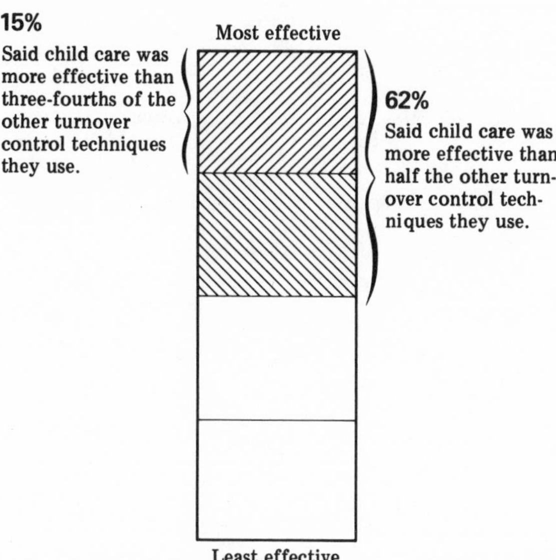
15%
Said child care was more effective than three-fourths of the other turnover control techniques they use.
Most effective
62%
Said child care was more effective than half the other turnover control techniques they use.
Least effective

Figure 2-3 Comparison of Factors That Reduce Turnover. (Number of companies reporting: 114) Companies were not asked which other turnover control methods they used, but typical methods include: • Competitive salaries and benefits • Job restructuring • Internal promotions • Participative management • Complaint procedures.

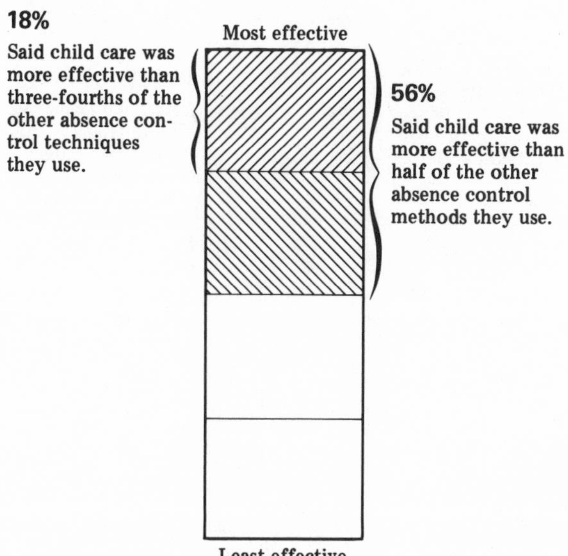
18%
Said child care was more effective than three-fourths of the other absence control techniques they use.
Most effective
56%
Said child care was more effective than half of the other absence control methods they use.
Least effective

Figure 2-4 Comparison of Factors That Reduce Absenteeism. (Number of companies reporting: 95) Companies were not asked which other absence control methods they used, but typical methods include: • Disciplinary counseling • Suspensions • Rewards for good attendance.

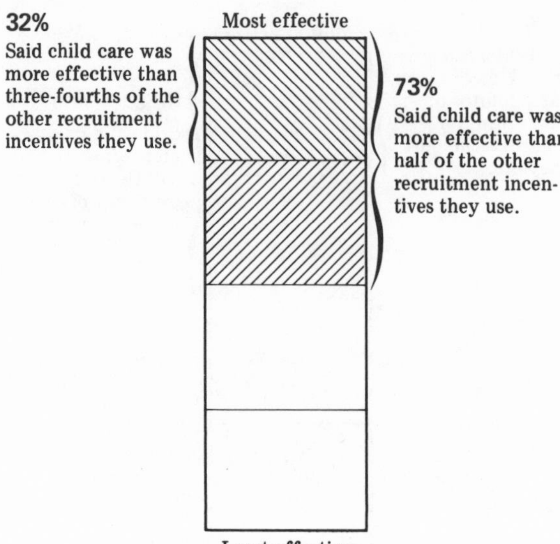
32%
Said child care was more effective than three-fourths of the other recruitment incentives they use.
Most effective
73%
Said child care was more effective than half of the other recruitment incentives they use.
Least effective

Figure 2-5 Comparison of Factors That Recruit Workers. (Number of companies reporting: 150) Companies were not asked which other recruitment incentives they used, but typical methods include: • Competitive salaries and benefits • Bonuses • Relocation benefits • Entertainment.

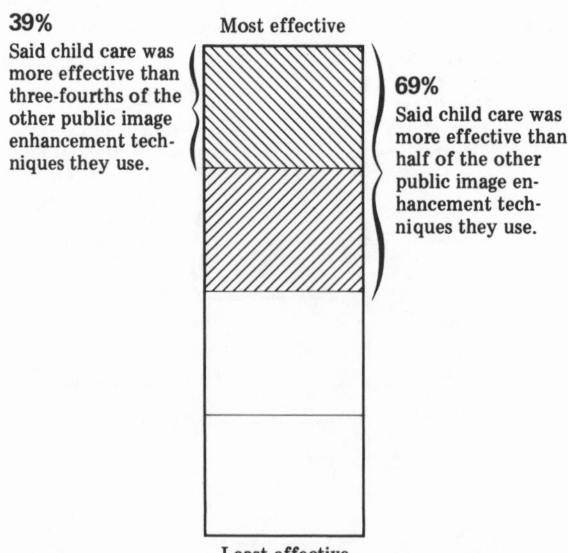
39%
Said child care was more effective than three-fourths of the other public image enhancement techniques they use.
Most effective
69%
Said child care was more effective than half of the other public image enhancement techniques they use.
Least effective

Figure 2-6 Comparison of Factors That Enhance Public Image. (Number of companies reporting: 153) Companies were not asked which other public image enhancement techniques they used, but typical methods include: • Advertising • Charitable contributions • Community service.

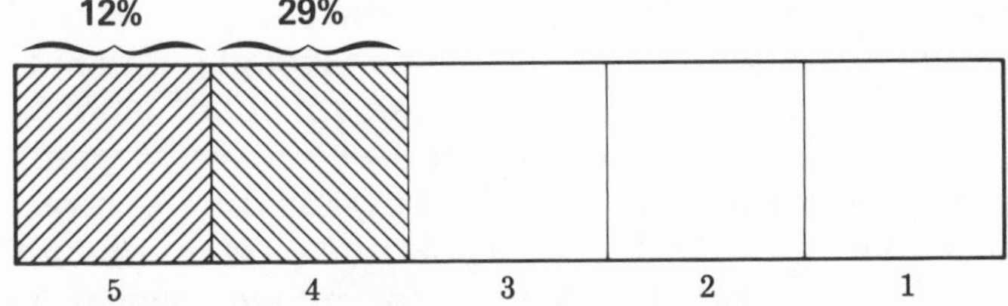

Figure 2-7 Comparison of the Effect of Employee Benefits on Productivity. (Number of companies reporting: 51) 41% of companies reported that child care improved productivity more than most other benefits. Companies were not asked which other employee benefits they offered, but typical other benefits that may affect productivity include: • Vacations and holidays • Health care • Profit sharing.

Program Characteristics

The following describes the programs from the National Employer Supported Child Care Project in greater detail. Table 2–1 categorizes programs by their primary type of child care service, although some organizations have more than one type of service.

Overall, more than half of the organizations surveyed had their own child care centers. Another quarter (123) supported community child care programs, most of which were existing child care centers supported by corporate money and in-kind services. The remaining quarter were involved with family day care, reimbursements, information and referral, or educational programs for parents.

The distinction between company child care centers and support of community child care programs was defined by the

Table 2–1 Company Type

Program Type	*Business/ Industry*	*Health Care Organization*	*Public Agency*	*Union*	*Total*
Child care center	42	152	13	4	211
Family day care	0	5	0	0	5
Reimbursement program	10	7	0	0	17
Child care information and referral	19	17	0	0	36
Parent education program	23	0	0	0	23
Support of community programs	103	14	4	2	123
Total	197	195	17	6	415

closeness of the relationship between the company and the program. Most firms with company centers thought of the program as "their own," ran it as an in-house function, gave it more support, and established it on or near the work site. Organizations that supported existing community programs often contracted for child care with an already existing outside service, although they may also have provided money and/or in-kind services. In these arrangements there was a much looser relationship between the company and the child care facility.

Organizations that support child care were for the most part those with a predominantly female work force. They averaged 74% female workers. A number of companies with child care, however, had predominantly male workers and many of the male employees also used the service. Seventy-four companies with programs reported that over 25% of the employees using the program were male. Thirty companies reported that 50% or more of the employees using the program were male.

Programs were found in almost every state, excepting only Alaska, Delaware, and Utah. The highest concentation of companies with programs were found in California (51 companies), Minnesota (41), Texas (36), Missouri (32), Massachusetts (26), New York (25), Pennsylvania (17), Wisconsin (14), Ohio (11), and Washington, D.C. (11).

The majority of programs were less than five years old. Sixty companies had child care programs over ten years old, and eighty had programs less than one year old.

Most companies had between 1000 and 5000 employees at the location where child care was offered. Only ten companies with less than 100 employees had child care.

Many of the companies shared their sponsorship of child care with other companies; 125 reported that another company was involved in supporting the child care service, including those which purchased services as well as those involved with other companies through consortium arrangements. In addition 95 companies reported that their programs received some kind of public assistance to support operation. For many, this support took the form of monies from child nutrition programs, Title XX programs (receiving public funds to serve low-income children), or local public agency funds.

Case Studies

The following case studies selected from participants in the National Employer Supported Child Care Project describe the benefits of child care for four separate companies. The types of industries and work forces vary, but each has found that the total savings attributable to child care outweigh its cost. These particular cases were selected because their records allowed the most complete analysis of the value of child care to a company. Each is a well-established quality program and each receives a substantial contribution by the company toward its operating costs. All case studies are of firms with a company center; no other type of program had compiled this level of data on child care related benefits. Together these four cases give a more substantive and vivid picture of the total impact of child care and the interplay of its effects. The benefits that companies can receive from child care, however, are not necessarily restricted to child care centers. Many forms of child care assistance can accomplish similar goals, serving, for example, as recruitment and retention tools and contributing to a positive corporate image.

CASE #1 A TEXTILE FIRM

Neuville-Mobil Sox, Inc.,
Performance Hosiery Mills
Hildebran, North Carolina

Neuville-Mobil Sox, Inc. sells and distributes hosiery. In January of 1981 a finishing plant, Performance Hosiery Mills, was added at their rural Hildebran, North Carolina plant, and an on-site child care center was opened. Management wanted an extra incentive to attract the best workers in an area with relatively low unemployment (1.5%–3%) and they also wanted a retention tool to avoid the high turnover rates characteristic of their industry. They decided to try child care as an experiment and to carefully weigh the results.

The company has 87 employees, half of whom are blue collar workers and the other half white collar; 26% of the employees use the child care center, which serves a total of 39 children. Parents using the program are divided equally between the blue and white collar groups. Children of all ages attend the center: infants, preschoolers, and school-age children (before and after school and in the summer).

The center was established at the same time as the new finishing plant, so a before-and-after comparison of its effect on the company cannot be made, but industry and area norm comparisons are possible.

Many favorable developments have been noted by the company since the child care service opened. Company management believes that they have resulted from three factors: salaries 15% above the going rate, a competitive benefits package (25% of wages), and the child care center. Steve Neuville, the company president, reports that the child care center is at least as important in bringing about these improvements as are the salaries and benefits. Economic conditions may also have affected some of the areas of change, such as turnover, although the reductions in turnover that Neuville-Mobil Sox reports are much greater than those comparable industries were experiencing during the same period.

TURNOVER

Rates: A primary company goal in offering child care was worker retention. According to Neuville-Mobile Sox, industry turnover rates averaged 50%–100% (voluntary and involuntary combined) for companies of comparable size, industry type, and location. In 1981 the turnover rate at Neuville-Mobil Sox was 7%–8%. No turnover was observed among parents using the center. In 1982 the third year, overall company turnover and the turnover rate of parents using the center were both 5%–6%.

Cost: The company reports costs of $1,000 each to train production workers and $2,000 each to train office workers.

Savings: Management reports achieving an estimated gross annual saving of $23,625 from reduced turnover of production workers. The company made this calculation by comparing their production department turnover rate of 7% with the low industry average turnover rate of 50% at a training cost per worker of $1,000 plus employee benefits at 25% of wages. The company reported saving an additional estimated $25,000 annually from reduced turnover of office workers. The company made this calculation by comparing the office staff turnover rate of 5% with the average turnover rate for office workers of 30% (estimated conservatively by Neuville-Mobil Sox) at a training cost per worker of $2,000 plus employee benefits at 25% of wages.

About $12,600 of this savings is estimated to come directly from current users of the child care programs, who are distributed equally between the production and office departments. It should be noted, however, that the company believes the turnover rates of other employees are affected by the center as well. Parents stay with the company who are not currently using the center but who plan to use it in the future or who feel good about the company because they have used it in the past.

An additional $9,840 was saved on federal and state unemployment taxes that would have been paid if its turnover rates had been as high as the industry norm.

RECRUITMENT

The second major goal of the center was to recruit a quality work force. During the first week the center was advertised, the company had 200 applicants for 50 positions. At the time unemployment in the area was only 1.5%–3%, and because textile or furniture manufacturers represented over 80% of the local industries, there was stiff competition for the kinds of workers the company needed.

During the first two months of the center's operation the Personnel Office conducted an informal survey about its effects on recruitment efforts. Ninety-five percent of applicants surveyed reported they were attracted to Neuville-Mobil Sox by the child care center.

OTHER PRODUCTIVITY

Management reported saving between six and ten additional production workers who would have been needed if the company's productivity were comparable to other industries in the area. Because the company is more productive than the industry norm, however, these workers are unnecessary. Because of increased productivity the company reported also saving on employee benefits for unnecessary workers. The reported savings amounted to $14,464–$24,107 for 6–10 workers earning a base pay rate of $4.92/hour and a benefit level of 25% of wages for 49 weeks/year. Other companies paying hourly wages instead of piece rate would also save the salaries of the workers not required, as well as some overhead savings since less machinery and utilities were needed (for the machines). Overhead savings in this case were felt to be minimal and therefore were not quantified.

When the increased productivity of workers is figured in conjunction with the lower turnover, the company reports saving an additional $3,000–$5,000 annually. This figure is the result of reducing turnover by 3–5 employees per year (about 50% of the 6–10 extra workers not needed) at a training cost savings of $1,000 per production worker.

ABSENTEEISM

The company's absenteeism rate in the beginning of 1983 was 1%. The local industry average is estimated by Neuville's President to be at least 5%–10%. One factor related to this low absenteeism rate is the company policy not to pay workers for sick days. Bob Szalanski, Vice President of Operations, states that the child care center has also been an important factor in lowering absenteeism among working parents. He cited the following examples: The center van picks up school children on snow days and brings them to the center so that parents do not have to leave work to do so. When children are suspected of coming down with a slight illness, parents are close and can check in on them during work breaks. Families can thus make better judgments about when children are actually too ill to stay at the center and avoid some of the false alarms inherent in children's illnesses.

PUBLICITY

The center has been featured in a number of national magazines, such as *Business Week*, *U.S. News and World Report*, and *Industry Week;* local and trade publications such as *North Carolina Magazine* and *Modern Knitting;* and television news shows. Because this company does not sell directly to the public, the value of this media coverage is less direct than it would be for other types of companies. Companies that advertise their products to consumers, for example, would have had to pay approximately $1,000 for advertising the size of the *Business Week* coverage of Neuville-Mobil Sox and about $5,500 for advertising the size of the *U.S. News and World Report* article. "We have become known as a company that cares about its employees and their families. The day care center has definitely had a positive effect," said Bob Szalanski, Vice President of Operations, and Alan Goodman, Controller.

MORALE

Management reports that the child care center has been good for the morale of the company as a whole in a number of ways. Workers feel a sense of attachment to the children. Children have a bigger "extended family" than most, and they know company executives by name. Both parents and other employees can visit the children at break time and lunch hours. The company reports that child care center thus furthers another company goal, that of maintaining a family atmosphere. "It adds an extra dimension to working, I think everybody is a little happier. The kids are around laughing and the mothers don't divorce themselves from their families during an 8-hour period of working," said Steve Neuville, President. "We believe the satisfaction of the mothers affects the other employees to create a good working environment," added Bob Szalanski, Vice President of Operations, and Alan Goodman, Controller.

OTHER BENEFITS

The following additional areas were positively affected by the child care center:

- Overtime, temporary help, and scheduling flexibility: when workers are needed overtime and on Saturdays, the center adjusts its schedule to serve them.
- Quality of products.
- Production down time.
- Employee work satisfaction, morale, commitment, and motivation.
- Quality of life: "Employees at our company live differently. Most of the mothers take this opportunity to strengthen their bonds with their children," said Beverly Neuville, Child Care Center Director.

PROBLEMS

This company, like many others, was concerned about problems with legal liability, insurance, and fluctuating need. Once the program opened, however, they found that liability and insurance issues presented no actual difficulties. Neuville-Mobil Sox has experienced periods of fluctuating need and consequently has established a policy of accepting children from other companies with whom they do business when enrollment is low. This policy has given them the necessary enrollment cushion and brought additional good will as well.

COMPANY COSTS

Start-up: An initial investment of $42,500 to renovate and equip the building for the child care center was made by the company.

Operating: The company partially subsidizes the center's operating cost at a rate of $1,000 annually per child, for an annual total of $30,000 for the infants and preschoolers of company employees. The school-age care program does not receive a subsidy, but it pays for itself through parent fees. The inclusion of children from other companies will bring the Neuville-Mobil Sox cost per child down, to under $1,000 per child for fiscal 1982–83.

PARENT COSTS

In assessing the impact of the center on the company, it should be noted that the program does not necessarily cost parents less

Neuville-Mobil Sox, Inc. Cost/Benefit Summary (1981)

I. *Benefits*		
A. Due to child care alone		
Tax savings	$15,500	
B. Due to child care and other factors:		
Reduction of turnover	$48,625	
Reduction of unemployment	9,840	
Increased productivity	17,464–29,107	
Total B	$75,929–$87,572	
Child-care-related benefits (1/3 of B)	$25,310–$29,191	
Total child care related benefits		$40,810–$44,691
II. *Cost*		
A. Operating costs (company portion only)	$30,000	
B. Start-up costs of $42,500 spread over 15 years	2,833	
Total annual cost		$32,833
III. *Summary*		
Net cost of program after tax benefits	$17,400	
Net benefit of program		$7,977–$11,858

NOTE: Released with permission from Neuville-Mobil Sox, Inc. There may be other costs and benefits associated with the program that have not been identified.

than they would pay on the average for care in the community. Parents at the company center pay $25 per week for care that could be purchased in the community for $18 to $25.

TOTAL BENEFITS

Even with estimates that management characterizes as conservative, the company has saved between $76,000 and $88,000 from improvements which they attribute to child care and two other factors, higher salaries and benefits. Child care accounts for at least one third of these savings ($25,000–$29,000), causing management to consider it as important a factor in these changes as the other two. Child care thus has more than recovered its total cost and clearly made good business sense.

CASE #2 A MEDICAL DEVICE MANUFACTURER

Intermedics
Freeport, Texas

Intermedics was having difficulty attracting workers to its Freeport, Texas plant. Management was also taking a serious look at the turnover rate, which had been climbing steadily. A single underlying cause for its turnover was pinpointed by the company: There was a high percentage of young parents in the work force of 1,000, and only a few of them had been able to find adequate child care.

In November 1979 the firm opened a child care center four miles from the plant. The center, which had room for 260 children, was full on opening day. The center has been in such demand and the company considers it so successful at achieving company goals that it has been expanded to accomodate more children (now 292). Further, plans are under way to build another center for 500 children within the next two to three years. The company, whose work force has grown to almost 2,000, believes that the center gives "more benefit to the company per dollar than any other employee benefit," according to Alice Duncan, Child Care Center Director.

Although the center is large, it is committed to high-quality care. It maintains a favorable teacher/child ratio, has a sound educational curriculum, and employs a stable staff having training in early childhood education.

The center is open only to Intermedics employees and serves children from 6 weeks to 6 years old, weekdays from 7:00 a.m. to 6:00 p.m. It offers additional support services to parents, such as a preventive health care program administered by an R.N.

The company pays four-fifths of the program cost, with the balance of the funds coming from parent fees. The center is operated as a wholly owned subsidiary of the company and the funds contributed by the company are declared as a business expense. Parents pay $25 per week per child, significantly less than the $60 per week for infants and $45 per week for preschoolers estimated by the director as the average child care cost in the community.

The company reports the following effects since the inception of the child care center:

TURNOVER

Intermedics manufactures heart pacemakers and other medical devices that must be made with great precision. A stable as well as highly skilled work force is required, and turnover therefore is a particular concern. According to management, turnover rates had been rising steadily prior to the center's opening. About two months before it opened, as word of the child care center circulated, the turnover rate began to drop. Company turnover decreased 9% in the first six months of the center. In the center's first two years, turnover at the company decreased a total of 60%, 23% the first year and 37% the second year. The turnover rate for parents using the center is currently one sixth the rate of the rest of the work force. The company reports saving over $2,000,000 in reduced turnover since the beginning of the child care service. "Experience has shown that once a parent has children in the center, he/she is 84% less likely to leave the company," said Alice Duncan, Child Care Center Director.

ABSENTEEISM

Management observed a savings of 15,000 person hours in reduced absenteeism in the manufacturing section of the company alone during the first year of the center's operation. The center is reported by the company to be one of the most effective factors in this accomplishment.

The center's role in reducing absenteeism caused by illness is largely the result of the preventive health care program. For example, 702 worker hours were saved annually because the center nurse takes the children to the doctor for their immunizations. Illness rates among workers and their children have declined steadily since the center opened. For example, in the second year of the center's operation, 32% fewer children from the center were sent home due to illness than during the first year, despite a 75% increase in flu and flu-like symptoms in Texas during the same period (January 1, 1981 to December 31, 1981).

RECRUITMENT

Since the opening of the child care center, the personnel manager reports that the company has not had to advertise locally for employees, and only 20% of the previous recruitment effort is now necessary. Attracting workers to Intermedics had been somewhat difficult in the past because of its fairly isolated rural location, but the company says that the child care center has now given them the needed recruitment edge.

PUBLIC RELATIONS

The company has been featured in national magazines and newspapers such as *Business Week, Money, The Wall Street Journal,* the *Washington Post,* and has been on television several times. It appears on an average of 63 times per year in the media. This positive publicity has been valuable in monetary terms, and is thought to be critical to Intermedics' image and to the marketing of their product. The company is projected as one with a special concern for people, a valuable image in their industry.

PROBLEMS

Although Intermedics anticipated problems with legal liability, insurance, and complicated regulations in the program establishment, there were none in these areas. The company's existing insurance policy was adequate to cover the center without additional premiums. The only problem the company reported was that demand for the center exceeded its capacity. The expansion plans that are under way will remedy this problem.

OTHER BENEFITS

Management reports that benefits of the program outweigh the costs:

- When considering both start-up and operating costs.
- When considering measurable effects.
- When considering only immediate benefits, not future advantages.

They also report that child care positively affects the following areas:

- Quality of overall work force.
- Use of overtime.
- Quality of products and services.
- Employee work satisfaction, morale, commitment, and motivation.

- Scheduling flexibility.
- Ability to offer equal employment opportunity.
- Ability to attract affirmative action target groups.

WHO USES THE CENTER?

209 employees use the center. Approximately 10% of the parent users are male; 36% of the users are single parents.

Intermedics Cost/Benefit Summary

Benefits	*1982*
Reduction of turnover (estimated by Intermedics)	over $2,000,000
Costs	
Set-up and operating costs (estimated by National Employer Supported Child Care Project)	1,500,000
Net benefits	+ $ 500,000

NOTE: Released with permission from Intermedics. All these costs and benefits are related specifically to child care. There may be other costs and benefits associated with the program which have not been identified.

CASE #3 A PHOTOGRAPHY COMPANY

PCA, Inc.
Matthews, North Carolina

PCA, Inc. (formerly Photo Corp. of America, Inc.) is a photography company specializing in portrait shots, primarily of children. PCA has portrait studios in K-Mart, Woolco, and other large stores. It is headquartered in Matthews, North Carolina, and has a work force there of 1,150.

In 1972, when the company was young, the work force was young also, and many employees were experiencing child care difficulties. A child care center seemed the logical solution. The work site center began in one empty room and was administered by a recent college graduate trained in early childhood education, the daughter of the company's founder. The center has proved to be such a useful service for employees that it has expanded its facilities twice since it opened (from serving 46 children to its current licensed capacity of 175), added an administrator, and assumed a comprehensive educational focus.

The center is open only to PCA employees and serves children from infancy up to 9 years old. School-age children are cared for after school and during summer and Christmas vacations. The center is open from 7:45 a.m. to 12:30 a.m., covering two work shifts on weekdays, and is also open Saturdays as needed.

The company currently pays 49% of the center's total annual operating costs of $380,000. This percentage represents a reduction in the company's portion of the bill down from 69% since the program began. A company study showed that child care constituted 9% of the total benefit package.

The fee paid by parents for care in the center is much lower than what they would pay for comparable care in the community. At PCA parents pay $30/week for infants, $38/week for toddler and one-year-olds, and $34/week for two- to nine-year-olds, with a cost reduction if they bring the child's food to the center.

The company reports the following benefits as linked to the child care center:

TURNOVER

Turnover among parents who use the center has been reduced so dramatically that their rates amount only to a fraction of the turnover of other employees at the company. The annual turnover rate of the parent group since the company began keeping records in 1976 has been less than 1% of the overall company turnover rate. The company did not release the overall company turnover rates; however, it states that even though turnover has fluctuated, the center has remained in a stable relationship at less than 1% of overall company turnover. Parents using the service amount to 17% of the total work force. The company conservatively estimates savings of 25 turnovers per year through the child care center. They estimate the cost savings at $2,000 per turnover, considering recruitment and training costs, for a total turnover savings annually of $50,000. Since children generally leave the center at 6 years of age, it is apparent that most employees stay on with the company at least as long as the child is in the program, a factor which has a significant effect on retention figures.

After childbirth, more mothers are reported to return to PCA, and new mothers return to work quickly because care for infants is available.

MODELING FEES

"We are a photography company specializing in color portrait shots (primarily of children)," says Joan Narron, Child Care Center Director. "Child models get up to $45 an hour, but with their parents' written permission, we use our children as unpaid models for advertising and testing portrait backgrounds. As a result, PCA saves about $10,000 a year on modeling fees and parents get free portraits."

ABSENTEEISM

Absenteeism due to child care related problems has been reduced "because we are here and we are open," continues Joan Narron.

RECRUITMENT

The center is estimated to be worth $30,000 as a recruitment aid. The company reported receiving 4,300 unsolicited applications for employment in fiscal 1979-80. In fiscal 1980-81 they had 3,500 walk-in applicants in a labor market with an unemployment rate of only 2%–3%. Other local companies had very few non-recruited applicants. "We attract employees who want to work for a company that cares this much about their children," says Joan Narron. Even the Vice President of Human Resources was indirectly recruited as a result of the child care center. He felt that a company that cares so much for children must care for all its employees and would be an attractive company in terms of corporate policies.

PUBLIC RELATIONS

Management estimates the value of publicity from the program at $30,000 annually. They have received unsolicited positive publicity in numerous newspapers and magazine articles, including the *Christian Science Monitor* and trade publications, as well as television and radio coverage.

MORALE

PCA reports that parents experience improved morale because they are confident about the care their children are receiving. In April 1976 an opinion survey administered by the company showed that the parents with children in the center ranked their level of satisfaction at 4 out of a possible 5. "Parents of a young child feel guilty if they must go to work. When the parents can see their child during the workday, it relieves some of the guilt and anxiety," said Joan Narron, Child Care Center Director.

OTHER BENEFITS

"Human relations is the number one benefit to the company. Parents with children in the center are more secure. Our facility is a point of pride, not just for the employees who use it, but for all our employees," concluded Joan Narron.

WHO USES THE PROGRAM

About 40% of the children's parents work in the laboratory; 60% are operations personnel who work in a variety of departments, and 8%–10% are male employees.

PCA, Inc. Cost/Benefit Summary

Benefits	*1982*	
Reduction of turnover	$50,000	
Modeling fees	10,000	
Improved recruitment	30,000	
Improved public relations	30,000	
Tax savings @ 49.25%	91,700	
Total benefits		$211,700
Costs		
Operating	$186,200	
Total Costs		$186,200
Net Benefits		+$ 25,500

NOTE: Released with permission from PCA, Inc. All these costs and benefits are related specifically to child care. There may be other costs and benefits associated with the program that have not been identified.

CASE #4 A HOSPITAL

Sioux Valley Hospital
Sioux Falls, South Dakota

Sioux Valley Hospital is a community general hospital with Nursing, Radiology, and Medical Technology Schools. In August 1980 it opened a 135-child capacity child care center at the hospital for infants and preschoolers, and school-age children needing before and after school care. The center's hours accommodate the special scheduling needs of the health care industry, being open 365 days a year from 6:00 a.m. to midnight and during the night shift occasionally as needed.

The center is subsidized by the hospital. The hospital's projected contribution to the operating costs for 1982–83 are expected to be $150,000. Parent fees are $1.25/child/hour for 6½ to 13 hours and $1.65/child/hour for less than 6½ hours a day. The cost for the second and successive children in a family is two-thirds that of the cost of the first child. The center has a high-quality program with teacher-to-child ratios of 1:4 for children under three, 1:6 for three-year-olds, and 1:8 for children four years old and older. An average of 8 children are in each group and the program has an educational emphasis. The program, which is considered highly successful from the company's point of view, reports the following benefits:

TURNOVER

Turnover has decreased company-wide: a 65% monthly decrease or 7.8% annual decrease has occurred since the establishment of the child care service. The overall company turnover rate has declined from 35% to 33%. In 1982 parents using the child care program had a turnover rate of 24%, compared with an average of 33% for the rest of the company. Prior to the opening of the child care program, the turnover rate of parents eligible for the program was 40%. The company estimates that it has saved a total of $239,400 since the program opened, or $159,600 annually through the reduced turnover of parents using the center. "The average age of our employees is approximately 30," said Vice President Human Resources, A. W. Scarborough. "We have many young mothers at work who continued to work for us now that we have a child care center."

ABSENTEEISM

Overall company absenteeism has decreased since the child care program opened. Management estimates the value of the reduced absenteeism of child care users to be conservatively worth $89,856 annually, figuring a difference in absenteeism of 3% for 180 employee families at an average rate of pay for the hospital overall of $8.00 per hour. The actual savings may be higher, because a proportionately larger number of professional employees use the service than are found in the total work force, and the average salaries saved accordingly are actually higher than the overall hospital average. The absenteeism rates of program participants have decreased from an estimated 6% to 1% since the child care program opened, while absenteeism of other employees is estimated by company management to have remained the same at 4%.

RECRUITMENT

The child care center has helped the hospital recruit people for targeted jobs such as registered nurses, medical technicians, and radiology technicians. Child care is a "real plus since we were first in our city to do so!" said A. W. Scarborough, Vice President Human Resources. Child care is "a tremendous asset for retention and for recruitment of a large number of female workers in short supply (RN's, LVN's, Medical Techs, and X-Ray Techs)," he added.

PUBLICITY

The hospital reports that the child care program has had a positive effect on its public image and has attracted publicity in both magazines and newspapers.

OTHER BENEFITS

The hospital says that benefits of the program outweigh the cost:

- When considering both start-up and operating costs.
- When considering only measurable effects.
- When considering only immediate benefits.

Management believes that the return on investment from the child care program has increased since it opened because of improved utilization (higher enrollment) and other internal changes. The center has moved twice since opening in response to increased demand for additional space.

The company reports that the center also has had a positive effect on:

- Quality of overall work force.
- Productivity.
- Quality of service.
- Employee work satisfaction, morale, commitment, and motivation.
- Ability to provide equal employment opportunity.
- Ability to attract affirmative action target groups.
- Scheduling flexibility.

PROBLEMS

Although insurance coverage and complicated regulations governing establishment of the programs were expected to pose problems, neither was found to cause significant difficulties. The costs of start-up and operation were found to be high, as expected, but management indicates that benefits from the program far outweigh the costs. The company reports no other significant problems with the program.

WHO USES THE PROGRAM

Program participants come from the following job categories: 15% are supervisory/professional personnel; 60% are other white collar workers; 15% are skilled blue collar workers; and 10% are unskilled.

Sioux Valley Hospital Cost/Benefit Summary

	Fiscal 1980–81	
Benefits		
Reductions in turnover	$159,600	
Reductions in Absenteeism	89,856	
Total benefits		$249,456
Costs		
Total operating costs	$324,220	
Revenue	-92,866	
Net cost (company subsidy only)	231,354	
Total costs		$231,354
Net benefit of progam		$ 18,102

NOTE: Released with permission from Sioux Valley Hospital. These are costs and benefits related specifically to child care. There may be other costs or benefits associated with the program that have not been identified.

Conclusion

Evidence from the National Employer Supported Child Care Project suggests that child care programs have benefited companies in a number of important ways. Many different types of firms have realized benefits and have supported different types of child care programs. The complete statistical data accumulated by a small group of companies further supports the positive impact of child care. In fact, each of the four case studies suggests that the benefits of child care can outweigh program expense.

In summary, companies with child care programs consider them an effective management tool that serves the goals of both the company and the program participants well.

Chapter 3

ESTIMATING THE BENEFITS OF CHILD CARE

Chapter 2 suggested that child care can yield important benefits to companies. This chapter deals with quantifying the cost and benefits of a program to the organization (rather than to the employee user of the service). It is designed to help companies or employee groups considering child care for the first time to decide whether a program can be of value to them. The material will be most useful to those who are beyond the initial stage of considering child care and are ready to study the costs and benefits of one or more program options. A rationale for evaluating corporate benefits is discussed, many of the benefits that child care services can provide are described, a formula is given for determining how child care may affect turnover and absenteeism, and the characteristics shared by programs affording the greatest corporate benefits are listed.

How to Compare Costs and Benefits

Companies or groups that want to conduct a financial analysis of a potential child care program, comparing the expected costs with benefits, may have different purposes:

- To estimate whether a program can pay for itself and to determine the expected net benefit or net cost of the service.
- To compare the expected net costs or net benefits of several alternative programs.
- To estimate which of several programs is the most cost effective to implement and would bring the greatest return to the company for a given expenditure.

Whatever the purpose, it is necessary to quantify all possible costs and all possible financial benefits that will be experienced by the company, attaching a dollar value to each item. Possible costs of child care include those for start-up and operating, as well as future expenditures required by the program and "opportunity" costs (that is, the value of the best alternative use of resources). Possible benefits of child care—for example, reduced turnover, improved recruitment, and tax benefits—are discussed in the following section, "Factors to Consider." Also a positive value is the equity in the land or building used for the program.

Once the costs and benefits have been quantified, a cost-benefit analysis or a cost-effectiveness analysis can be done. The application of these two methods for comparing costs and benefits of child care is described in detail in Appendix C, where precise definitions and procedures are given with examples. Also discussed is a discounting procedure that can be used to account for benefits to be received in the future. The balance of the information needed to complete a financial analysis is provided in the text, including a complete description of possible costs and benefits from which a company can select those appropriate to its situation. The cost analysis of each program option is described in detail in separate sections of this manual.

Factors to Consider

Let us consider some of the possible benefits that child care can bring and explain why and for whom child care can have these effects. The benefits became apparent in several phases of the National Employer Supported Child Care Project during the national survey of programs, site visits to programs, and interviews with company personnel. Some of them may not ordinarily be recognized by companies as child-care-related. Some benefits have been observed formally, and some informally. Not all were experienced by each company, but a comprehensive list was compiled across several companies. This list can be the basis for a thorough examination of the following potential benefits of child care:

1. Turnover.
2. Absenteeism.
3. Recruitment.
4. Employee/management relations and morale.
5. Public relations.
6. Equal employment opportunity.

7. Tardiness.
8. Scheduling flexibility.
9. Other productivity factors.

Child care can have effects on both male and female employees in the above areas. With the increasing numbers of two-worker families and single-parent fathers, as well as changing life styles, child care is becoming a responsibility shared by men and women. Companies that employ working parents can therefore experience benefits from child care programs. Let us now consider in detail the two major areas: turnover and absenteeism.

Turnover

Voluntary Turnover. There are some child-care related problems that may directly cause a parent to leave the company—for example, when costs increase significantly or when the traditional support sources of friends, neighbors, and relatives become unavailable. [1] Child care can indirectly cause a parent to leave when the strain of balancing problematic multiple responsibilities takes its tool; when the worker feels there is little chance for advancement because he or she cannot work overtime, travel, or relocate; or when parents are not satisfied with the quality of care available to them. The role that child care plays in such a decision may not be fully realized by either the worker or the company.

Involuntary Turnover. A worker may be terminated because of excessive absence due to illness or other causes. A worker's illness rate may include days missed because of a child's illnesses, often not reported as such because sick leave policies in most companies do not allow leave for family illness. Other absences may occur when the regular child care provider is not available, the child care center is closed temporarily, or the child has health care appointments. These absences are often charged to the company as "sick" days.

The Turnover of Employees Beyond the Current Child Care User Group. The turnover rate of parents who currently use child care may affect the turnover rates of potential future users and non-parents as well. High turnover rates within a work group can have a ripple effect because of the strain on the remaining employees, who have to train replacements and absorb work not completed by exiting employees. Reducing the turnover rate among parents therefore may lessen the strain on other employees and thereby cut down on burnout and turnover.

It should be noted, of course, that reduction of turnover is not always considered desirable. Some companies prefer high turnover to avoid the higher compensation levels required for employees with long job tenure.

Extent of Impact. In a 1979–80 survey by the Bureau of National Affairs,[2] personnel executives were asked about the reasons for employee separations. The three leading causes of turnover among all groups of employees were:

39% Personal problems (including family, transportation, and poor health)
34% Dissatisfaction with compensation
22% Dissatisfaction with job opportunities

A child care service can have a positive impact in all three areas:

- *Personal problems:* A child care service can solve some child-related problems, including transportation, when children need to be conveyed to and from child care or school.
- *Dissatisfaction with compensation:* A child care service that reduces the cost of care to parents either through a cash allotment or through a company-subsidized program can increase the disposable income of parents. If the child care service qualifies as a Dependent Care Assistance Plan under the Economic Recovery Tax Act, the child care benefit is non-taxable income. Additionally, the employee can take a tax credit for employment-related and dependent care expenses up to a maximum of $2,400 for one child and $4,800 for two or more children.
- *Dissatisfaction with job opportunities:* A child care service may open up promotions and new job opportunities to an employee if it provides the flexibility for overtime and travel.

Absenteeism

Unscheduled Absenteeism. Parents may miss work when children become suddenly ill or when regular child care providers become unavailable at the last minute.

Scheduled Absenteeism. Even when parents know in advance that regular child care will be interrupted, as during school vacations, absences may still result if alternate care is unavailable.

Size of Impact. A survey by the Bureau of National Affairs asked companies to name the primary cause of absenteeism. Three of the four causes cited could be connected with child care difficulties. The causes, in order of the frequency with which they were named, included: (1) illness, (2) personal problems or personal business, (3) inclement weather, and (4) family illness, transportation problems, inadequate child care, and alcohol abuse.

Absences reported to supervisors as being caused by illness or personal problems may in some cases be the result of an underlying difficulty with child care. Child care difficulties are considered the fourth largest cause of absenteeism. Their impact may be even greater when one considers the cases in which child care difficulties are not recognized or reported as such.

Research on absenteeism indicates that a small proportion of employees account for a large percentage of the problems. As with turnover, solutions found for those employees with significant absenteeism can have a large beneficial effect on the company's total problem.

Recruitment

An employer who provides a child care service is more attractive to potential applicants than competing employers who do not provide such a service. Potential employees may perceive child care as an additional benefit or additional compensation. They may view the company commitment to child care as an indication of a humanistic administration. And they may also see child care as a practical solution that can ultimately improve the quality of their life.

Child Care Can Attract New or Returning Workers into the Labor Force. Workers who cannot find or afford adequate child care frequently are single parents, mothers on maternity leave, or fathers on paternity leave. Wives are more likely to work if their husband's income is in the middle range than if it is either very high or very low. The second income in the family must result in an adequate net gain after the cost of child care and other work-related expenses or working will not be economically worthwhile.

Child Care Can Improve the Quality of the Applicant Pool. By advertising a child care benefit, a company can increase the number of total applicants from which it can select new employees. Some companies report that a high-quality child care program can attract more responsible workers. Workers who display a strong sense of responsibility to their families may also be more responsible employees.

Child Care Can Serve as an Additional Attraction to Induce Employees to Work in Hard-to-Staff Locations or on Difficult Schedules. Changes in labor force composition have occurred as a result of lower fertility rates, delayed child bearing among some women, increases in female labor force participation, and the sheer numbers produced by the baby boom. During the next decade, there will be more workers than ever in the age group between 25 and 44 years; they will account for one-third of the population, an increase of approximately nine percentage points since 1970.[3] This trend means that employee incentives and benefits will be more important for this age group than in the past.

Employee/Management Relations and Morale

Child Care Can Improve Labor/Management Relations and Morale. It provides a practical service that has the potential to benefit a large group of employees. Nearly all workers will at some point in their lives be parents.

Productivity Factors

Child care can have the following positive influences on productivity:

- Reduce the work hours lost when workers leave to handle child care emergencies.
- Reduce the number of personal phone calls made by workers to check on children left at home alone—for example, calling school-age children before and after school.
- Increase the worker's ability to concentrate by removing the worry and frustration of having children in an inadequate care situation.
- Increase employee motivation to perform well by offering a benefit not available in all companies.
- Increase the energy level of parent workers by reducing the excessive drain caused by inadequate child care arrangements.
- Reduce the production lag time resulting from absenteeism and turnover due to child-care-related problems.

From the economist's point of view, it is difficult to identify precisely the reasons for productivity declines. Theorists include the following as primary causes: changes in labor force composition, a shift from high-productivity industries to low-productivity industries in various sectors of the economy, inadequate capital investment on the part of business, and lower personal savings in the population at large. Some people disagree that there has been a recent decline in productivity in this country and insist that it is simply not being measured properly.[4]

Popular thought, however, credits decline and increases in productivity to "employee attitude." Business executives in a U.S. Chamber of Commerce-Gallup business confidence survey conducted in the fall of 1978 were asked for their explanations for recent productivity declines. Worker attitude was ranked second among all causes, following federal regulations as the primary cause. When asked what changes had the potential to effect the greatest improvement in performance and productivity, these executives ranked worker attitude as having the greatest potential for change. Several sections of this manual discuss the possible impact of a child care benefit on worker attitude.

Public Relations

Child care can help shape a company's image as being concerned with human issues and as being innovative. *It can also help the company attract valuable media coverage* in business and popular magazines, trade publications, and national and local newspapers, as well as on television and radio. Business organization newsletters and publications such as those of the U.S. Chamber of Commerce, American Management Association, The Conference Board, and Bureau of National Affairs are also potential sources of publicity.

Equal Employment Opportunity

Child care can accomplish the following desirable objectives:

- Allow part-time workers the opportunity to take full-time jobs offering greater potential for promotion.
- Retain workers in the company long enough for them to develop promotion potential.
- Make it possible for workers to work overtime, vary their work schedules, travel on business, and participate in additional schooling or training sessions after regular work hours.
- Make the labor market accessible to workers who are not working at all because of difficulties with child care.

Tardiness

Positive effects of child care services on tardiness depend on proper scheduling of the program, its location, and back-up supports. With proper planning, the following causes of tardiness can be reduced:

- Commuting delays when child care is inconveniently located.

- Delays when the child care center does not open on time or when the child care provider is late.
- Time taken to make emergency arrangements for child care.

Scheduling Flexibility

Child care can allow workers who have been restricted by the schedules of their existing child care programs to work more flexible hours including overtime, weekends, and evenings. Traditional child care is very seldom available much beyond regular working hours. Often workers have barely enough time to pick up their child if they leave work promptly at 5:00 p.m. Community child care programs also are generally open only on week days. Child care schedules can be matched to employee work schedules through company programs and cooperative agreements between companies and local child care programs.

Estimating the Value of Reductions in Absenteeism and Turnover

One of the most critical components of cost/benefit analysis in child care is the accurate projection of potential savings. Many companies underestimate the costs of problems such as turnover. Some weigh only direct costs such as worker salaries and advertising for replacements. In fact, direct costs can amount to less than half of the total cost of turnover. (See the cases discussed in Appendix C.)

Several methods are described here to quantify the cost of turnover and absenteeism. These methods are easy to use, are inexpensive, and can yield substantial information regarding the real value of potential savings. Assessing the potential value of savings in turnover and absenteeism involves the following three distinct steps.

Turnover

Step 1. Determining the Present Rate of Turnover. Turnover can be defined as a function of termination in a given month relative to the average number of employees on the payroll during a typical week of that month in the following formula.[5]

$$\frac{\text{Separations in a given month}}{\text{Average number of employees on payroll}} \times 100 = \text{Rate of turnover}$$

Although turnover rates can be analyzed by examining voluntary and involuntary separations separately, it may be wise to consider these categories simultaneously because of the potential effects of child care on both.

Step 2. Determining the Cost of Turnover. A cost estimation developed by Thomas E. Hall has been included in Appendix C because of its completeness in identifying the cost factors of turnover. It gives detailed instructions for completing the model and identifies both direct and indirect costs, crucial factors in pinpointing the total cost of turnover. It also allows for a distinction to be made between exempt and nonexempt employees. Finally, the results in five companies that have used the model are presented. These results underscore the point that it is easy to underestimate the cost of turnover if a systematic model is not used.

Step 3. Estimating the Potential Rate Change Brought about by Child Care. To project the potential effect of child care on turnover a company can begin by reviewing the research data presented in Chapter 2. In order to make a projection for a particular company, several considerations should be included in the analysis. First, characteristics of the company, of the programs, and of the affected workers will influence the change in turnover brought by the child care program. Company characteristics that are important include industry type, geographic location, work force characteristics, and employment situations.

Characteristics of the program and the child care problems that it solves or leaves unsolved will affect the work place as well. For example, where the existing supply of care in the community is not sufficient to meet the demand, a referral service alone will probably be less influential in the retention of workers than care provided directly by the company (in homes or in centers). If care is provided only for preschoolers, for example, there will be an impact on fewer workers than if children of all ages are eligible for the program. The degree of impact in any particular case is affected by:

- The extent of the worker's child care problem. A worker with a severe child care problem will be more likely to quit.
- The differences between the company child care service and other such services already available to workers.
- The child care problems relieved by the service (cost, supply, convenience, quality, or information on where to find care, as well as access to preferred types of care).

The number of workers who use the service will also have an impact on how much turnover is reduced. One must take into consideration the number of current employees who use it as well as changes in the applicant pool over time attributable to the availability of the child care service or to other factors that influence the proportion of employee users.

The number of employees who would be affected by the service can be determined as part of a larger information-gathering process discussed in Chapter 5 of this manual. Several methods requiring direct questioning of employees are presented, as well as methods that use existing company records. Exit interviews that explore the reasons for an employee's leaving may be helpful in evaluating the effect of child care. However, special interview questions that are sensitive to child care related terminations may be required in order to ensure the accuracy of such information. Workers' child care problems can be identified and a productive match between workers' child care needs and proposed child care service can be formulated by using the materials in Chapter 5.

Care should be taken to project accurately the population of potentially affected workers. Life styles are changing. Today parents often share more responsibility for child care. That men are assuming more responsibility for the care of their children is illustrated by the increasing frequency with which men gain custody of their children; work part-time, jobshare, or leave the work force to raise their children; participate more in the raising of their children; and are involved in child care arrangements when both parents work outside the home. All of these factors contribute to child care rate change projections that must be fed into the cost estimation model.

Absenteeism

Step 1. Determining the Rate. Absenteeism is most frequently defined as "scheduled, paid, or contractual absence (paid vacations, jury duty, holidays, etc.); long-term absence due to illness or medical leave; and unscheduled casual or incidental absence (short-term illness, family emergencies, etc.)" The employee whose absenteeism may be potentially reduced by child care will be those who need or use child care either regularly or for emergencies. Such employees include those with children from infancy through early adolesence who may still need supervision of some type when not in school, both during the school year and during summer vacation.

Step 2. Determining the Cost. The Bureau of National Affairs (BNA) index measures absenteeism in terms of the number of work days lost in a month through worker absence, divided by the product of the average number of employees and the number of work days per month in the following formula:

$$\frac{\text{No. of work days lost per month}}{\text{Average no. of employees} \times \text{No. of days per month of work}} = \text{Rate of absenteeism}$$

Child care difficulties have the greatest potential impact on unscheduled casual or incidental absences, but they can influence long-term absences as well. For example, a childhood illness lasting two weeks can require the parent to miss two weeks of work to care for the child. Leaves of absence taken during Christmas vacations and summers can be the result of child care unavailability, as can extended time out of the work force after childbirth.

Figure 3–1 provides a set of decision rules for measuring absenteeism costs and lists the factors that should be taken into consideration when estimating them. A second and more detailed method is given by Frank E. Kuzmits in "How Much Is Absenteeism Costing Your Organization?"[7] Acme International, a fictional medium-size steel manufacturer employing 1,200 people, was used to provide an example for computing absenteeism costs. The form for computation shown in Figure 3–2 is accompanied by explanations from the article on how to collect appropriate information and make the necessary calculations.

Step 3. Estimating Potential Rate Changes. To project the potential rate of change in absenteeism, first determine the current rate of absenteeism for the company overall and, if possible, the current rate for workers with children from birth to 11 years old. Look also at the past trends of growth in the absenteeism rates.

If the absentee rate of participating parents cannot be readily identified, they can be assumed to represent the same proportion of the absentee problem as they do of the work force. This method will not be precise, of course, because absentee problems are usually not spread evenly thoughout the employee population; rather, a small group of employees is generally responsible for a large share of the absences. It is dangerous to make assumptions. Any single group of employees—for example, parents—may actually be causing a larger or smaller portion of the absentee problem than one might expect.

Once the workers whose absenteeism may be affected by child care have been identified, there are a number of ways to estimate the size of the potential effect. Existing company records are one source of information, but caution should be exercised in taking

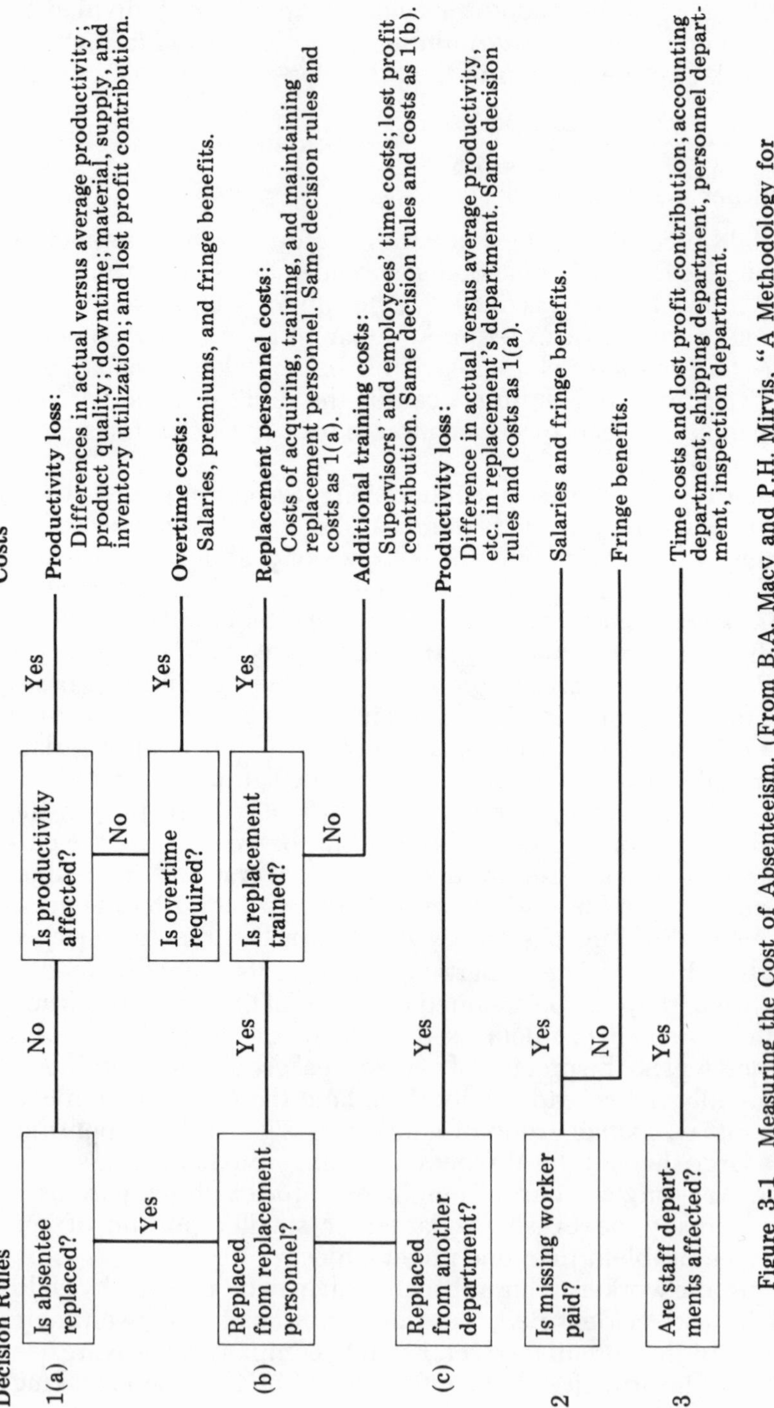

Figure 3-1 Measuring the Cost of Absenteeism. (From B.A. Macy and P.H. Mirvis, "A Methodology for Assessment of Quality of Work Life and Organizational Effectiveness in Behavioral Economic Terms," *Administrative Science Quarterly* (1976), pp. 212-226.

Figure 3-2 Total Estimated Cost of Employee Absenteeism

Item	*Acme International*	*Your Organization*
1. Total man-hours lost to employee absenteeism for the period	78,336	
2. Weighted average wage/salary per hour per employee	$4.32	
3. Cost of employee benefits per hour per employee	$1.90	
4. Total compensation lost per hour per absent employee		
A. If absent workers are paid (Wage salary plus benefits)	$6.22	
B. If absent workers are not paid (benefits only)		
5. Total compensation lost to absent employees (total man-hours lost X 4.A or 4.B, whichever applicable)	$487.250	
6. Total supervisory hours lost on employee absenteeism	3,840	
7. Average hourly supervisory wage, including benefits	$9.15	
8. Total supervisory salaries lost to managing problems of absenteeism (hours lost X average hourly supervisory wage—item 6 X item 7)	$35.136	
9. All other costs incidental to absenteeism not included in the above items	$38.500	
10. Total estimated cost of absenteeism—summation of items 5, 8, and 9	$560.886	
11. Total estimated cost of absenteeism per employee *(Total Estimated Costs)* / (Total Number of Employees)	$560.886 / 1200 = $467.41 per employee	=

these records at face value. Many absences that are actually child-care-related are never reported as such because of employee attitudes or company policies. Employees often assume, in keeping with traditional beliefs regarding work and family roles, that the interference of family obligations with job performance will be viewed more negatively than other types of problems and thus may choose to report a reason for absence other than the real cause. A typical company policy that can result in such misreporting is one prohibiting sick leave to care for ill family members. In such circumstances, workers may report a child's illness as their own in order to qualify for sick pay.

Another way of obtaining information is to explore with employees, in a non-punitive way, the extent to which their absences may be related to child care problems. This information can be gathered as part of a broader needs assessment process, such as that described in Part Three of this manual. This process can include the use of small discussion groups or surveys.

Also relevant to the size of the possible impact are potential changes in the work force over time as a result of child care program's availability. A child care program may attract more workers with children, so its long range impact on absenteeism might be significantly higher for the future work force than for the present one.

The nature of worker's child care problems should also be considered. Child care problems generally fall into five broad categories: cost, quality, supply, convenience, and information about appropriate facilities. Which of these are the current cause of absenteeism and which could be solved by the proposed child care service should be considered. The relative difference between the proposed service and arrangements workers now have is also important.

The impact on absenteeism often depends on how the child care program is designed. For example, if the program being proposed provides care for ill children or has a preventive health care component that reduces illnesses, absenteeism caused by sick children is likely to be reduced. If, however, transportation for school-age children needing care before and after school is not part of the proposed service, then absences due to transportation problems will not be reduced.

Maximizing Benefits

Several characteristics were shared by the child care programs reported as the most beneficial to companies. These similarities were noted in the National Employer Supported Child Care Project, particularly during site visits with company administrators. They were also common characteristics of the programs selected as case studies, all of which were reported to be highly successful from the company's point of view. The following list of characteristics, which was compiled from these site visits and interviews, can apply to a number of types of programs. They may, for example, apply to community centers or family day care homes as well as to programs operated by employers.

1. *High-Quality Programs.* Companies report that high-quality programs generally have a greater potential to attract and retain workers and to maintain high morale. These programs also have a greater public relations value, attract more positive media coverage, and give a company a better image within the community. High-quality programs have an age-appropriate educational program, a well-trained staff who enjoy working with children, adequate staff-child ratios, and relatively small group size.

2. *Comprehensive Programs Serving a Variety of Employee Child Care Needs.* Broad programs are more likely to be successful in reducing turnover and absenteeism and in attracting workers. Those that help with the child care needs of infants and school-age children as well as preschoolers, for example, have a more pervasive effect than those serving preschoolers alone. Programs that make child care more affordable, accessible, and available affect the work force more than those accomplishing only one of those goals.

3. *Programs Adequately Supported by the Company.* Support from the company takes many different forms, including financial contributions, in-kind service donations, and donations of space or products. In many cases a higher level of support from the company provides more benefits to parents by lowering tuition cost, by improving the quality of programs, by making it economically feasible for programs to be open during extended hours, or by making possible capital expenditures to expand the size of the program and make child care available to more workers. All of these program improvements made possible by corporate subsidy have beneficial effects for the company, in turn, because of the solutions they represent to the workers' child care dilemma.

4. *Programs Designed to Complement Community Resources.* Programs that fill gaps in community child care services rather than duplicate existing services are most beneficial to companies. Employers who do not consider whether such services are already available sometimes find their program utilization rates low and its appeal to employees less than desired.

5. *Timing.* The first programs established in a community tend to offer more of a recruitment and retention advantage. Early programs also have a greater potential for attracting publicity and influencing a company's image within the community.

6. *Programs Designed According to Employee Preference and with Employee Involvement.* Tailoring programs to accomodate employee preference for types of child care generally results in programs that are maximally used. Employee involvement in the planning process often reduces the risk of employees having unrealistic expectations about the scope of the program and enhances its value for labor-management relations.

Conclusion

Both potential and realized benefits have been discussed in this chapter, along with suggestions for maximizing the benefit potential of a child care program. The benefits experienced by a company will depend on whether the child care service adequately addresses the workers' care needs and whether the program is efficiently designed. Parts Three and Four of this book give the information needed to determine whether a child care service would be appropriate, to select the best type of service, and to design a program that will enhance company goals as well as provide a benefit to employees.

Endnotes:

1. Average annual center care costs nationally were about $2,000 per child in 1980. See Richard R. Ruopp and Jeffrey Travers, "Janus Faces Day Care: Perspectives on Cost and Quality," in *Day Care: Scientific and Social Policy Issues*, eds. E. F. Zigler and E. W. Gordon (Boston: Auburn House, 1982), p. 5.
2. Bureau of National Affairs, Inc., *Job Absence and Turnover Control, Personnel Policy, Forum No. 132* (Washington, D.C.: The Bureau of National Affairs, Inc., 1981), p. 13.
3. G. Masnick and M. J. Bane, *The Nation's Families: 1960–1990* (Boston, Mass.: Auburn House, 1980), p. 65.
4. Personal communication with Mary Young, Economic Analyst, Austin Families in Austin, Texas (June 3, 1983).
5. *Personnel Management: Policies and Practices*, Loose Leaf Service (Englewood Cliffs, N.J.: Prentice-Hall, Inc., 1966), p. 5402.
6. T. Stone, "Absenteeism Control: Is Your Company a Candidate?", reprinted from the September 1980 issue of *Personnel Administrator* (Berea, Ohio: The American Society for Personnel Administration, 1980), p. 79.
7. Kuzmits, F. E., "How Much is Absenteeism Costing Your Organization?", *Personnel Administrator* (June 1979), p. 31.The American Society for Personnel Administration, Berea, Ohio.

Chapter 4

TAX CONSIDERATIONS

This chapter is a general summary of the current federal tax provisions relating to child care. Employers and employees should consult their own attorneys or other tax advisors about their individual tax situations, the applicability of state and local tax provisions, and changes in the law. Tax planning can maximize the financial benefits to the company and employee, help anticipate and resolve potential legal and tax problems, and establish the program on a solid organizational base.

Employer Tax Considerations

Deductions and Credits

Profit-making employers who support child care programs can receive the benefit of tax deductions that are unavailable to non-profit organizations. Child care expenditures are deductible as business expenses when they are intended to benefit the employer's business by reducing absenteeism and turnover (Rev. Rul. 73–348 1973–2 C.B. 31). The costs of goods and services used currently are all deductible in the year in which the expenditure is made. For example, the entire cost of subsidies to parents or providers, the annual costs of operating a child care center (but *not* capital costs such as those for building and major equipment), and the costs of operating or contracting for information and referral services are generally deductible business expenses in the year they are spent.

NOTE: This section was written by Kathleen Murray, Attorney at Law, Child Care Law Center in San Francisco and Ann Mitchell, Director of Child Care Consultation Services, Bank Street College in New York.

When an employer establishes a child care center, capital costs may be incurred for real property such as buildings and renovation, as well as for personal property such as playground equipment, vehicles, classroom equipment and office furniture. The cost of these items is depreciable over a period of years, with only a portion of the cost deductible each year. For federal tax purposes, capital expenditures are subject to the Accelerated Cost Recovery System (ACRS) in IRC Section 168. Under ACRS the annual deduction is based upon statutory recovery periods and annual percentages rather than on the actual period of time the property is to be used. Real property is deductible over a 15-year period; child care personal property is generally deductible over five years. If a new business and a day care center are started simultaneously, the employer may have the opportunity to deduct certain "start-up" and "investigatory" costs over a five-year or longer period rather than deduct them in the year incurred (IRC Section 195.) This may be an advantage to some employers whose expenditures meet the qualifications.

Certain personal property is eligible for the investment tax credit, a credit against the value of the investment that may be claimed during the first year the property is placed in service by the employer.

Voluntary Employee's Beneficiary Associations

A voluntary employee's beneficiary association (VEBA) is a separate tax-exempt entity organized pursuant to IRS Section 501(c)(9) for the purpose of providing benefits to the members of the association. A VEBA may provide for the payment of life, sickness, and accident insurance and other benefits, including day care.

Charitable Contributions

Employers who make gifts to qualified tax-exempt organizations (such as many child care centers, child care information and referral agencies, and other community organizations) can deduct them as charitable contributions. The entire amount of a contribution may be deducted in the year in which it is given. If strings are attached to the gift, such as preferred admission status or a reduced fee for employer children, the donee's tax exempt status may be jeopardized. (*Baltimore Health and Welfare Fund*, 69 T.C. 554 (1978))

Dependent Care Assistance Programs (DCAP)

Employers considering implementing a child care benefit or service should be aware of the provisions of IRC Section 129, Dependent Care Assistance Programs (DCAP), which establish the mechanism through which an employer can offer child care as a tax-free benefit to employees. If the cost of employer-provided child care does not qualify as a DCAP, the fair-market value of the service is most likely taxable to the employee.

Under a DCAP the employer may actually provide child care, may contract with third parties for child care services for its employees, or may reimburse employees for child care expenses. To establish a program, the employer must prepare a separate written plan that is communicated to employees. The program may not discriminate in favor of officers, owners, or highly compensated employees. Members of a collective bargaining unit may be excluded, however, if dependent care benefits were the subject of good faith collective bargaining between the employer and the union. No more than 25% of the amount paid by the employer for child care may be paid on behalf of a group of persons each of whom owns more than 5% of the profits or capital interest in an unincorporated employer.

The amount of benefit an employee can receive as a non-taxable benefit is limited to an amount equal to the earned income of an unmarried employee or, if the employee is married, the earned income of the spouse with lower earnings, even if that spouse is not employed. Consequently, an employee with a non-working spouse will have to pay taxes on the value of any child care benefit received from the employer. A spouse who is a full-time student for at least five months a year or who is disabled will be assumed to have earned $200 per month if there is one child, or $400 per month if there are two or more children. Thus, a student or disabled spouse may accrue up to a maximum of $2,400 or $4,800 worth of excludable income.

The caregiver may be any person except a person for whom the employee or the employee's spouse is permitted to take a personal exemption deduction or a person who is the employee's child under the age of 19. Thus, the caregiver cannot be the spouse of the employee or an older sibling of the child.

If the child care program serves seven or more children, it must meet applicable state and local licensing laws and regulations. Thus programs with six or fewer children (family day care homes or child care centers) do not have to meet state or local licensing laws in order to qualify for a DCAP (IRC Section 129, 44A). In order to operate legally, however, these small programs must be in compliance with all applicable state and local laws.

A DCAP may be one of the benefits offered in a *cafeteria plan* under which an employee may choose among two or more benefits. If the *cafeteria plan* meets the requirements of the IRC Section 125, the benefits under the DCAP will be non-taxable to the employee who chooses it.

Amounts provided under a DCAP are not subject to employment taxes or withholding. A sample dependent care assistance plan follows. Employers should consult their own tax attorneys or advisors with respect to adoption and implementation of any dependent care assistance program.

MODEL DEPENDENT CARE ASSISTANCE PLAN* ABC CORPORATION

1. *Purpose.* ABC Corporation (the "Company") wishes to assist its employees in the care of their qualified dependents and therefore has adopted the ABC Corporation Dependent Care Assistance Plan (the "Plan") set out herein for the exclusive benefit of those employees who are eligible to participate in the Plan. The Plan is intended to qualify as a dependent care assistance program under Section 129 of the Internal Revenue Code of 1954, as amended (the "Code") and shall be construed to comply with Code Section 129.

2. *Definitions.* The following terms are defined for purposes of the Plan and are indicated by capitalized initial letters wherever they appear in the Plan:

a. "Dependent" shall mean (i) any child of an Employee who is under age 15 or who is physically or mentally incapable of caring for himself or herself and with respect to whom the Employee is entitled to claim an exemption for Federal income tax purposes or who is in the custody of the Employee for at least six months during the calendar year; and (ii) a spouse of the employee who is physically or mentally incapable of caring for himself or herself.

---

*Additional plan provisions will apply and other considerations will pertain if the plan is an "employee welfare benefit plan" as defined in Section 3(3) of the Employee Retirement Income Security Act of 1974, as amended.

This model plan was prepared by Barbara B. Creed and Deene Goodlaw Solomon of the San Francisco law firm of Pillsbury, Madison and Sutro. Ms. Creed and Ms. Solomon are tax attorneys who specialize in employee benefits and compensation.

b. "Employee" shall mean any person employed by the Company any portion of whose income is subject to withholding of income tax and/or for whom Social Security contributions are made by the Company, as well as any other person qualifying as a common law employee of the Company.

c. "Dependent Care Expenses" shall mean amounts paid for the care of a Dependent in the Employee's home or at a dependent care facility which meets all applicable requirements of state or local law or is exempt from such requirements under the state or local law in question and amounts paid for related household services, except that the following items shall not be considered Dependent Care Expenses.

(i) Amounts paid to a person with respect to whom the employee or his or her spouse is entitled to claim an exemption for Federal income tax purposes;

(ii) Amounts paid to a child of the Employee who is 18 years of age or younger; and

(iii) Amounts paid for or reimbursed under another plan of the Company or to which the Company contributed on behalf of the Employee, under any Federal, state or local program of dependent care assistance, or by an employer of the spouse or by an educational institution where the spouse is an enrolled student.

3. *Effective Date.* The plan shall be effective on__________.

4. *Eligible Employees.* All employees of the Company shall be eligible to participate in the Plan.

5. *Reimbursement of Expenses for Dependent Care.*

a. Upon application of the Employee, accompanies by a bill, receipt, cancelled check, or other written evidence of payment or of the obligation to pay Dependent Care Expenses, the Company will reimburse the Employee for Dependent Care expenses incurred in order to enable the Employee to be employed by the Company, subject to the limits of paragraph b. The Company reserves the right to verify all claimed expenses prior to reimbursement.

b. *Limitation on Benefits.* The maximum amount of Dependent Care Expenses which will be reimbursed under this Plan shall be of the lowest of:

(i) $ ______________ per calendar year; or

(ii) If the Employee is single or is married and earns less than his or her spouse in a calendar year, the compensation paid to the Employee by the Company as reflected on his or her Form W-2 for the year; or

(iii) If the Employee is married and the earned income of his or her spouse is less than the compensation paid to the

Employee by the Company in a calendar year, the earned income of the spouse. If the spouse is a student or is physically or mentally incapable of caring for himself or herself, the spouse will be deemed to have earned income (for each month that the spouse is a student or incapacitated) of $200 per month if the Employee has one Dependent for whom care is provided and of $400 per month if the Employee has two or more Dependents for whom care is provided.

The Company may require that the Employee and/or his or her spouse certify to the Company the amount of such spouse's expected earned income for the calendar year in question and may require that the Employee provide documentary evidence of the amount certified in the form of an employment contract, paycheck stub, medical records (if the spouse is incapacitated), or a school enrollment form (if the spouse is a student).

c. *Direct Payment in Lieu of Reimbursement.* The Company may, in its discretion, pay any Expenses for Dependent Care directly to the dependent care provider in lieu of reimbursing the Employee in satisfaction of its obligations under the Plan.

d. *Limitations of Benefits Paid to Prohibited Group.* No more than 25% of the benefits paid under the Plan in any one calendar year shall be provided for the class of individuals (or their spouses or dependents) each of whom owns more than 5% of the stock of the Company, determined in accordance with Code Sections 1563(d) and (e) without regard to Code Section 1563(e)(3)(C), on any one day of that calendar year. If the benefits payable under the Plan to such class exceeds the limits of this paragraph, the benefits paid to each individual member of the class shall be reduced proportionately.

6. *Funding Method.* The benefits provided under the Plan are funded entirely out of the general assets of the Company.

7. *Notification of Terms of Plan.* A copy of the plan shall be given to all Employees.

8. *Statement of Benefits.* On or before January 31 of each year, the Company shall furnish each Employee who received benefits under the Plan a written statement showing the amounts paid or the expenses incurred by the Employer in providing Dependent Care Assistance under the Plan for the prior calendar year.

9. *Amendment or Termination.* The Company may amend or terminate the Plan at any time; provided, however, that any such amendment or termination shall not affect any right to benefits arising prior to such amendment or termination or shall cause

benefits paid hereunder not to qualify as dependent care assistance under Code section 129.

10. *Governing Law.* This Plan and the rights of all persons under the Plan shall be construed in accordance with and under applicable provisions of the Internal Revenue Code of 1954, as amended, and the laws of the State of California.

[Note: The following provisions should be added if the plan is an "employee benefit plan"]

11. *Fiduciary Responsibility and Plan Administration.*

a. *Plan Sponsor and Plan Administrator.* The "plan sponsor" and the "administrator" of the Plan, within the meaning of the Employee Retirement Income Security Act of 1974 ("ERISA"), is the Company.

b. *Named Fiduciary.* The Company is the named fiduciary responsible for the operation and administration of the Plan.

c. *Assignment of Duties.* The duties of the Company hereunder shall be carried out in its name by its executive committee, officers, and employees. The Company may designate any person to carry out fiduciary responsibilities under the Plan pursuant to a written instrument which specifies the fiduciary responsibilities assigned to each such person. Any person may serve in more than one fiduciary capacity with respect to the Plan.

d. *Employment of Advisors.* The Company or a fiduciary designated by the Company, may employ one or more persons to render advice with regard to its fiduciary responsibilities under the Plan.

12. *General Plan Information.*

a. *Employer Identification Number.* The Employer Identification Number assigned to the Company by the IRS is:

________________ .

b. *Plan Number.* The Plan Number assigned to the Plan by the Company is: ________ .

c. *Plan's Fiscal Year.* The date of the end of the year for purposes of maintaining the Plan's fiscal records is: ________ .

d. *Agent for Service of Legal Process.* The agent for service of process with respect to the Plan is: ________________

____ .

TO RECORD THE ADOPTION OF THE PLAN, the Company has caused this document to be executed by its duly authorized officer this ____ day of ________ .

ABC CORPORATION

By ____________________________

Employee Tax Considerations

Because so few companies have implemented dependent care assistance programs, the primary tax benefit available to parent employees is the federal child care tax credit, IRC Section 44A. Many states also provide a state child care tax credit.

The federal child care tax credit provides a credit for certain employment-related child and dependent care expenses up to a maximum of $2,400 for one child and $4,800 for two or more children. The credit may be applied against the costs of care for dependent children under the age of 15, as well as for a dependent of any age, including a spouse who is physically or mentally incapable of caring for himself. The amount of the credit is determined by the adjusted gross income shown on the federal income tax return of the employee.

Employees with adjusted gross incomes under $10,000 receive the largest credit, 30% against eligible expenses. Employees with incomes between $10,001 and $28,000 receive a sliding credit ranging from 29% to 21%, the credit being reduced by 1% for each $2,000 of family income or fraction thereof over $10,000. Employees with incomes in excess of $28,000 receive a flat 20% credit. Table 4–1 presents the percentages and maximum allowable at various income levels.

To claim this credit, the taxpayer must be employed with income in excess of the expense limits of $2,400 or $4,800, depending on the number of children. The child care expenses of married employees are limited to the amount of income earned

Table 4–1

Adjusted Gross Income	*Percentage*	*One Child or Dependent*	*Two or More Children or Dependents*
Up to $10,000	30%	$720	$1,440
10,001–12,000	29	696	1,392
12,001–14,000	28	672	1,344
14,001–16,000	27	648	1,296
16,001–18,000	26	624	1,248
18,001–20,000	25	600	1,200
20,001–22,000	24	576	1,152
22,001–24,000	23	552	1,104
24,001–26,000	22	528	1,056
26,001–28,000	21	504	1,008
28,001 and over	20	480	960

by the lesser-earning spouse. Thus, if a married mother with two children in day care earns only $3,500 (and her husband earns more), their child care expense for purposes of the credit will be limited to the $3,500 she earned. Students and disabled spouses are subject to the same rules set forth in the section describing dependent care assistance plans. Child care programs that serve seven or more children and dependent care centers for seven or more adults must comply with state and local laws and regulations in order for the costs of care to be eligible for the credit.

If an employee receives a tax-free benefit through a dependent care assistance plan, the credit is not allowed with respect to the value of the benefit received through the plan. For example, if an employer pays $1,000 of an employee's total child care costs of $2,400, the employee may take the credit against only the $1,400 paid by the employee.

The credit is non-refundable, which means that the IRS will not issue a refund to a taxpayer whose child care credit exceeds the amount of the income tax owed. For example, a taxpayer whose tax liability is $300 and who is entitled to a $480 child care tax credit can use the credit to offset the entire $300, thus paying no tax for the year. However, the taxpayer will not receive a $180 refund for the "unused" portion of the credit.

Beginning with the 1983 tax year, taxpayers claiming the credit will be able to file the short form and attach the 2441 Dependent Care Credit form. Until then, taxpayers must file the long form to claim the credit.

Employers can *assist employees with child care needs* by helping them to take advantage of the child care tax credit, informing them of the existence of the credit and its provisions. Employers can also help their employees receive the benefit of the credit throughout the year by assisting them to amend their form W-4 (Employee's Withholding Allowance Certificate). (See Appendix B.)

Part Three

HOW CAN THE NEED FOR CHILD CARE BE DETERMINED?

Chapter 5

DATA COLLECTION AND DECISION MAKING

Information about the nature of supply and demand for child care services and the implications of unmet needs for the company will help employers determine whether to become involved. It will also help a company identify which of the many possible services would be most appropriate for it to implement. This chapter describes a practical process for gathering and analyzing information in order to decide whether and how to become involved in child care. Sample materials that illustrate this process are included in Appendix D.

The diversity of possible child care services makes it possible for companies to design programs that achieve corporate goals while serving company employees. The following factors are important to consider in a child care decision: (1) the supply of existing care, (2) the demand for care among company employees, (3) the relationship between supply and demand, and (4) the company's motivation for involvement in child care. Let us briefly discuss the relevance of each of these factors to company decision making.

What Information is Needed?

The Supply of Care in the Community

It is important to have detailed information about both the supply of and demand for child care to design a successful program. The type of information needed about the supply of existing care includes types of community facilities, number of spaces available, number of children on waiting lists, geographic distribution of available care, ages of eligible children, operating hours, quality indicators, and cost. This information is pertinent for both family day care homes and centers.

Program design may also be influenced by trends in community supply and demand. For example, is the supply of community care dwindling, static, or expanding? Are others planning to offer direct services that might compete or coordinate with the company's own plans? Is community redevelopment attracting young families to the area and increasing the demand for existing services?

Companies will usually not have to collect such information about the community child care market themselves. It may be readily available from such sources as the local United Way office, child care information and referral services, and child care licensing or registration agencies. However, in locations where there are not such agencies or other experts on local child care services, a telephone or mail survey of licensed child care centers and registered family day care homes can provide an estimate of community supply and demand. More specific suggestions regarding information gathering are presented later in this chapter.

The Demand for Care in the Company

Companies often want to know how many employees have children, how these employees are distributed throughout the company, and how many children need care. To design an appropriate program, they need to know about employee's current child care arrangements and difficulties, what services are needed, and how much parents can afford to pay.

Information about the demand for care within the company can be obtained in a variety of ways. A rough estimate of child care needs might be derived from labor force demographics available in company personnel and health insurance records, although some companies have found this information inconvenient to access and too outdated to be useful. If the company already holds parent seminars and discussion groups or provides child care referrals for employees, information on parents' needs may be collected while providing these services. Questions about child care may also be added to exit interviews, annual reviews, or general employee benefits surveys. The most direct and frequently used method, however, is to ask employees about their child care needs in a survey, interview, or focus group discussion specifically designed for this purpose. Detailed explanations of several methods are presented later in this chapter.

A child care program is likely to be successful over a longer period of time if the program design takes into consideration an estimate of future demand. Projection of future recruitment needs and labor force trends can provide an estimate of future child care needs within the company.

Effects on the Company of Unmet Needs

In addition to assessing supply and demand, a company may also want to ascertain how the gaps in services are affecting the company and what benefits a company-supported child care service might be expected to bring. The potential effects of unmet child care needs cover a broad range, from the high telephone bills of employees calling home to check on children left without supervision and absenteeism due to unreliable care or lack of care for sick children, to the loss of women employees who cannot return to work as soon as desired after childbirth for lack of infant care. Evidence of such effects may be available through personnel records and supervisors' reports or directly from employees via surveys, interviews, and group discussions. Companies considering child care may want to examine the benefits experienced by other companies, as reported in the case studies presented in Chapter 2.

The Effect of Company Goals on Data Collection and Program Design

The choices to be made in child care depend not only on existing supply and demand but also on the company's rationale for considering child care in the first place. Companies establish child care services for many reasons. Each has its own unique pattern of motivation, which may include a general concern for employees and their families, a desire to be in the forefront of the employee benefits field, or the desire to achieve corporate goals such as reduced turnover, improved morale, and better community relations. Clarification of a company's goals helps determine what information is needed for decision making and also facilitates selecting and tailoring the company's child care program to achieve desired objectives. For example, if better community relations is a goal, the company may want to investigate how existing employer-supported programs have helped their companies achieve this goal. Employers contemplating child care might also examine variations in program design that could contribute to accomplishing company goals. For example, to maintain good community relations, a company may establish a child care consortium in partnership with other businesses or agencies, and it may consider providing a program that serves children in the community as well as employee children.

The data collection and decision process in a company consists of three major phases:

I. Preliminary Planning:
- Establish task force.
- Clarify corporate goals.

II. Assessment of Need:
- Assess demand.
- Assess supply.
- Assess effects of the gap on the company.
- Synthesize.

III. Analysis and Decision Making:
- Consider alternatives.
- Estimate costs and benefits.
- Identify resources.
- Select program.
- Plan evaluation.

Let us consider these phases in detail as follows.

Phase I: Preliminary Planning

Establish a Task Force

The major purpose of a task force is to gather and analyze information so that management can decide whether the company will start a child care service and, if so, to plan the type of program to be established. It is advisable that the task force represent all significant groups in the company that would be affected by the proposed service, since planning is more efficient if a broad range of interests and viewpoints are incorporated early in the process. Also, eventual changes in policies or practices may be more readily accepted if all significant groups share ownership of the project.

The effectiveness of the task force depends in part on its members' influence within the company. Recommendations are more likely to be respected if members enjoy the trust of senior management as well as other employees. Typical task force members include the following:

- An influential representative of senior management.
- The personnel director and/or human resource accounting representative.
- A representative of the planning department.

- A representative of labor (whether organized or not) who is influential through status or seniority.
- The director of the largest department or a department that is most likely to be affected by child care-related absenteeism, turnover, or recruitment.
- Parent employees who are potential users of the service.
- A representative of the public relations department.
- An attorney familiar with company taxes and liability.

The size of the task force will depend on the size and organizational structure of the company; however, small groups of 6–8 members usually find it easier to meet and accomplish tasks. In addition, small group size and confidentiality of discussions help minimize the risk of prematurely raising employee expectations.

The task force may want to consult with specialists at various stages of the decision making and planning process. Often a company has personnel skilled in data collection, processing, and analysis who can assist the task force. Few companies, however, have anyone on staff with expertise in selecting and planning employer-supported child care services, so the task force may want to solicit counsel from an outside specialist at some point in the process. Of the 93 companies in the National Employer Supported Child Care Project who sought help outside their company in developing programs, the most common sources of assistance were consultants (used by 78 companies) and non-profit child care firms (used by 17 companies.)

Some local child care information and referral agencies and child care coordinating councils (often known as "4-C" organizations) are able to provide technical assistance and information. If the company is concerned about unduly raising employee expectations while investigating the need for services, the task force may want to gather data on employee needs in conjunction with such an outside agency. Their involvement may highlight the research aspect of the process and minimize implications that a specific service will be created. Child care agencies may also be able to provide lists of model programs to visit, other companies interested in developing programs, and child care centers or homes that might be interested in providing services to company employees. Specific information or technical assistance may also be available from existing employer-supported programs at other companies. One resource for potential contacts is the list of employer-supported child care programs in Appendix E.

While help from external specialists is frequently desirable, both the company and child care program will benefit if several task force members educate themselves about child care issues and services. In this way, after a program is in place and the outside consultation is complete, company employees remain knowledgeable enough to fine-tune the program from time to time to keep it operating smoothly.

Clarify Corporate Goals

The task force must clarify the company's objectives in providing child care service. Companies consider involvement in child care for a number of reasons—for example, to help employees balance home and work responsibilities, to achieve personnel goals such as enhanced recruitment or reduced absenteeism, to maintain good community relations, and to obtain favorable publicity.

Careful delineation of goals sets the stage for appropriate data collection and program design. For instance, a company that wants to contribute to the community and maintain a positive image may prefer that its program serve the community as a whole by addressing the gaps in community supply and demand rather than the more specific needs of its own workforce. Data collection would thus focus on the community rather than company employees. Another company's goal might be to recruit more young skilled technicians. If it were found that such employees tend to need infant care and could afford its high cost, that company might choose to organize an infant program emphasizing convenience and high quality rather than low cost.

Since there are many ways in which companies can provide child care services, the task force will want to be familiar with the full array of possibilities. A broad perspective is particularly appropriate prior to data collection. After the information on child care supply and demand is collected and analyzed, the task force will be able to narrow its focus to those options that best match the gaps in services and offer the opportunity to achieve certain corporate goals. See Part Four for detailed descriptions of possible child care programs.

Phase II: Assessment of Need

Collecting and analyzing data from employees and the community will help management decide whether to become involved in employer-supported child care and, if so, which programs would be preferable. Companies approach these decisions in various ways. Some document the general level of employee need and the effect it is having in the work place before committing time and effort to collecting the detailed information on needs and community services that is useful in designing a program. Other companies prefer the efficiency of collecting all the data at one time. They may feel confident in proceeding this way because they already have some informal evidence of employee need, or they may want to develop a program even if the current level of need is relatively low.

A major duty of the task force is to decide what specific information to collect and how to collect it. The ultimate consideration at this stage is the decisions that will be made as a consequence of the information gathered. The lack of a clear plan for using information can result in the accumulation of insufficient or inappropriate information. Interesting but unnecessary data can mask crucial information and thereby make the final decision more difficult instead of facilitating it. A useful rule of thumb is to limit the information collected to that which can pass the "So what?" test.

Assess Demand

In most cases one of the company's goals is to meet the child care needs of its employees (rather than providing a service solely for community families), so the task force will want to assess the needs of current and future employees. As a first step, it is essential to define the employee population about which information is to be gathered. Most companies expect current parent employees to be the users of a child care service. It is also important, however, to anticipate the needs of future users in order to plan a program that will not become outdated. The personnel department or the human resource department projections of future recruitment needs and labor force trends can give some indication of future needs. Will there be more employees of child-bearing age? More single-parent workers? More workers from dual-career families? More women in full-time positions? More women preferring to take shorter maternity leaves? More men staying home to care for sick children or requesting paternity leaves? It is also relevant to note how long workers tend to remain at the company. For example, if current employees with small children are expected to stay at the company for 10–15 years or more, it might benefit the company to anticipate their needs for school-age care. Several companies with employer-supported programs have noted a tendency for employees to remain with the company at least as long as their children are eligible for the child care program. The broader the age range served, the longer the employees stayed with the company.

If a company expects future employees to differ significantly from present employees in ways that could affect use of the child

Table 5-1 Major Methods for Obtaining Employee Data

Written Survey	Focus Group Discussion	Analysis of Record Data on Employees' Child Care Referrals
DESCRIPTION: Written questionnaire (primarily multiple-choice questions).	Group discussion with 10–15 people in each group led by skilled group leader. Comments recorded for later analysis.	Data collected from users of child care referral service (in-house or external agency) over 9–12 months).
PURPOSE: 1. Determine needs. 2. Design program.	1. Determine needs. 2. Design program.	1. Determine needs. 2. Design program.
DATA CAN INCLUDE: • Demographics. • Quantitative description of current child care arrangements and problems. • Ways child care arrangements affect work. • Preferences for child care and company services. • Personal comments.	• Similar to survey but provides generalized view, not specific numbers for each variable. • Indepth information on individual problems and experiences. • Intensity of concerns.	• Demographics on users. • Current child care arrangements (actually used, not self-report). • Problem leading to need for referral. • Requests for specific arrangements. • Personal comments.
MAJOR ADVANTAGES: • Can collect comprehensive, detailed data from many people in short time. • Can obtain inforamation on whole work force through representative sampling. • Data can be easily quantified and analyzed. • Easy to compare groups of respondents. • Employee respondents can be anonymous. • Lets employees know company cares.	• Gives good overall "feel" if groups selected are representative sample of whole work force. • Individual comments provide concrete illustration of needs. • Interactive method allows flexibility in data collection; can pursue details and cover broader scope.	• Quantifiable data. • Easy to compare groups of respondents. • Gives good information on gaps in existing services and what care users find acceptable; usage data is more reliable than self report but, cannot be assumed same as preference. • May be used as unobtrusive measure; avoids raising employee expectations. • Can structure questions to get information on child care problems and effects on work behavior. • Can only use if referral data on employees is available.

MAJOR LIMITATIONS: • Overt data collection may raise employee expectations to unrealistic levels. • Self-report measure is subject to bias towards socially desirable answers.	• Overt data collection may raise employee expectations. • Data more qualitative than quantitative—e.g., will not know average days missed due to care problems. • Data may not accurately reflect total need, although it may be sufficient for the purpose in small company. • Self-report measure is subject to bias toward socially desirable comments. • Employees are not anonymous; may not reveal real problems even if reassured.	• Data subject to unknown degree of bias since it reflects only those who use referral service (during time data collected). No information on parents who do not use service—e.g., who, how many, reasons not using it, problems, effects on work. If use referral data to select and design program, first determine representativeness of referral service users. May need to supplement with data on other parent employees. • Expressed preferences may be limited by what is available.
POPULATION: • Population may include all employees, a random sample, or a specific target group—e.g. employees at a specific work site.	• Same as for survey (but hard to include ex-employees).	• Population is limited to users of referral service, (not representative sample of parents in workforce).
RESULTS SENSITIVE TO: • Information communicated to employees prior to survey (vocabulary, purpose of, company's intent, anonymity, etc.) • Composition of survey (clear, concise, unbiased). • Response rate may vary tremendously—e.g., 10%–80%, depending on pre-survey PR, perception of company's intent, survey composition, anonymity, etc.	• Information (same as survey). • Group leader's skills and knowledge of child care and company goals. • Participation rate (depends on advance PR, perception of intent, freedom from negative reaction, group rapport, etc.)	• Availability of sufficient choices in child care arrangements and parents' knowledge about them. • Scope of information collected; interview and referral skills of staff. • Type of employees and needs served by referral service.

care service (for example, age of children or preference for type of care), it would be important to the program's success to estimate those future employees' needs and preferences. This estimate would be particularly pertinent if a company wanted to use the child care service to attract new workers.

Some companies may have a specific group of employees to which they wish to target their program. For instance, they may want to recruit certain highly skilled workers, to retain trained low-income employees, or perhaps to improve morale and productivity at a certain branch office. In such a case, the task force may decide to collect data on these employees only or to give special weight to the data from this group when analyzing the needs of the entire workforce.

A rough estimate of current need may be gleaned from company personnel and health insurance records, although some companies have found this information inconvenient to access and not timely enough to be very useful. Discussions at parent seminars or employee lunch programs may also be used to collect relevant information. Where still more accurate and detailed information is needed, especially for designing a program, a company can obtain it through a more formal needs assessment process.

For many people the term "needs assessment" is synonymous with "survey." However, there are several data collection possibilities, each with its advantages and limitations. The two major methods are the written survey and the focus group discussion. Employees may also be interviewed individually; because this technique is time consuming, however, it is more often used as a supplemental method than as the primary data collection technique. Still another technique, using data collected by a child care referral agency or in-house referral office for company employees, is also possible if such a service exists. To decide which methods to use, the task force can compare their characteristics and select those which are most efficient and feasible, given the time, expertise, and resources available.

It is often desirable to use two or more methods to collect information on employee needs. Using more than one method dissipates the bias of the assessment techniques and obtains a better estimate of a "true" need. A combination of methods may also provide a more complete perspective on the complex issues involved. Following is an overview and comparison of the three most commonly used methods: written survey, focus groups, and referral record analysis. A more detailed description of each method is then presented. See Appendix D for further guidelines and sample materials (such as a sample survey and cover letter) for gathering employee need and preference information using these three methods.

The Written Survey. The written survey is the most frequently used method of collecting data when companies consider creating a child care program. Of the 147 companies in the National Employer Supported Child Care Project who reported completing a feasibility study prior to program implementation, 85 surveyed all employees and 40 surveyed selected employees.

A primary advantage of the written survey is its ability to collect extensive information from many people in a short period of time. A survey can provide a demographic description of respondents, including information about the worker's job (for example, job title, shift, department) and personal characteristics (for example, number and ages of children, type of care used or desired, mode of transportation to work, marital status, income level). This information can be of value in several ways, including the following:

1. Identify empolyees who might use child care services. For example, a large proportion of those with child care needs might tend to work in a certain department or on a particular shift that is hard to staff.
2. Help determine important program characteristics. For example, working parents who use public transportation to get to work may prefer child care located close to home rather than commuting with their children.

The written survey can provide a complex, quantified picture of current and preferred child care arrangements and child care problems. This information is essential to defining the gap between supply and demand in order to design a practical, realistic program. A survey can also quantify some of the ways in which employees perceive their child care problems affecting work (for example, the number of work days lost annually due to child care problems). Some company decision makers are particularly interested in this type of information.

Another important advantage of the written survey, as opposed to the focus group method, is its ability to preserve the anonymity of respondents. For many reasons, employees tend not to be candid about their child care problems unless assured that their information will remain anonymous.

The written survey does, however, have several limitations. As a self-report measure, it is subject to the bias that people tend to give socially acceptable answers that do not reflect their true needs. Also, when employees are aware that the company is collecting data, a survey may raise their expectations. And, as a written instrument, a survey offers no chance for questions or dialogue. Thus, a survey's validity and reliability depend on its being well-structured in terms of length, wording, directions, and format. A poorly constructed survey may prove worthless, and a poorly administered survey—even if well written—is likely to provide inadequate data.

Focus Groups. Focus groups are small groups of employees who voluntarily meet with a skilled group leader to discuss common concerns. To investigate employee's child care needs, the discussions should focus on their child care arrangements, problems, and needs, how the company is affected (for example, with regard to absenteeism and productivity), and what sort of services would be helpful. Usually a company would collect data from several groups. The total number of participants can be fairly small (for example, 5%–10% of the employee population) and still provide a good estimate of the concerns of all the workforce if the participants are selected randomly. In order to analyze results, the discussion can be recorded either with tape recorders or manually.

The small-group process has been used far less than the written survey in needs assessments. Only 24 out of 147 companies in the National Employer Supported Child Care Project reported that they used small groups when doing a feasibility study prior to program implementation. However, the small group process, often called "focus groups" or "1-in-5s," is popular with many companies for such purposes as developing new product ideas and organization development. As more companies familiar with the process become involved in child care and share their experience with others, it is possible that focus groups may become a more popular needs assessment tool.

Although providing less quantifiable data than the survey, focus groups give a good overall "feel" for the nature and intensity of child care problems, richly supplemented with specific examples. One of the advantages of this method, particularly over a written survey, is its interactive nature, which allows the group leader a great deal of flexibility during the data collection process to pursue problems, details, and feelings as they unfold.

The limitations of focus groups are similar to those of the survey. By the nature of the process, employees know the company is exploring child care concerns, and their expectations may be raised. Also, the information collected in groups, as in surveys, is subject to the respondents' tendency to give socially desirable responses. In addition, group participants cannot be anonymous within the group. Hence the task force members and group leader will want to create a comfortable and confidential environment to encourage honest and complete participation.

The administration of focus groups is a critical factor in their effectiveness. Experienced companies emphasize the need for both solid group leading skills and knowledge of child care issues and services. This compound need may necessitate two or more people working closely together to elicit appropriate information. For example, one company used focus groups successfully by arranging for a child care professional and the director of human resources to view the groups from a nearby room with participants' knowledge. During breaks they met with the group leader to discuss which comments to follow up and which issues to probe further. Thus, by combining their skills, they were able to gather comprehensive data from a small number of groups.

Referral Records. A third method of collecting data on employee needs is reference to the records of the child care referral program serving company employees. Sometimes companies have worked out an arrangement with a community referral agency whereby the company recommends the agency to its employees and the agency provides child care referrals and keeps records for the company on employees' needs and usage. Some companies have established their own in-house referral service and keep their own records on employees' needs and preferences to determine if additional services should be established in the future.

The type of data collected through the referral process usually includes current care arrangements, problems that led to the need for referral, the number and ages of children, and preferences in child care. The referral technique may be adapted to suit the company's need for additional information. For example, the referral staff can also obtain employees' perceptions of how their unmet child care needs affect the work place. Thus, good counseling and interview skills are important prerequisites for the referral staff.

The use of referral records has several advantages. Companies hesitant to raise employee expectations with a survey or focus group can use the referral data in an unobtrusive way. In addition, the interview part of the referral process is a flexible technique, and the interviewer can pursue details of problems or needs as seems appropriate. Furthermore, the purpose of a referral service is to help parents find acceptable care. Thus, referral staff deal on a daily basis with the child care needs that parents experience. This information may provide a perspective that is somewhat different from the written responses given in an employee survey.

Companies that use referral record data, however, will want to take into account the fact that the employees who use the service may not constitute a statistically representative sample of the total parent population within the company. This is true because they are a self-selected group. Not all employees who use or need child care will use a referral service for a wide variety of reasons. For example, they may not know it exists, they may think it will not protect their privacy, or they may find it inconvenient to use. A company can estimate the representativeness of its referral data by conducting a brief written or telephone survey of a small, statistically random sample of the workforce to determine if this group differs significantly from the referral service users in ways that would affect program design (for example, number and ages of children and preferences for child care services).

The Value of Advance Communication. The effectiveness of data-based decision making depends on both the completeness and the quality of information collected. For both the survey and focus group methods, these aspects can be influenced to a great degree by good advance communication. Employees can be alerted to expect the survey or focus groups, can be encouraged to participate honestly and fully, and be reassured that their answers will be kept confidential. Such communication also gives the company the opportunity to make it clear that the data gathering is an exploration of child care concerns and not a promise that a program will be established.

A final purpose of advance communication is to present the vocabulary and issues of employer-supported child care prior to the actual gathering of information so that the results accurately reflect employees' true needs and preferences. If employees misunderstand the concepts and vocabulary of the survey items or group discussions, the data will not be very useful in decision making.

Some suggestions for enhancing advance communication are as follows:

- The company's chief executive officer can direct a letter to supervisors and department heads, supporting needs assessment and requesting complete cooperation.
- Small group meetings can be held to inform and motivate mid-management and other employees.
- Written information can be disseminated through the company newsletter, flyers, and posters (see Appendix D for samples).
- Personal communication can take place during office gatherings, a "child care fair," meetings, brown bag lunches, and one-to-one conversation, preferably with local child care experts on hand to discuss the issues.
- A network of supportive people can be established in each department to publicize, encourage, and answer questions.

- Task force members who are familiar with the issues and assessment process can be given the opportunity to field questions.

Several of these methods may be used throughout the month or quarter preceding the focus groups or survey to promote wide interest.

Assess Supply

Information on available child care services in the community is useful for several reasons:

1. To verify employee's perceptions of needed services in order to determine the gap between supply and demand and thereby target the company's involvement in child care appropriately. For example, employees may need information and help in making better use of existing resources rather than being provided with new services.
2. To identify other organizations in public, private, and voluntary sectors with whom child care services can be coordinated.
3. To determine whether community families are available to utilize a company child care service—for example, as a possible cushion for enrollment fluctuations in a company center or family day care homes.

Approximately half of the 147 companies in the National Employer Supported Child Care Project who completed a feasibility study surveyed the available care in their area prior to implementing their programs. The information a company would want about local services often has been inventoried already by community agencies such as:

- Local United Way offices (United Way funds some child care resource and referral agencies and sometimes does its own research on child care needs).
- State day care or licensing agencies.
- Local child care information and referral agencies, often called Child Care Information Service, Children's Home Society, Child Care Coordinating Council. (Referral agencies may be listed with United Way, the State Department of Education, and the local Department of Social Services, as well as in the phone book.)
- "Umbrella" organizations of family day care homes, which may be located through referral agencies or community colleges.
- College departments of education, early childhood education, or social welfare.

If these types of organizations cannot help, the task force can conduct a telephone or mail survey of child care centers, including nursery schools, preschools, and licensed day care homes in the area.

The type of information that is useful in an inventory of community services includes the following:

1. Information on direct services, such as centers, family day care homes, before-and-after-school programs, summer day camps, and care for ill or recuperating children:

   - Ages served and associated requirements (for example, whether young children must be toilet-trained).
   - Hours of operation, especially with respect to how they match with company hours and shifts.
   - Days of operation vis-à-vis company schedules, school holidays, and summer vacations.
   - Location relative to location of working parents' homes and the company.
   - Capacity, enrollment level, waiting time.
   - Cost and availability of financial assistance for which company workers would qualify.
   - Measures of quality such as teacher-child ratio, level of education or experience of staff, staff salaries, staff turnover rate, and educational aspects of program.
   - Whether facility is licensed or registered.
   - Sponsorship and related limitations (e.g., sponsored by another company but open to public).
   - Financial assistance programs: requirements, limitations, sponsorship. (Who qualifies, where and how can funds be used, how can employees obtain funds, how much funding is available, and how long can a family use it?)

2. *Information on auxiliary service:*
   Referral services:
   - Geographic area served. (Does it include areas where most employee parents live?)
   - Type of information provided (facts only, evaluation or counseling).
   - Format of information (written, phone, personal interview).
   - Costs, if any, to users.
   - Range of available referrals (type, cost, locations, licensed, facilities, etc.) that are likely to be useful to company employees.
   - Frequency of updates and accuracy of information.
   - Follow-up provided.

- Location, hours that service is available, and accessibility to company parents.

Parent education:

- Type of information provided.
- Format.
- When and where provided.
- Cost.
- Quality of information and presentations.
- Sponsorship of service and limitations on who can use service.

To target their involvement, many companies examine the trends in community supply and demand that could affect their plans. For example, what other companies in the area are considering child care involvement and what services are they planning or likely to implement? Are there other companies that would like to form a consortium to sponsor services jointly? Are there any plans for increasing the supply of child care under the auspices of another company or some other organization that would make child care more available, accessible, or affordable to employees? Is there business development planned for the area that will increase demand for community child care and thus make it less accessible for company employees?

Sources for such information include city planning committees, the chamber of commerce, voluntary agencies such as the United Way, social service agencies, child care experts who may be contacted through local colleges, child care councils, professional organizations for early childhood educators such as local chapters of the Association for the Education of Young Children, and local child care centers.

Assess Effects

For some companies, decisions about child care involvement will be facilitated by evidence that child care services would help the company attain personnel or public relations goals. In this case, the task force can gather evidence that links child care services with the corporate goals that are defined by the task force. Several sources of such information are located within the company itself:

- Employees' self-reports through survey, interview, focus group, or referral interview can provide insight into such factors as the number of days absent due to child care arrangements, frequency of calls home or to care provider, and aspects of job performance such as traveling, overtime, or transfers that are limited by child care arrangements. This information may be collected when the company explores employees' child care needs. See Appendix D for a sample survey that includes questions for both purposes.

- Supervisors' perceptions of work place behaviors affected by child care, including turnover in their departments caused by child care problems and difficulties in covering work of employees absent because of child care problems.
- Personnel records including exit interviews and annual reviews that mention work problems associated with child care needs—for example, repeated absenteeism precipitated by unreliable child care arrangements and resulting in demotion or firing.

The task force may also wish to obtain information about how other employer-supported child care programs have affected their supporting companies. See Chapter 2 for several case studies and a description of the numerous potential benefits these companies have experienced with their current child care programs.

Synthesize

After collecting relevant information, the next order of business is to compare the profile of employee needs ("demand") with the inventory of available community services ("supply") to identify gaps in services. If the task force thinks that any services are needed, management will probably want a summary of how many or which employees need what kinds of services and a summary of evidence that unmet child care needs are affecting the work place. After weighing this information, management can decide whether the task force should proceed with further investigation of a specific service or services that appear to be most appropriate for company involvement.

Phase III: Analysis and Decision Making

Consider Program Alternatives

Using the data gathered by the task force and the information on program alternatives presented in Part Four of this book, the task force can now describe each of the alternative services or variations of a service that match employees' unmet needs and corporate goals that management would seriously consider implementing. Such proposals generally cover type of service;

eligibility; whether and how community services, resources, and families might be involved; proposed hours, location, and other details determined by the needs assessment to be important characteristics of the new program; possible administrative structures; and relevant legal and insurance issues.

Project Costs and Benefits

Costs can be estimated at this point. They should be made specific to each option, with general estimates of start-up and ongoing costs. Estimated savings through achievement of corporate goals and tax incentives associated with each option under consideration are also critical to consider at this point because they can significantly reduce the net cost of the program. Thus, selection of the most cost-effective program is facilitated by accurate estimates of costs and benefits. Information and procedures for making these projections are found in Chapters 2 and 3.

Identify Resources

Identify the type and amount of resources available from the company and from outside sources. Company contributions can take the form of space, technical assistance, products, and in-kind services, as well as financial contributions. Possible structures for making these contributions should also be considered—whether, for example, they will be considered as part of the cost of doing business or as a charitable contribution.

The structure by which the contribution is made can affect the level of management at which approval must be obtained. In large companies one-time financial contributions to a local child care program can often be decided at a local level, whereas a new company-wide child care policy would often require high-level approval. Both kinds of programs could be designed to solve the same type of child care need, but the possibility of different arrangements allows companies important flexibility.

The level of income that can be reasonably expected from parent fees should be projected. The payment required from parents will determine which parents will be able to use the program and ultimately impact the program's real effect on child care supply and demand.

Select Program

It is at this point that major decisions are made regarding what program is to be implemented and what company resources may be tentatively committed to it. Recommendations are made to the decision-making body about the type of program that should be implemented. A report should be drafted to management covering the following items:

1. The make-up of the task force, its mandate, the process used, and reasons for selection of the process.
2. Relevance of child care needs and services to company goals and priorities.
3. Recommended program (or alternatives):
   a. How it fills the gap between assessed employee needs and community resources.
   b. Complete description of proposed program (or alternatives of each) with relative merits and limitations.
   c. Costs and benefits.

See Appendix D for a sample outline of a task force report. The resources in Appendix F of this book also include a few additional examples of such reports. Program design can be finalized after a decision to implement child care has been reached.

At this point the task force can expand the preliminary program description in order to guide the program's implementation. It should describe exactly what services are to be offered, who will be eligible, how information will be distributed, and what services will be delivered. A detailed budget needs to be spelled out, including the start-up investment and operating budget, if any. Since centers or family day care homes may take a year or more to reach full enrollment, the task force planning such direct services may want to draw up a separate budget for the first year to allow for an initially small program that can be expanded during this period. Informational programs or financial assistance programs also require some time to reach full utilization. The task force can benefit greatly by utilizing the expertise of qualified child care professionals at this stage to ensure a high-quality program at a reasonable budget. Thoughtful planning and full awareness of the many factors that affect quality will help the task force plan a practical, efficient, effective, and affordable program.

The most effective specialists in designing and setting up new child care services are usually those with directly relevant experience. A person who has operated a successful center may not have the somewhat different expertise necessary to design and set up a new center. Likewise, a person who has set up a new center may not have the necessary skills to establish a group of family day care homes or a referral service.

However, for designing and operating all types of programs, it is generally necessary to have knowledge and expertise in the three basic areas of business administration, child development, and early education, so that the program is appropriate from these perspectives. Depending on what consulting resources are available, companies may want assistance from more than one person in designing or operating their programs.

Certain skills or experience are particularly valuable in setting up each of the different types of programs. For example, in setting up or operating a center, a person with experience in full-day center care may provide more appropriate assistance than a person familiar only with morning "nursery school" programs or someone with experience only in public school teaching. Center care for infants and toddlers also requires relevant experience beyond that of the usual preschool program. Setting up any center involves expertise in designing appropriate environments indoors and out, staff selection, policy development, and curriculum development. Setting up family day care homes is significantly different from setting up a center, and a company would benefit from the assistance of a person with direct experience in the field of family day care, including selection, training, and monitoring of providers. The person setting up a referral service, voucher program, or company support of community programs ought to be knowledgeable about community child care services and the issues concerning quality child care. In addition, the effectiveness of referral services depends in part on the counseling and communication skills of the referral staff. Accordingly, staff selection and training are particularly important areas for the specialist setting up a referral service.

Plan Evaluation

If there is a desire to document the new program's benefits to the company, the task force may want to lay the groundwork for a future evaluation. For example, to assess the effects of the program on employee absenteeism, the rates of one group of working parents during a period prior to program implementation might be compared with the same group's rate after they have been using the established program. This comparison would necessitate collecting some of the data prior to the beginning of the service, so the evaluation planning would need to be completed in advance.

Part Four

WHAT OPTIONS DO COMPANIES HAVE AND HOW ARE THEY IMPLEMENTED?

Companies can use a number of different arrangements to help employees with child care. The array of available alternatives makes it possible to design a program that uses resources efficiently, yields maximum benefits, and allows for the degree ofcontrol and involvement desired in any particular case. A child care program can at the same time fit the specific needs of parent employees and complement community resources. The following chapters describe in detail program options ranging from those requiring a small amount of company involvement to those requiring substantial commitment.

Child care options fall into four categories. First, flexible personnel policies often can help employees reduce the need for out-of-home child care. They include, for example, flextime, job sharing, and part-time work. Second, informational programs help employees locate existing child care and other related resources, including child care information and referral programs and educational programs for parents. Third, financial assistance programs are designed primarily to lower the cost of child care. Assistance can take the form of child care reimbursement or a corporate contribution to community child care programs. And fourth, direct services constitute the most familiar form of employer assistance. Such programs may be managed by the company or contracted to an outside firm. They include child care centers, and family day care homes.

The following chapters focus on the basic child care program options within these four categories. Suggestions for variations and combinations of services are given, and guidelines are provided for tailoring program alternatives. Specific information is presented on setting up each type of program and identifying the costs involved. These program options can be tailored or combined to fit the specific needs of the employer as well as employees and to complement community child care resources. It is by considering child care from these three perspectives—the employer, the employee, and the community—that the most successful programs are designed. A general discussion of these perspectives is presented here to assist companies in selecting the most appropriate type of child care involvement for their situation.

The Company Perspective

Both the amount of support that a company will give to child care and the form it takes can be adapted to a company's type of resources. It is not always necessary, for example, to give large financial contributions in order to help with child care. Companies can give direct financial assistance or support child care through donations of space, equipment, products, or in-kind services. Some of the more commonly donated services include legal advice, accounting, copying, printing, payroll or other financial services, and maintenance supplies and services. Donation of such services, equipment, or space can often achieve the same goals as direct financial assistance because it lowers program overhead and ultimately reduces the cost to parents. It can also improve the quality of the child care services and be relatively simple and inexpensive to provide.

Companies also have different preferences as to their degree of administrative involvement in child care. These preferences can be reflected in the option chosen and its design characteristics, as well as the decision to initiate the service alone or in concert with others. Companies that prefer close involvement in order to have maximum control over decision making may choose an in-house program; those that prefer not to be involved in the ongoing administration can have an outside agency run it for them. Those wanting to share program responsibility with others can make cooperative agreements for the establishment and/or the operation of the program with other businesses, unions, non-profit organizations such as community agencies or colleges, child care management firms, or employee groups.

Companies that want to use child care as a management tool can include management goals in the program selection and design. Some may want to use child care to attract and retain workers, reduce absenteeism, improve productivity, or achieve a number of other goals discussed in Part Two. To gain an exclusive recruiting advantage, for example, they may decide to operate a company center exclusively for employees' children. Other companies, whose goal is to enhance their community image, may prefer a program that can be used by the public as well as by employees.

The Parent Employee Perspective

Tailoring company resources to the particular needs of the work force makes the most effective use of company resources and ultimately brings the greatest return on investment to the company. The needs of one workforce can be very different from those of another. In order to design programs that match parents' needs and preferences, the following five distinct care requirements should be considered.

Adequate Supply. There is a shortage of child care in most communities today. Some types of care are more likely to be in short supply than others. For example, shortage of care for infants and school-age children (before and after school) is generally more acute than shortage of care for preschoolers. Some communities may also have less care available in particular geographic areas.

Reasonable Cost. Very few families can afford the full cost of good child care. Even middle-income families may have difficulty affording care because it is such an expensive service, particularly when families have more than one child. In many parts of the country, care for an infant costs $75–$150 per week, care for a preschool child costs $45–$95 per week, and care after school for six- to twelve-year-olds costs about $25 per week. The problem that such costs present to most families—particularly, low-income and single-parent families—is clear. The result of these high costs is that, even when child care is available, many parents cannot afford to use it.

Information on Existing Services. Parents need to know how to find the care that is available. Child care centers are the easiest to locate, although some are not advertised or listed in the telephone book. However, the most frequently used form of care outside the parents' home is family day care, and these homes are more difficult to find. They are rarely well advertised, and parents have to rely on word of mouth to find them. States that require family day care homes to be licensed have a listing of licensed homes with the licensing agency, but parents are usually unaware that such a list exists. Most day care homes are unlicensed, and there thus is no central listing. The frequency with which these more informal arrangements change increases the difficulty of locating them. A few communities have developed information and referral agencies to give child care information, but most have not.

Convenience. Parents need convenient and accessible care, including hours and days that match work shifts. Many parents have difficulty finding care available early enough in the morning or late enough in the evening to care for the child during work hours and to allow for commuting time. Scheduling difficulties are particularly acute for parents who need care during night or evening shifts and on weekends, for almost no child care is available during those times.

Child care arrangements also should be in a location that does not cause transportation problems for the working parent. Some parents must travel an additional 20 miles or more at each end of their work day in order to transport their children to and from care. Parents with school-age children or other children using two or more different arrangements face even more complicated logistics. The resulting stress and increased likelihood of missing a part of the work day are of concern to employers as well as employees.

Quality of Care. Parents want care that meets their own standards of quality. If it does not, they will not use it. Parents constrained to settle for care that they are uncomfortable with experience anxiety and stress. Research on child care centers has shown that there are three important factors in assessing quality: (1) an adequate ratio of staff to children, (2) relatively small numbers of children in each group, and (3) caregiver training in child development and early childhood education.[1] Indicators of quality are discussed in each of the following chapters. Employer support can be an important factor in increasing the quality of the child care available to parents.

The Community Perspective

The child care supply in the community has a direct impact on the design of a successful employer-supported child care program. Care that duplicates existing services may have utilization problems and is not likely to have the same appeal to employees as one that fills a gap in community services. In many cases it is possible to identify community programs that need only some alterations to better match worker child care needs; thus the company would not have to start an entirely new program.

A company that does initiate new services, however, will be wise to use information about community resources and design its program to complement existing services. For example, in a community where there is space for children in existing programs but workers cannot afford the cost, a child care reimbursement system may be the most cost-effective approach. Conversely, in a community where there is an insufficient supply of child care, a reimbursement system would be ineffective.

* * *

Integrating the needs and resources of the company, the employee, and the community does not have to be complicated, but it is necessary to consider all three aspects to maximize the effectiveness of the program.

Endnotes

1. R. Roupp, J. Travers, F. Glantz and C. Coelen, *Children at the Center: Final Report of the National Day Care Study* (Cambridge, Mass: Abt Associates, 1979).

Chapter 6

FLEXIBLE PERSONNEL POLICIES

Many companies offer their employees flexibility in work arrangements. Variations include alternative work schedules, job sharing, permanent part-time employment, voluntary work time reductions, leaves of absence, and work at home. The findings in the General Mills American Family Report (1980–81) illustrate a growing acceptance among major corporations of personnel and work policies geared to the needs of working parents. For instance, 60% of the benefits officers who participated in the study reported that their companies had policies allowing employees to return to work at the same pay and seniority after a leave of absence. Forty-eight percent allowed them "the right to refuse a relocation or transfer with no career penalty." Many benefits officers also reported that they expected their companies to adopt more flexible policies by 1985, including job sharing (expected by 70%), freedom to set a work schedule as long as employees work 70 hours every 2 weeks (expected by 66%), a choice between a 7:00 a.m. to 3:00 p.m., 8:00 a.m. to 4:00 p.m., or 9:00 a.m. to 5:00 p.m. workday (expected by 60%), and a shorter workweek with less pay (expected by 51%).[1]

This kind of flexibility is especially important—and sometimes essential—for employees who have children. Even parents who already have reliable arrangements for their regular child care often need flexibility when children are sick, have medical appointments, or require school visits. Parents who share child care with a spouse, relative, or friend need flexibility to schedule convenient work hours. Employees in companies that support direct child care services probably use their flexible time options less often because the services may be specifically designed to accommodate these special instances. But most parents need

Table 6-1 Flextime Options

Options	*Starting Times*	*Who Sets Start Times*	*Start Time Variability*	*Duration of the Work Day*	*Hours in the Work Day*
Staggered shifts	6:30–9:30 a.m.	Employer sets start times at spread intervals	Employees must report at the same time each day	Work hours and lunch period fixed	No carryover from day to day
Employee-chosen staggered starts	"	Employees choose their own start times	"	"	"
Flexible starts	"	"	Employees can vary their start times from day to day	"	"
Flexible hours	"	"	"	The length of the lunch period can vary	"
Flexible days	"	"	"	"	"Credit" or "debit" hours can be carried from day to day

NOTE: The compressed work week transforms the full-time five-day week into 4½, 4, or 3 days. The most common form is the 4-day week, 10 hours per day. Three-day weeks involve 12 or 12½ hour schedules, and a recent innovation provides biweekly schedules of 9-hour days for 9 days, with the tenth day off.

flexibility for emergencies or when child care arrangements fail. Flexible personnel policies can help by giving parent-employees alternatives that allow them to maintain their own delicate balance between work and family life. Sections of this chapter describe how four kinds of flexible policies can help parents make and maintain workable child care arrangements.

Alternative or Flexible Work Schedules

Employers give employees choices about their work schedules in a number of different ways. Under "flextime" arrangements, the employee can choose which hours (but not how many) to work. Some approaches give the employee very little control (for example, staggered work shifts, when the employer sets the possible shift starting times). Others give the employee a great deal of individual choice (for example, flexible starts which set different starting times each day, and flexible days, which carry credit or debit hours over the work week). New Ways to Work, a nonprofit research and resource organization on work alternatives, developed the chart shown in Table 6–1 to illustrate the differences between many of the flextime options.[2]

According to one study, 12.8% of all nongovernmental organizations with 50 or more employees used flextime in 1977.[3] In others words, about 2.5 to 3.5 million workers could choose flexible work schedules in this country in 1977. Flextime has become a relatively well-known alternative for companies that want their employees to have some flexibility in adapting work and personal life schedules. The concept is probably more workable for some types of workers than for others, it is more widely used in office and professional settings than in production or assembly line settings. There is some concern among union representatives that flextime may undermine the guarantees of the 8-hour day and adequate compensation for overtime work. Although the idea is becoming more popular in some places, it may not be available to the majority of working parents within the foreseeable future.

Flextime clearly does not offer the solution to the child care concerns of all working parents, but it can be useful in some situations. Flextime may be especially helpful to parents who share the responsibility of caring for children at home. It can work well, for instance, if one parent cares for the children in the morning before school and the other picks them up from school in the afternoon. It also may allow parents some latitude in matching the work day with the schedules of local child care providers (for instance, allowing parents to use a center that opens slightly later than the normal starting time). Because flex-time does not cut the number of hours in the work day, however, it generally does not lessen the need for child care services or cut down on the child caring tasks of working parents.

Permanent Part-Time Employment and Job Sharing

Many parents would like to be able to work part time during their children's younger years. Many of today's mothers cannot afford to take unpaid time off after maternity leave, and they return reluctantly to full time work. Others try to plan so that children are born between jobs or at timely points in a career, but it is very difficult to give a full share of attention to both jobs and children. For many women, and for a growing number of fathers, part-time work offers a valuable temporary or long-term solution.

Traditionally, the majority (about 70% in 1977)[4] of part-time workers in this country have been women; they have also been in low-status jobs with poor wages and no benefits. Increasingly companies are realizing the value to both employer and employee of providing opportunities for less than full-time work that includes job security and benefits. One way to structure permanent part-time jobs is through job sharing, when two people voluntarily share the responsibilities of one full-time position, with prorated salary and benefits. Job sharing seems to work especially well for couples and friends; people who have known each other before and are compatible are able to adjust to the responsibility of sharing a job. Job sharing work also offers companies the benefit of the energy, credentials, and expertise of two people for the price of one.[5]

Another way to create part-time positions is to allow employees to voluntarily reduce their work time through a time-and-income tradeoff. Employees may choose to work, for example, 10%, 20%, or 30% less than full time by reducing the number of hours per day or days per week worked. It is especially important that employees who choose this plan be protected from work speedups and be guaranteed adequate fringe benefits.

Permanent part-time employment is one of the options most sought by parents. A reduction in the number of hours worked per week allows parents to maintain a reasonable family income while spending the necessary time with their children.

Leaves of Absence

Employers can also help parents by allowing extended maternity or paternity leaves with an assured return to the job at the same salary and seniority level. A four- to six-week maternity leave given under most insurance plans may not be enough time to get the child settled into the family and arrange adequate child care services. Some companies offer new parents the opportunity to return to work with reduced hours after a maternity leave. First Interstate Bank in Los Angeles, California developed a modified work plan in response to the suggestions of a number of middle-level managers who were pregnant at the same time and who worked out an acceptable plan with the bank. Such non-traditional solutions can make a big difference for professional or managerial employees who do not want to leave their careers even when their children are very young.

Another modification that companies can make is to expand their "sick leave" policies to include "family leave" time which parents can use to care for sick children or other family members.

Work at Home

Many professionals have long had the option of working at home at least part of the time—for example, college professors, writers, and computer programmers. Continental Bank in Chicago, among others, established an experimental program where word processing was done on the employee's home terminal. Many parents would be delighted to have the option of working in the electronic cottages envisioned by Toffler in *The Third Wave* or Deken in *The Electronic Cottage*. Others who view work as a chance to get out of the house would not find at home work appealing. Although it may have limited appeal, work at home is an important concept and a helpful policy for some working parents.

Flexible personnel and work scheduling policies can help parents find solutions to the difficulties involved in balancing work and child rearing. Finding the right balance can be difficult, particularly if there are not many child care resources in the community. But companies that are aware of the problems faced by parents, that offer some flexibility in scheduling and arrangements and that support needed child care services reap the beneits of a more productive work force.

Endnotes

1. General Mills American Family Report—1980–81, *Families At Work: Strengths and Strains* (Minneapolis, Minn.: General Mills, 1981).
2. New Ways to Work, 149 Ninth Street, San Francisco, California 94103.
3. S. Nollen and V. Martin, *Alternative Work Schedules, Part I: Flextime* (New York, New York: American Management Association, 1978).

4. R. Smith, *Women in the Labor Force in 1990* (Washington, D. C.: Urban Institute, 1979).
5. Information on job sharing is available from the National Job Sharing Network through New Ways to Work.

Chapter 7

INFORMATION AND REFERRAL PROGRAMS

Child care information and referral services give employees general information about child care, suggestions for selecting good care, and referrals to specific local child care providers. Such information can be made available through distribution of printed materials, by referrals on the telephone, or in personal interviews. Parents may receive general information (for example, a simple checklist of what to look for or names of some local programs) or staff may individualize the service for each parent, matching specific family needs with providers who have available openings.

Selecting a Program

The type of child care information and referral program developed by an employer will depend, at least in part, on the amount of child care information available in the community. There are two types of information and referral services: (1) generic information and referral services that offer information about a range of services in the community, and (2) programs limited to child care information and referral. During the past two decades, many communities have developed generic information and referral systems to help people find and utilize the services they need. These programs consolidate information about social services in a particular community; they have "a single comprehensive base of information about all of the services available in a community."[1] In contrast to the generic approach, child care information and referral services concentrate specifically on child care. The information in this chapter refers to specialized child care information and referral services (CCIR's).

In addition to providing basic information on local child care programs, information and referral services may also help parents understand the complexities of the child care market and give them the information needed to make informed choices, work with child care providers to improve the quality of care in the community, and act as child care advocates in the community to promote the development of needed services.

In areas where there is no existing information and referral service, any information that the company can provide may be helpful to parents, whether it is made available in lists or directories for all employees or by retaining a consultant or staff member to provide individualized services. Where child care information and referral agencies do exist, referrals may be available to employees of local companies. However, a company may want to supplement or expand existing services by giving additional information, focusing on a specific location or service type, determining how well existing child care facilities meet the needs of the company's employees, or following up with parents to ensure that they find adequate care within a reasonable amount of time.

A high-quality child care information and referral service requires comparable information on a large number of providers and a system for cross-filing entries so that information can be accessed easily. Where such systems do not exist, employers with expertise in microcomputer technology may assist the child care community to establish and operate systems serving employees and the whole community.

Minneapolis was the first city to develop a computerized child care information and referral service, supported by the contributions of Honeywell, Inc., Williams Steel & Hardware, Northwestern National Life Insurance Company, General Mills Foundation, and others. The rationale for developing the system was twofold: The community needed a comprehensive system available to all citizens and decision makers needed access to the kind of information generated by an automated system. Data are distributed throughout the community to assist public and private sector decision makers in child care decisions.[2]

Efforts to develop such computerized CCIR's are underway in other cities.[3] In Portland, Oregon, for example, a project sponsored by the Portland State University is using computer technology to profile child care supply and demand throughout the community. In a segment of the project funded through the Administration for Children, Youth, and Families, U.S. Department of Health and Human Services, the child care needs of 13 employers and 7,000 employees will be surveyed. Employer support of these kinds of efforts could make a substantial impact on the effectiveness and efficiency of child care information and referral for the entire community.

Child care information and referral services are becoming more and more important in urban areas, because they help make the child care market work better by linking consumers to sources of supply, maximizing consumer choice, and promoting informed decisions.[4]

The National Employer Supported Child Care Project identified 36 companies whose primary child care program was information and referral and an additional 6 who offered CCIR in combination with another primary child care service. Most of the companies with in-house programs utilized one or two staff people to run the service; employers who contracted for the service with an outside agency generally had access to all of the referral staff of that agency.

The average number of families served per month by these programs ranged from 2 to 601. The methods used to distribute information also varied. All of the companies provided names of potential providers, basic information on the types of child care available, and information on parenting. In addition 20 evaluated potential providers, 15 posted information on child care, and 33 followed up to see if the child care found was satisfactory.

Following are examples of child care information and referral services developed by or for companies:

Gillette Company; First National Bank of Boston; John Hancock Mutual Life Insurance Company; Federal Reserve Bank of Boston, Mass.

These companies contract with the Child Care Resource Center in Cambridge, Massachusetts, a non-profit agency, to provide information and referral for individual employees.

Mills Memorial Hospital; Peninsula Hospital Medical Center; Sequoia Hospital, Burlingame, California

These hospitals contract with the Expanded Child Care Referral Program of the Child Care Coordinating Council of San Mateo County for referral. Employees receive information beyond that generally available to the public from this agency, including evaluation of potential providers, follow-up to ensure appropriate placement, and recruitment of providers for odd-hours and weekend care.

MASCO, Boston, Mass.

A consortium of six health care agencies and two schools contributed to start this information and referral service geared to the needs of medical personnel. MASCO is a service organization for hospitals that brought together the Harvard Community Health Plan, Joslin Diabetes Clinic, Children's Hospital Medical Center, New England Deaconess Hospital, Harvard Medical School, Harvard School of Public Health, Sydney Farber Cancer Institute, and Beth Israel Hospital to institute the service.

Prime Computer, Inc., Natick, Mass.

The company produces and distributes a booklet with information about choosing child care and provides the names and descriptions of local providers.

Steelcase, Inc., Grand Rapids, Mich.

Child care coordinators who are company employees provide information and referral, technical assistance to existing providers, advocacy and parent education through individual conferences, workshops, and written materials.

South Community Hospital, Oklahoma City

The Community Connection program provides in-house information and referral.

Mountain Bell, Denver, Colo.

A full-time staff consultant provides information and referral and runs seminars for employees on parenting and child care issues.

Lankenau Hospital, Philadelphia, Pa.

In addition to a child care center for infants and preschoolers, the hospital provides information and referral for employees who need other types of child care.

Program Advantages and Disadvantages

Advantages	*Disadvantages*	*Solutions*
Short start-up time. Relatively low cost. Utilizes existing child care services. Provides information on employee child care needs and use. Can be initial stage of larger child care initiative.	Does not improve the supply, quality, or cost of existing care.	Combine information and referral with other program types, such as donations to existing programs. Use child care information and referral as a springboard for a more comprehensive child care program.

Program Development Decisions

Administration. Employer-supported information and referral programs have been arranged in several ways as mentioned above. The company can contract with an existing agency, such as a child care information and referral agency, or in-house staff can be used. The company also may contribute to the development of a centralized child care information and referral for general use by the community.

The Information Offered. In small communities with few child care resources, parents may only need the names of all of the local providers. Employers can gather and furnish this information quite simply in lists or directories. In large communities where choices are more complex, the information and referral services generally identify parent preferences, check the available resources, make an appropriate match, and give the parent names of several providers. Parents may also receive information about how to select an appropriate program for their child.

This referral information may be sufficiently detailed that parents can select programs based on complete information. (For instance, the parent may want to know about all of the people who care for infants within a mile of one location, or all of the afterschool programs that serve a local school.) If there are many options in each category, more detailed information may be needed. (For instance, the parent may want to know which preschool centers open until 6 p.m., which charge less than $50 per week, or which have an immediate opening for a two-year-old.)

The basis of the referral service is information kept on each local child care provider which gives the information and referral service the ability to (1) report on each individual provider; (2) cross-index provider information by location, type, or any other variable of interest; and (3) look at the overall supply of child care in the community. For instance, information and referral programs can conduct ongoing assessments of the adequacy of child care supply by comparing facility data with requests made by parents. They can also use this information to promote changes or expansion in the supply of care. Companies can use their information to promote changes themselves or they can work with other agencies to do so.

Combined Programs. Child care information and referral programs often work well in combination with other child care options because information is a basic necessity for choosing care. It works well with reimbursement plans; employees can be referred to appropriate programs and get help paying for them if needed. It works well with parent education because parents often need other information about child rearing and community resources than is generally available through CCIR's. It can be a first step in developing cooperative arrangements with local programs as the company recognizes the child care needs that are not being met in the community. Information and referral records can be structured to give a clear account of the kinds of child care services desired by employees, the problems they encounter in finding adequate care, and the local gaps in supply.

Starting a Program

Ways of Contracting. A company that wants to contract with an outside agency to provide information and referral for employees can (1) arrange to have agency staff provide the services on site by being available at the work site full time or for specified days and times; (2) arrange to reserve specific hours for telephone contacts between employees and staff at either the agency's regular number or a special hotline number; or (3) arrange for employees to meet face-to-face with referral staff off site at the agency offices or in another convenient facility where workers can feel relaxed and comfortable away from the job. The company can pay monthly or yearly fees or a fee per employee served.

Staff Qualifications and Job Tasks. Referral staff should be familiar with all kinds of child care, understand the child care resources in the community, be able to organize and manage large amounts of detailed information, and have good communication skills. There are five major tasks of referral staff as follows:

First, to provide referrals to individual parents and to talk with employee groups about the information and referral service program and about child care in general.

Second, to establish an information system with the capability of reporting clearly on individual providers, groups of providers, and other variables of interest, as well as on child care in the community.

Third, to establish a data bank by:

- defining the service area—i.e., identifying the parts of the community that are covered.
- defining the individual pieces of data required for each provider.
- identifying all providers and collecting information on each.

- organizing the system of record keeping and retrieval.
- updating files regularly.
- developing a system to track parent inquiries, referrals, and outcomes.

Basic information generally kept on each child care facility includes:

- provider name
- address, zip code
- telephone number
- contact person
- type of facility (day care center, nursery school, head start center, family day care, after school, camp)
- program curriculum
- program focus (extended day programs, infant programs, drop-in care)
- number of children served
- ages of children served
- hours of operation
- cost
- special services available (for handicapped or sick children, evening or weekend care, overtime)
- capacity
- whether licensed or registered
- special restrictions
- staff qualifications
- accreditation by professional associations (such as NAEYC)

Information kept on parents who contact the program includes:

- parent name
- address, zip code
- telephone number
- number of children
- ages of each child
- other job-related information (department, job status, etc.)
- hours and days of care needed
- special services needed
- preference for type of care
- special restrictions
- other demographic information (marital status, family income)

This information will help answer important questions about employees' child care needs, such as:

- Who needs child care (their locations, job titles, departments)?
- What child care problems do they face (finding infant care, after school care, or paying for care)?
- Does supply match demand?
- What are the kinds of care that cannot be found?

After collecting this information over a period of time, the company may decide to provide direct child care services or to share information with local child care providers and planning groups.

Analysis of this information about parents, along with the information about providers, will allow the staff to facilitate future analysis of supply, demand, and the degree to which the CCIR actually helps employers meet child care needs. It may also help companies decide whether to provide child care supports in addition to the referral service.

The fourth task is to work with licensing departments and other local agencies in sharing data and resources.

And finally, the fifth task is to work with the Human Resources Department (or other company staff) to publicize the information and referral service.

Information and Referral within Employee Assistance Programs. Companies can consider placing their child care information and referral service within an employee assistance program (EAP). Although most EAPs were developed primarily to provide counseling for substance abuse and emotional problems, they also play an important preventive role by helping people get the information they need about a range of issues *before* a serious problem develops. For instance, Steelcase's Counseling and Referral Service regularly deals with problems of two-paycheck and single-parent families, including questions about household responsibilities, time priorities, finances, and child care. The drawback of placing child care within an EAP, however, is that employees may associate the stigma attached to other EAP services to child care as well and thus may hesitate to use it. It also may be less visible to them, because they may not think to look for child care in an EAP.

Costs. Companies in the National Employer Supported Child Care Project reported that they support in-house information and referral programs with money and in-kind services. Nine of the companies reported that they provided start-up money to get their information and referral service going and other companies have given in-kind supports such as space, administrative services, and supplies. Fourteen reported that they pay for contracted services based on the number of individuals served.

Parent Choice of Providers. CCIR's do not directly advise parents as to which facility would be best for their children. They do, however, provide parents with information on how to select a good child care program and generally attempt some degree of quality control, such as referring only to licensed facilities, following up on complaints and other feedback from parents, and stopping referrals to providers with whom there consistently are problems.

To the extent that each parent has his or her own criteria for care, a referral program providing the most factual data about each program enhances parental choice.

*Liability.** Although operating a child care resource and referral agency is not a high-risk venture, there are some unique areas of liability. For example, companies are often concerned about the liability for a referral made to a child provider who subsequently endangers the health and welfare of the child. The following short-run steps can be taken to minimize risk: refrain from providing quality recommendations regarding any child care provider; issue a disclaimer of warranty with each referral; and require that providers carry adequate liability insurance in order to be listed by the agency. Longer-term solutions include devising and procuring malpractice insurance for negligent referrals (group insurance would be the most cost-effective) and petitioning the state legislature for a grant of statutory immunity. Immunity statutes for lawyers and other professional services currently exist in many states and could provide the model for such legislation. Referral agencies are also exposed to potential liability from providers whom they exclude or delete from their files. Agencies should use good business judgment, establish standard referral policies, operate in a non-discriminatory fashion, and provide a reasonable level of due process such as notice and an opportunity to appeal an exclusion or deletion from referral files. More information is available from the Child Care Law Center publication, "Protection from Liability for Child Care Resource and Referral Agencies."

This summary is provided as a brief description of selected liability concerns. Employers should consult their own attorneys for assistance in identifying and resolving their individual liability issues.

Endnotes

1. M. G. Cline, "Generic Information and Referral and Specialized Child Care Resources and Referral," *Project Connections* (unpublished, December 1981), p. 3.
2. Letter, Lauren P. Weck, General Mills Foundation, P.O. Box 1113, Minn., Minn. 55440.

---

*This section was written by Kathleen A. Murray, Attorney at Law, Child Care Law Center.

3. In Cambridge, Massachusetts, the Child Care Resource Center is developing software that could be standardized and used in agencies across the country to make it possible to start up a system quickly and at a reasonable cost. Contact CCRS, 24 Thorndike Street, Cambridge, Massachusetts 02141.
4. J. A. Levine, "The Prospects and Dilemmas of Child Care Information and Referral," in *Day Care: Scientific and Social Policy Issues*, eds. E. Zigler and E. Gordon (Boston, Mass.: Auburn House, 1982), pp. 378–399.

Chapter 8

EDUCATIONAL PROGRAMS FOR PARENTS

Some employer-supported programs are designed to give working parents information on parenting and local resources and to provide recognition and support for employees who feel the stress of balancing work and family roles. Research, such as the American Management Association's study of executive stress, has shown that problems at home can have negative repercussions at work.[1] The reasoning behind the development of educational programs for working parents is that helping employees to become better parents also helps them to become better workers.

Parents want to know what to expect from children of different ages and how to reward, discipline, and teach their children what to do in times of crisis or difficulty. Fewer of today's parents can find this information in the traditional ways by talking to neighbors and relatives or by watching family members and friends raise their children. Family life has changed substantially over the past decade, and there are increasing numbers of working mothers and high rates of divorce and remarriage. Parents need help in dealing with all of these developments. Increasingly, fathers are assuming more responsibility for parenting. Parents of both sexes are faced with difficult situations involving child-rearing roles, custody, step-parenting, and changing family relationships. Parents need basic information on child rearing, explanation of different kinds of parenting, and help in finding community resources such as child care, health care, and family counseling. Finally, many need to be able to discuss these problems with other parents.

Selecting a Program

Although educational programs are not direct child care services in the same sense as the other major program options discussed in Part Three, they provide an important service that many parents need. Furthermore, they can be used as a transition for companies considering other possible child care services. A program may have one or several of the following purposes:

1. To provide *basic information* about parenting, child care, and other community resources for parents; to stimulate discussion about the problems and benefits of being a working parent; and to provide information about existing company policies and programs that benefit parents.
2. To *help assess the family support and child care needs* of the working parents in the company in preparation for the development of another child care service, or to stimulate discussion among management and parent employee groups about company options in helping working parents.
3. To *supplement another kind of child care service,* such as a reimbursement or information and referral, by offering information needed by parents in a more structured way.

Since parent education is not a direct child care service program, no effort was made by the National Employer Supported Child Care Project to identify all of the companies that currently support educational programs. However, a sample of companies with parent education programs was included in the survey. Twenty-three reported that parent education was their primary or sole child care service. The size of these programs ranged from 4 to 98 families per month; of the 28 companies that provided enrollment figures, 8 served fewer than 20 families per month and 20 served 20 or more families. The majority of companies reported that they used more than one method of presenting information to parents, including seminars, lectures, discussion groups, and posting of information.

The following examples illustrate programs serving employees in different kinds of companies:

Citibank NA, New York, N. Y.

The Staff Advisory Services Department runs small group education workshops on topics such as dual-career families and parenting and refers employees to community child care resources.

Society National Bank, Cleveland, Ohio

The bank contracts with the Center for Human Resources for a series of four working-parent workshops.

Mountain Bell, Denver, Colo.

A full-time staff consultant runs seminars for employees on parenting and child care issues, as well as providing information and referral.

Steelcase, Inc., Grand Rapids, Mich.

Child Care Coordinators provide parent education through individual conferences, workshops, and written materials, as well as information and referral, technical assistance to existing providers, and child care advocacy.

Honeywell, Inc., Minneapolis, Minn.

The Corporate and Community Responsibility Department designed the curricula for a series of six seminars for employers, in addition to providing support for other child care programs.

COPE, Boston, Mass.

The agency, whose initials are an acronym for Coping With the Overall Pregnancy/Parenting Experience, organizes "Parent Fairs" in shopping malls, office parks, and companies. The fair, which lasts one or two days, includes materials on over 100 local agencies and services for parents and parents to be. Topics include pregnancy, health and safety, child development, special needs, fertility, adoption, adolescence, after-school and summer programs, and local child care services. Employees can use their break time to peruse the exhibits and talk with the 3 to 4 professionals who run the fair and who are available to facilitate discussion and answer questions.

Program Advantages and Disadvantages

Advantages	*Disadvantages*	*Solutions*
Relatively inexpensive, requiring a small amount of staff time, a group leader, space, and time for employees.	Not a direct child care service.	Link programs with direct child care.
Adaptable, easily changed to reflect parent and company concerns.	Varying utilization.	Use parent information programs as a springboard for a more comprehensive child care program.
Supplements other company programs—for instance, supports employee assistance or employee relations efforts.		Use parent input to help determine content and times of meetings.

Program Development Decisions

The major decisions involved in developing a parent education program have to do with type and amount of information offered, format, and management of the program.

The type and amount of information offered will vary with the needs of parents. The following formats have been used by companies responding in the National Employer Supported Child Care Project:

- Written information: posted for employees to read; printed in company newsletters, magazines, or other publications; or set forth in a more formal document that outlines company policies and local resources.
- Presentations in group discussions or seminars: using "expert" presenters, facilitated by company staff or consultants, ranging from formal lecture format to informal, ongoing discussion group.
- Information presented in a "fair" where employees can get information from brochures or representatives of local service agencies on all kinds of services, including child care and other parent services.

Programs are often managed in-house using staff from the personnel, human resources, or employee assistance departments. Or they may be developed and managed by outside experts under contract with an individual consultant, child care agency, human services agency, college, or other educational institution.

Starting a Program

Companies that use staff to run in-house parent education programs may structure the program as an adjunct to another service—that is, as part of an in-house information and referral service or as part of an existing employee assistance program. In these cases, the staff already has the expertise needed to develop and run a program.

Companies that do not have this kind of in-house expertise can contract with one of the many existing qualified community groups or agencies providing educational services for parents. It is often more cost-effective to make use of the existing expertise in the community than to develop an in-house service, unless the company sees parent education as a way to open the door for other child care services. In the latter case it may be important to develop company expertise on the needs, preferences, and problems of employees.

Examples of agencies that are currently providing employer-supported seminars include the Texas Institute for Families in Houston, Texas; Wheelock College in Boston, Massachusetts; Parents at the Workplace in St. Paul, Minnesota; and the Center for Human Resources in Cleveland, Ohio. Other local organizations such as child care advocacy agencies, colleges, child care management groups, and non-profit human services agencies are also resources for companies that want to contract for this service.

The staff member or consultant who develops written parent education materials will gather information from local agencies, write appropriate descriptions, and distribute materials. The person who is in charge of group meetings also needs a background or interest in parenting and child care issues, group facilitation skills (ability to include participants, elicit comments, and help the group focus on important topics), and the ability to summarize content for the group and for company administrators.

The program can be designed to fit the needs of the particular parent group being served. There are seven major considerations in designing programs with a group or seminar format:

1. *The number of sessions needed.* Single sessions can be useful for presenting targeted information such as where to find child care in the community. A series of sessions has the advantage of giving the participants time to feel easy in the group, to give and receive information, and to be involved in discussions with other parent participants. In the companies studied, a series usually consisted of 4 to 6 sessions.
2. *The kind of presentations.* The basic content can be presented in a formal lecture or in discussions. If the lecture method is used, parents should have time to talk about the issues and ask questions. Sessions can be divided into a brief formal presentation period and a longer period for guided discussion and perhaps problem solving, using a case study or experiences of the participants as examples. In the discussion format, the leader is prepared to elicit certain kinds of content from participants or to guide the discussion so basic points are covered.
3. *Scheduling.* It is possible to plan sessions that occur during employee break time or on release time. In planning the time for meetings, it is important to consider the desires of the employees. Some prefer sessions right after work or in the evenings because they do not want to take time out of a busy

schedule. Lunch time meetings are popular with some employees. Break time combined with a small amount of work time has also been used successfully.

4. *Group size.* Appropriate group size depends in part on the format. Informal discussion and group participation requires a smaller group—generally between 10 and 20 people. More formal presentations, such as a lecture by a visiting expert, can accommodate a much larger group.
5. *Written materials.* Written materials can supplement material presented in group meetings. Such materials might include reprints of articles, lists of effective parenting techniques, or descriptions of local resources.
6. *Topics.* Possible topics for parent education meetings can include handling work and family problems, discipline, local services for families, information on how to select and evaluate child care, local activities for families, the stages of child development, parent development, single- and stepparenthood, and how to work effectively with a child's babysitter or teacher.
7. *Follow-up.* Group leaders can contact participants to determine whether the meeting was useful to them and to answer additional questions. This can be done individually or using a standard form that includes questions about the value of the information provided and suggestions for the next time. At the end of a session or series, parents may give additional information that would be useful to the company in planning services, including the kind of child care currently used and programs for dealing with child care problems and needs. The leader might write a report for company management outlining employee reactions to the program, their suggestions for the future, and the leader's suggestions for changes for the next series. This kind of feedback helps management evaluate the effectiveness of the program and informs it about employee needs.

Educational programs for parents are relatively inexpensive. For example, the cost of a seminar lasting from one to two and a half hours ranged from $50 to $300 in 1981. No start-up expenditures are required other than those associated with hiring a staff member or consultant. Direct ongoing costs include the preparation of materials for distribution and salary or session-by-session payment for group leaders.

Educational programs are a relatively inexpensive way for companies to express concern for employees' quality of life, and they are sufficiently flexible that a company can tailor them to its own goals and workforce. At the same time they give families new resources and guidance in handling parenting dilemmas and a forum for mutual support.

Endnotes

1. A. Kiev and V. Kohn, *Executive Stress* (New York: AMACOM, A Division of American Management Associations, 1979), p. 2.

Chapter 9

REIMBURSEMENT PROGRAMS

The primary problem with child care for many parents is that available services cost more than they can afford. Employers who wish to help their employees meet the cost burden of child care may offer a reimbursement or subsidy plan to cover some or all of the cost. This alternative may be attractive for companies that do not want to provide direct services themselves but do want to provide support for employees who choose their own child care services. It is also particularly attractive to very small companies and those with a widely dispersed work force. Reimbursements work best in communities having an adequate supply of convenient quality care. In most communities, however, care is often substandard or in low supply. It is, therefore, also important to help upgrade the quality and/or increase the supply in order for reimbursement to be effective.

Reimbursement can be part of the flexible benefit plan discussed in Chapter 11, or it can be given in addition to benefits already offered. It performs the same function as certain corporate contributions (discussed in Chapter 10) which lower tuition costs to parents or purchase child care spaces. Each of these mechanisms—reimbursements, corporate contributions, and purchase of spaces—are ways of giving financial assistance which differ only slightly in their design.

Child care reimbursements can pay for care in child care centers, in family day care homes, or with neighbors or relatives. The payment can be made for the program ordinarily used by the employee or it can be made available for selected programs that match employer specifications regarding location, quality, and service. Reimbursement schedules can be at whatever intervals the parties arrange—that is, so much per month, week, or hour or even on an annual basis. Payment can be made to the employee or directly to the child care provider. The purpose remains the same: to lower the cost of child care for parents.

Selecting a Program

Reimbursement systems can serve particular groups of employees or the total employee population. Major variations in the program that allow for individualization include the amount of payment to differently situated employees, the amount of verification and paperwork required, and the types of care for which parents can receive reimbursement. Programs can be tailored to a particular company, and they are basically simple to set up and operate. The cost depends almost entirely on the company's rate of payment and the number of users; administrative costs are minimal.

Seventeen companies with reimbursement programs participated in the National Employer Supported Child Care Project study. Program size varied from one serving 2 children to one serving 139 children. The average number of children served by these programs was between 23 and 24. Eleven companies reported that they had no restrictions on eligibility for the reimbursement program; eight restricted use based on the type or level of employee, six had use restrictions based on employee salary levels, and thirteen required employees to use certain types of care (for example, licensed care). The average subsidy paid also varied. Four companies reported that they paid between $11 and $20 per week, 5 paid between $21 and $30, 4 paid between $31 and $40, 2 offered between $41 and $70, and 2 paid over $70 per week per child.

The following brief descriptions of existing employer-supported reimbursement programs illustrate the many different kinds of companies that successfully use this approach.

Title Data, Denver, Colo.

The company reimburses 50% of the cost of any kind of child care that employees choose. The employee presents a bill at the end of the month and is reimbursed for half of the monthly cost of care, except for a prorated amount deducted for sick days.

Horsham Hospital, Ambler, Pa.

The hospital pays 50% of the cost of *licensed* care. Any full-time employee is eligible. Payment is sent directly to the provider. Currently only center care is being used, but employees using licensed family day care homes are also eligible.

Children's Hospital; United Hospital, St. Paul, Minn.

Both hospitals offer a 50% child care reimbursement for nurses who work straight night shifts. (The hospitals also reported construction of a near-site child care center to be in operation at the end of 1982.)

Puget Consumer Cooperative, Seattle, Wash.

The company pays a flat hourly rate for up to two children under age 18. Both full- and part-time employees in all three stores are eligible.

KPFA Radio, Berkeley, Calif.

The company reimburses employees for all types of child care. Full-time employees are eligible for up to $100 per month reimbursement for child care expenses. Part-time employees are eligible for a prorated amount and volunteers receive an hourly reimbursement rate.

Burger King, Hartford, Conn.

The former manager of the franchise reimbursed employees for the full cost of care on submission of a child care bill. Although this program was recently discontinued when a new manager was hired, it demonstrates an effective approach for fast food businesses. The former manager reported that the child care reimbursement was a good incentive, that recipients were more productive, that sales were increased, and that the program worked extremely well in the fast food business.

Polaroid Corporation, Cambridge, Mass.

The program provides a subsidy to any employee whose family income is under $20,000, the amount of the subsidy being determined on a sliding scale. Employees using licensed child care centers or homes are eligible. The program is available to all employees nationwide.

Program Advantages and Disadvantages

Advantages	*Disadvantages*	*Solutions*
Easy to administer: can use current staff, is simple, quick start-up. *Low Cost:* low start-up cost, predictable on-going cost, no capital investment. *Wide Parent Choice:* parents select the child care program. *Flexible:* Responsive to changing needs. *Supports Existing Child Care:* The company does not "get into the child care business" and providers have an incentive to serve parent-employees. *Helps Parents:* Makes many types of child care affordable.	Depends on good existing care. Low company visibility. Company may support programs of poor or marginal quality.	Use when an assessment of the community shows an adequate amount of quality child care. Mount an educational PR campaign about the program for employees and the public. Set standards for acceptable care; help educate parents about choosing quality care.

Program Development Decisions

The major topics to be considered in the development of a child care reimbursement program are the amount of subsidy to be offered, the method of payment, the target group to be served, the eligible child care providers, whether a reimbursement alone is adequate to meet the company's child care needs, and the option of flexible spending accounts.

The Amount of Subsidy. The amount of the child care subsidy provided by the employer can vary from the full cost to a small portion. The employer may pay a flat amount to all eligible employees, a consistent percentage of the cost of care (for example, 50% for all employees), or an individualized rate determined on a sliding scale. Under any of these arrangements, employees often have to prove their eligibility according to company guidelines (for example, salary level, full- or part-time employment, or children of specified ages) and provide verification that care is being provided (for example, by showing receipts or checks made out to the providers). If a sliding scale is used, employees also provide supplemental information on their eligibility, such as family income and number of dependents. The sliding scale has been used by large companies as a way to target employees needing the most help and to contain costs.

Methods of Payment. There are several different ways of arranging the payment structure. Reimbursement payments can be made to parents or paid directly to the child care provider. Some companies give an annual contribution to a child care program instead of more frequent payments. The advantages of this arrangement are reduced paperwork and the fact that the amount can be predetermined. This arrangement seems more like a "contribution" and less like a child care "benefit." For employers who worry that a reimbursement program may be perceived as inequitable by childless employees, a lump sum payment may be easier to establish, manage, and justify.

Target Population. Reimbursements can be directed to specific employee groups such as those difficult to recruit (for example, secretaries, computer programmers, and nurses) or they may be offered at a specific work site. Thus, they can further specific company goals.

When sliding scales are used to determine eligibility, they usually take the total family income and number of dependents into account in determining the amount of reimbursement for which an employee is eligible. The cutoff point, the family (or individual) income level over which employees will receive no benefits, should be selected carefully to balance corporate goals with employee needs. Setting the cutoff point too low may make a group of employees who really need help ineligible for the voucher, as child care presents a cost problem even for middle income families.

Employer-supported child care programs must not discriminate on the basis of sex, race, ethnicity, or religious affiliation. In order to qualify under a Dependant Care Assistance Plan they also may not discriminate in favor of officers, owners, or highly compensated employees. But with these exceptions, targeting groups of employees for child care reimbursements is allowed.

In projecting potential costs it is important to note that not all eligible employees will use the program. A recent report on Polaroid's voucher system showed that only about 25% of those eligible to use their voucher program did so.[1] This usage probably reflects program restrictions on the types of care allowed (use of licensed providers is required), since many parents prefer to use informal arrangements with neighbors or relatives, as well as the difficulty that second- and third-shift workers have finding adequate child care of any type.

Eligible Child Care Providers. Companies have a number of choices about the type of care to be eligible for reimbursement. Some companies allow only the use of licensed care (in either homes or centers) while others allow licensed and unlicensed care to be used. Some also reimburse employees' relatives, who constitute the most prevalent suppliers of child care. The more choices given parents, the greater their opportunity to find the care that is most useful to them.

If the employer wants to establish the reimbursement under a Dependent Care Assistance Plan and make the contribution nontaxable income to the employee, there are certain requirements which are discussed in Chapter 4.

Combined Programs. A reimbursement system by itself provides a solution to employee child care problems where there is an adequate amount of accessible, high-quality, and convenient child care. In other communities a reimbursement system is most effective when paired with other forms of child care support. For example, when there is a shortage of a particular type of care, a one-time contribution to expand the capacity of local programs can be paired with an ongoing reimbursement system. Or, a company with an on-site child care center serving preschool children could also offer a reimbursement for infants or school-age children.

Flexible Spending Accounts. Some companies are experimenting with the idea of allowing employees to request money withheld from their salaries to establish a child care account. This means that employees set up their own child care reimbursement programs, which can operate in the same way as a company-funded program. This approach may be effective if the company does not offer a program, if certain employees are not eligible for or do not choose to use the company program, or if employees wish to add to the amount available to them through the company program. Salary set aside through such a plan is not taxed and the employee thus receives a higher net pay after taxes. The advantages are that some higher-paid employees not eligible for company child care reimbursement may fund their own accounts; that companies can set up programs relying on a combination of employee contributions and company dollars and therefore be eligible for some tax advantages; and that both the company and employees realize the benefits associated with good child care. Since arrangements such as these are not yet common, many questions about accounting and tax deductibility remain unanswered. In concept, it offers another source of flexibility for companies and employees cooperating to develop a variety of realistic child care options.

Issues

The central issue regarding child care reimbursements is that they directly impact only the cost of care and thus are not a far-reaching solution in a community that has additional child care problems such as low supply, low visibility, or poor quality. Properly designed reimbursement programs can, however, address these problems as well. For example, they can be paired with employer contributions to increase the supply as previously discussed.

They can also help to improve the quality of existing care if the reimbursement, along with parent tuition, represents a net increase in the total income to child care programs. This increased revenue can also help make the quality of care more consistent throughout the community, variability of quality being a concern often raised in relation to child care reimbursements. Additionally, employer eligibility restrictions can produce an incentive to programs to upgrade their quality.

Because reimbursement systems do not directly address the difficulty of employees in finding care, the most effective ones also often incorporate aspects of child care information and referral programs as well.

Employer sponsorship of this kind of program is increasing and employers report that such programs are very successful. Public agencies in California, Texas, and several other states have also developed larger-scale efforts that demonstrate the effectiveness of the reimbursement approach in selected settings.[2] These programs show ways of using both public and private dollars from different funding streams to support the many different kinds of specialized child care services needed to serve families.

*Liability.** Companies providing a child care reimbursement to employees who select and monitor their own child care providers may wish to acknowledge this fact in a written agreement between the employer and the employee. Such an agreement would clarify the nature of the relationship and alert employees from the beginning that the employer does not bear responsibility for injuries that may occur while child care services are being provided.

For companies that pay providers for child care services on behalf of their employees, a written contract between the company and the vendor can help to shift the responsibility for injuries to the vendor through an indemnification clause, coupled with an agreement that the vendor will carry insurance adequate to cover possible claims. A carefully written contract can also help prevent characterization of the relationship between the company and the provider as "employer-employee" rather than the "independent contractor" relationship most companies prefer. Of course, the provider must be a true independent contractor.

Companies that provide child care reimbursements to employees should be sure that their program qualifies as a Dependent Care Assistance Program under Internal Revenue Section 129. If it does not, the fair market value of the employer-provided care most likely is taxable to the employee, and the company must withhold payroll taxes.

This summary is provided as a brief description of selected liability concerns. Employers should consult their own attorneys for assistance in identifying and resolving their individual liability issues.

Starting a Program

Management. Child care reimbursement programs can be managed in-house by a child care coordinator or by the staff in departments such as personnel, employee benefits, public rela-

---

*This section was written by Kathleen Murray, Attorney At Law, Child Care Law Center.

tions, community affairs, strategic planning, or recruitment. To start the program, a written statement of eligibility, verification of child care use, and payment procedures are needed. The possible ways in which these procedures are handled have been discussed in other sections of this chapter.

The stipulations for eligible programs must be made clear—for example, whether continuing eligibility depends on a certain level of services or work hours. Companies may want to regularly reevaluate criteria such as location in relation to the employees' needs, services offered, hours open, cost of care relative to prevailing costs, and other factors that influence the utility of the child care program for the employee population. Agreements can include a provision that the company will pay to keep a certain number of spaces in the program open, even when not in use by employees.

Record Keeping. The paperwork involved in operating a reimbursement program is minimal. Initial records include information such as the child's name, age, enrollment date, hours of care, provider name, type, address, and telephone number. If the company wants to officially verify enrollment, the initial form must include the date of verification. Verification can be done over the telephone or with a short form signed by the parent and provider.

Other record keeping needed is a regular (perhaps monthly) recording of child care expenditures. This may be handled simply by presentation of a bill, receipt, or cancelled check. Or the employee may present a form to be signed monthly by the provider indicating that a certain number of days or dollar amount of care has been provided. Since most parents have to pay child care tuition in advance, companies may want to give advances for the care and then receive verification of care from the parent or provider.

Among the several other decisions to be made are the following:

1. Will the payments be based on full-time usage? If part-time child care is used (that is, the child attends morning nursery school and stays with the spouse in the afternoon), will payments be adjusted? Some companies establish a rule that those who pay more than the reimbursement amount will receive the full reimbursement and that those who pay less will receive reimbursement for their exact payment. Another solution is to prorate the reimbursement, so that the payment for part-time is based on a percentage of the payment for full-time care.

2. How many hours per week do employees need to work in order to be eligible for the reimbursement? Including part-time employees in the program is a good idea, since many mothers of young children work part time or make flexible hour arrangements while their children are small.
3. Will the company require that providers keep track of the exact number of hours used per child per month? This puts an additional burden on the providers. It may be adequate to ask the provider to attest that a child used at least a minimum number of hours of care during this month or child care worth a minimum dollar amount.

An example of a sliding scale that might be used to determine eligibility is that used by Polaroid (Table 9–1). Effective April 1981, the company subsidized the child care expenses of employees who earned $20,000 or less. The amount of subsidy was determined by the total family income and the number of people in the employee's family.

Costs. The administrative cost of a reimbursement program is relatively low, because the existing staff can usually manage the program along with other responsibilities. Almost all of the money spent goes directly into providing child care services.

One program that has kept records of costs since 1972, The Ford Foundation program, pays up to 50% of expenses for any kind of child care for staff with annual family incomes under $25,000. The Foundation has set maximum amounts for care based on rates set by the New York City Agency for Child Development. Annice Probst, a former consultant for the Foundation, says that the program has been "one of the least expensive fringe benefits offered." The average cost per participant varies each year, depending on the circumstances of the parents; that average cost per participant has ranged from a low of $386.13 in

Table 9–1 Percentage of Day Care Costs Paid by Polaroid Corporation.

Total Family Income	*Number of Family Members*		
	2 or 3	*4 or 5*	*6 or more*
Up to $ 9,500	50%	60%	70%
$11,000	45	55	65
$12,500	40	50	60
$14,000	35	45	55
$15,500	30	40	50
$17,000	25	35	45
$18,500	20	30	40
$20,000	15	25	35

1978 to a high of $624.64 in 1975. In 1980 there were 19 program participants, or 95% of the 20 nonexempt employees. The total expenditure for the voucher program has ranged from $15,676 in 1974 for 26 participants to $6,178 in 1978 for 16 participants. In 1980, the most recent year for which figures were available, the program cost $8,462, or an average of $445 per participant.[3]

Endnotes

1. Verna Brookins, Manager of Community Relations, Polaroid, speaking at April 1981 conference, New Management Initiatives for Working Parents in Boston, Massachusetts.
2. Governor's Advisory Committee on Child Development Programs, *Voucher Payment in California: A Review of the Public Policy Issues Raised by the Use of Vouchers as a Child Care Payment System,* June 21, 1977; and Terry Gillus, "Child Care Voucher Program of Austin Families Inc.," in *Shaping the Employer Role in Child Care,* ed. Dana Friedman, report of preconference session of NAEYC (November 1982).
3. "Employees Pleased with Child Care Assistance Plan" *Employee Benefit Plan Review,* 36–4 (October 1981), pp. 38–42.

Chapter 10

SUPPORT OF EXISTING PROGRAMS

Companies that want to help employees with child care without operating a program themselves often support existing child care programs in the community by contributing money, space, or in-kind services. Arrangements vary widely. Some contribute support with no strings attached, while others stipulate special treatment for their employees (such as priority admission or reduced rates). The other chapters in Part Four deal with employer support of child care programs specifically designed to serve the children of employees; this one focuses on charitable contributions to existing community child care programs as well as employer purchase of child care services for employees.

Selecting a Program

Employer support of community child care programs can have different purposes:

1. To reduce the cost of child care for employees.
2. To make admission to programs easier.
3. To assure that child care resources will be available to employees when needed.
4. To establish new child care resources.
5. To support the improvement of child care through planning and advocacy groups.

Many programs are intended to accomplish several of these purposes simultaneously. A company may serve its short-term objectives by purchasing services while it also supports long-term community planning to improve community wide child care.

When a contribution is designed solely to reduce tuition costs for parents, this type of program is similar to a child care reimbursement. Such donations are usually given as a charitable contribution rather than as an employee benefit, as is the case with reimbursements. For the most part, however, contributions to community child care programs are designed to do more than give financial assistance. They often also expand or improve the program or purchase preferential admission for the company's employees as well.

Many companies support existing child care programs; 123 participated in the National Employer Supported Child Care Project. These companies have many different kinds of arrangements, including purchasing services for employees at a local center, contracting with for-profit child care chains or other local providers to serve employees, and giving charitable contributions to local planning/advocacy groups for the development of additional community services. An additional five companies reported that they support existing child care programs in addition to supporting their primary child care service. More than half of the industries in the survey reported supporting local child care programs as their primary service, whereas only 14 hospitals, 4 public agencies, and 2 unions were included in this category.

Thirty-four of the companies in the survey supported more than one community program. When asked how their support benefited employees, 31 companies reported that the employees received cost reductions, 61 reserved access to the programs with no cost reduction, 18 purchased preferential admission for employees, and 17 reported that their support assured better-quality programs. Seventy-six of the companies supported programs that served both employee and community children, while 3 supported programs reserved for employee children and 17 supported programs used only by community children.

Supporting community child care programs makes it possible for a number of companies to jointly contribute to a single program. This concept, called a consortium, in its fullest sense involves several companies jointly initiating and administering a child care program. Consortia of this type are discussed in Chapter 16. Those discussed here are a variation on the theme, whereby companies jointly support an already existing program which is managed by an outside organization. The appeal of this variation is that it is simpler and less demanding for the supporting companies. Examples of this idea are included in the programs that follow, as well as other forms of employer support to community programs. The following examples illustrate the diversity of the programs that have been developed.

The Sunnyvale Service Center, Sunnyvale, Calif.

This comprehensive center program serves children of Sunnyvale residents and employees of local companies. The complex provides care for up to 64 infants and toddlers, 72 preschoolers, and 44 school-age children. The center was established and is operated by a private child care management company, Child Development Incorporated. The city of Sunnyvale holds the lease on the property and local companies (TRW Vidar, TRW DSSG, ESL, Inc., Aertech Industries, and Hewlett-Packard) make annual contributions. Some contributions allow employee families a discount or priority admission to the program.

Wesley Medical Center, Wichita, Kan.

The center reserves 50 slots, about half of its total capacity, for employee children in the Wesley Children's Center. The hospital gives both money and in-kind support, including printing and publicity. Employee parents pay through a payroll deduction arrangement. The center is open from 6 a.m. to 12:30 a.m. to serve both first- and second-shift employees.

Apex Oil; Metroplitan Life Insurance Co.; General Dynamics; Brown Shoe Co.; Clayton Times; Chamber of Commerce, and others in Clayton, Mo.

These companies support the Clayton Child Center. Initial loans from five local banks provided funds for the center's start-up. Ongoing contributions from these companies continue to support this private nonprofit center for 110 children from one year old to kindergarten age. Summer care is also offered for school-age children.

First Minneapolis Bank, Minneapolis, Minn.

The bank gives a corporate donation to Child Care Service, Inc., which provides care for sick children in their homes when their parents are at work. The program began in 1975. Health care personnel are experienced in child care and have been trained in first aid and CPR techniques. The program serves 10 to 20 families per month.

The San Juan Batista Child Development Center, San Jose, Calif.

The program received one-time donations for start-up from the Levi-Strauss and Hewlett-Packard Foundations to support the development of a program for sick children. The city of San Jose also gave a block grant to support the development of this program for children from 2 months to 14 years old.

Program Advantages and Disadvantages

Advantages	*Disadvantages*	*Solutions*
Leaves the "business of child care" to others.	Less control over programs.	Select carefully, purchase specific services, and work with the child care provider.
Program start-up is quick, easy, and low in cost.	Does not increase supply of care.	If the type of care needed by parents does not exist, encourage providers and planning groups to see the need.
Enhances community relations.		

Can help both employees and the community. Can contribute to better community-wide child care.	Less publicity than with own center. Parents feel they have less say about service than with company center.	Donations to providers for specific kinds of services (i.e., infant care) can encourage development of needed services. Help direct PR to educate people about the employee/community benefits of this approach. Keep communication between company and program active.

Program Development Decisions

Program variations have to do with the form and amount of support offered, purchasing mechanisms, the target group for the program, criteria for deciding which program to support, and potential liability issues.

Forms of Support. Companies can give financial or in-kind support to community child care programs. *Financial* support can be:

1. A contribution or loan to defray start-up expenses in a new program.
2. Contributions to offset on-going expenses for regular program operation.
3. Contribution earmarked for special projects such as refurbishing a playground or buying a new equipment.
4. Fees to assure available spaces, priority admissions, or cost reductions for the children of employees.
5. Contributions to community organizations or planning groups to support special functions such as training sessions for providers, equipment loan programs, or child care planning functions. For instance, the Levi-Straus Foundation has given money to an umbrella organization in Toronto to be used for start-up funds for new non-profit centers.

In-kind support is another form of employer contribution, helping indirectly to lower program overhead and thereby reducing the eventual cost to parents. In-kind supports include:

1. Services such as duplicating, printing, and indoor and outdoor grounds maintenance that companies regularly provide for themselves can be used to support a child care program.

2. Legal, financial and administrative advice: Many child care program directors do not have regular access to professionals for this kind of consultation.
3. Board Membership: For instance, representatives of Control Data and three other companies sit on the board of the Northside Child Development Center in Minneapolis, a program these companies helped establish in 1971. Their long-term interest in the management of the program has had a positive influence on the stability and direction of the program.
4. Equipment: Donations of office equipment help reduce overhead costs. Other kinds of equipment such as computers, record players, and tape recorders can enhance the classroom experiences of the children in the program.
5. Space: Some companies may have space that could be used for a child care program, but they do not want to develop or run the program themselves. Use of this space might allow a local child care program to expand its capacity or open a new program that would be convenient for employees.
6. Transportation: For some programs, transportation of the children to and from the program and on special field trips is a major problem. In programs for school-age children, transportation of the children between school and child care facility can be a disincentive to participation. Summer camps may also need bus or van service to pick the children up at places that are convenient for working parents. Companies can provide the vehicles for transporting children and help organize the scheduling. An example is the arrangement between the Houston General Insurance Company in Fort Worth, Texas and the local YMCA: Parents bring their children to work and buses from the Y pick up and return the children to the worksite.
7. Food: Companies with worksite centers often provide the children's food through the company cafeteria. They can have the same arrangement with nearby programs. Companies in the food industry may contribute products to local child care programs on a regular basis.
8. Products: For example, Stride Rite gives shoes to children in its day care center. In return the children "wear test" the shoes. Companies that make family-oriented products such as furniture, soaps, toys, and clothes can get maximum public relations value by donating products to community child care programs.

Amount of Support. Obviously, the amount of support offered to child care programs will vary depending on need and resources. Even when the support initially offered is minimal, company and child care program representatives working together can lay the groundwork for a lasting relationship. The time investment made by the company personnel who work with child care providers will be repaid by an increased understanding of community child care needs and resources.

One way to make limited money go further is to develop programs that utilize matching funds from other sources. For instance, the John Hancock Insurance Company in Boston, Massachusetts gave a $10,000 donation to the Child Care Resource Center in 1982. This donation was matched on a three-to-one basis by the State of Massachusetts, which gave $30,000 in matching funds to support the Center's information and referral program. This kind of coordination is an example of mutually beneficial cooperation between the public and private sectors. John Hancock has also made sizeable contributions to child care centers near the work site and has given special funds through United Way to support child care.

Purchasing Mechanisms. Buying specific services from providers in existing programs is relatively straightforward. In some communities, employers have the opportunity to purchase child care services through a centralized system. For instance, Children's World, a proprietary chain of child care centers, offers employers the opportunity to buy services for children in any of their local centers. Three companies have participated in this offer: Current, Inc. in Colorado Springs, Colorado; the Baptist Medical Center in Oklahoma City, Oklahoma; and the Miami Valley Hospital in Dayton, Ohio. Parents can choose which of the local centers is best for them. Quality Child Care, Inc. in Massachusetts is developing a similar kind of approach that would allow parents to choose a family day care home from among a group of providers.

In several cities, child care advocate groups are developing plans that would allow employers to contract with a central service to purchase the child care needs by each employee. For instance, this type of service might refer parents to existing child care facilities, investigate individual eligibility for federal or local financial aid, and/or administer reimbursement programs for employers. This idea is being developed in different ways in several cities:

- In Orlando, Florida the Employer Assurance Plan of Community Coordinated Child Care of Central Florida, Inc., has been approved by the IRS as a Dependent Care Assistance Plan for tax purposes.
- In Hartford, Connecticut employers and the United Way are

supporting the development of a centralized child care services agency.

- In Westchester County, New York, The United Way is studying the development of a centralized service purchasing mechanism. For many employers, this concept would provide a practical way to purchase existing child care services for employees and a chance to have a role in the improvement of services at the same time.

Employers who want to encourage providers to open new services in different locations, to modify hours, or to expand existing programs can also negotiate directly with providers. Employers can offer donations of space for a new program, low-interest loans for start-up, and charitable contributions as incentives for local providers to develop needed services. While charitable contributions do not buy specific services for employees, they can have a significant impact on child care for employees and other parents in the community.

Target Group. Who does the company want to benefit from the support given to a child care program? The target group will help determine the cooperative arrangements between company and program. The company may want a service for all parent employees or for a particular subgroup of parents. For example, the Sunnyvale Service Center receives a corporate donation in exchange for which secretaries from the company get a reduced tuition rate. Some companies may also want their support dollars to help provide child care services for other parents in the community.

Criteria for Supporting a Program. Companies develop their own criteria for deciding which specific child care programs to support. These criteria include: (1) the type of service offered (family day care, infant center, preschool, and so forth); (2) the ages of children served; (3) the quality of the program (staff/child ratios, group sizes, and teacher training requirements); (4) user satisfaction with the program; (5) location and hours of the program; (6) prices charged; and (7) current employees served and projected future utilization by employees.

By utilizing community child care programs, companies make the most cost-efficient use of existing resources. There is a great deal of choice in the amount and type of contribution companies make and their level of involvement in the programs. It is critically important that these arrangements address the variations in child care needs that differ from one company to the next. Thus, supporting community child care programs can be the most economical, adaptable, and efficient type of service in many situations.

Chapter 11

FLEXIBLE BENEFIT PLANS

Flexible benefit plans allow employees to choose employee benefits from a "menu" of benefit possibilities. The popularity of flexible benefits stems from a number of changes taking place in the workplace, including a move away from paternalistic management strategies toward greater worker participation in company decision making. Flexible benefit plans have particular appeal to companies considering child care because, under a flexible benefit system, the child care benefit is less likely to be perceived as inequitable: Every worker has the opportunity to choose benefits that fit his or her own needs.

Selecting a Program

If the child care services discussed in this book are to be offered as an employee benefit, they can—but are not *required* to—be part of a flexible benefit system. For example, child care reimbursement (discussed in Chapter 9) can be one of the benefit choices in a flexible benefit plan. Other forms of child care services can also be one of the benefit choices, although reimbursements are the most commonly accepted form of child care within flexible benefits.

Flexible benefits are a statutorially defined program with special tax advantages. The Dependent Care Assistance Act stipulates that child care benefits set up under a DCAP are non-taxable income and that a DCAP may be one of the benefits offered in a flexible benefit program. Thus, offering child care as an employee benefit rather than as an employee service or charitable contribution has particular tax advantages to both employer and employee.

Many flexible benefit plans increase the total amount of benefit dollars contributed by the company; others build flexibility without increasing the money spent on benefits. In either case, flexible benefit systems can make more economical use of benefit dollars for employees. They avoid the duplication of benefits encountered when two-income couples each have medical or insurance benefit coverage. Shared tax advantages for both employer and employee are discussed at length in Chapter 4. These plans also enable employees to select benefits that better meet their needs.

Possible sources of support for child care services include:

- Salary reduction, when the individual parent decides to have a portion of salary reserved for child care services. (This amount becomes non-taxable income under a DCAP; see Chapter 4.)
- Trading benefit dollars when the employee trades off other benefits to buy child care services.
- Additional company support when the company adds a certain amount of benefit "currency" to existing benefit levels or allows employees to use some portion of a salary increase to purchase additional benefits.

Different decisions about the three basic elements and financing can define very different flexible benefit plans, some of which give more options and cover a higher percentage of the actual cost of child care than others.

There are three elements in a flexible approach: First, the *inflexible portion* of the benefit plan is the "minimum level of coverage out of which an employee cannot elect."[1] The company decides that there is a baseline amount of coverage that each employee must maintain. The employee can not opt out of benefits, nor can he use the dollars which purchase these benefits for any other benefits.

Second, the employee is allowed a certain amount of *currency* to use in purchasing individualized benefit options. This currency may be available as flexible dollars, flexible credits, or choice pay.

Third, the employee uses his currency to buy additional benefits from among a range of *options*. Options may include cash or additional amounts of benefits that are part of the inflexible portion (for example, purchasing better health coverage or more insurance), or they may include benefits that are not offered at all in the inflexible portion. Child care benefits are among those that would not be included in the inflexible portion of the benefit package, because many employees would not need them.

Program Examples

Among the best-known flexible benefit plans are those established by the American Can Company in Greenwich, Connecticut; by TRW Inc.'s West Coast Systems Group in Redondo Beach, California; and by Northern States Power Company in Minneapolis, Minnesota. *American Can Company* established its flexible benefit programs in 1979 to allow each of its approximately 9,000 employees a range of choices about their benefits. Employees automatically receive a core of benefits. They select the balance of their benefits depending on the amount of "flexible credits" they have left. These flexible credits, which are expressed in dollars, represent the difference in value between the new core benefits and the level of benefits they received prior to the flexible program. The flexible credits are refigured each year based on the employee's age, pay, family status, and years of service. The employees "cost" for each benefit item (how many flexible credits an additional item uses) is also set differentially based on pay, age, and other factors.

Employees complete a form specifying their choices of benefit levels in five areas: (1) medical coverage, (2) life insurance, (3) vacation, (4) disability income, and (5) retirement/capital accumulation. After checking and processing, the individual benefits selections are entered into a computerized employee information system. American Can stresses that the plan has been successful in part because of the concerted employee communication effort that has accompanied the program, including materials sent to employees' homes, a newsletter, videotapes, and a telephone hotline to answer individual questions.

TRW, Inc. Electronics and Defense Sector implemented its program in 1974 after several years of research and design. The program, called Flexible Benefits, allows employees to select among a variety of hospital and medical plans and a number of insurance options. The basic core benefits are those the company offered before the Flexible Benefit program was implemented. The choices involved a "leaner" or "enriched" version of the core benefits. Taking a "leaner" hospital medical program allowed an employee to "enrich" his or her life insurance, for example. Choices may be changed annually.

Northern States Power Company's flexible benefit plan went into effect in 1981. It includes a basic package of four benefit areas: medical insurance, disability insurance, time off, and retirement pay. All employees have basic coverage in these four areas, but not at the same level. The dollar value of the difference is calculated in "flex dollars." Employees can add to their benefit dollars by taking payroll deductions or, if they do not spend them all, can take the difference in cash. For example, they may sell up to ten days of vacation to use the flex dollars for other things, or they may buy five more days of vacation.

Many more companies are now developing or considering implementation of flexible benefit plans.[2] Of the relatively small number of companies that now have flexible benefit plans, one of the first to include child care or dependent care assistance benefits as part of the plan was Highland Park Hospital in Highland Park, Illinois. This plan allows employees, depending on their length of service, to allocate up to $500 per year for care for children under 14 years old.[3] Northern States Power Company has also recently added a child care subsidy or reimbursement option to their flexible benefit plan.

In 1981 TRW conducted a formal evaluation of its flexible benefit program. An overwhelming majority of the employees surveyed (over 90%) reported that they were moderately to very satisfied with the program. Berwyn N. Fragner, Vice President Human Relations for the Electronics and Defense Sector, says, "The developmental costs of flexible benefits are dependent on many factors specific to the program choices to be implemented, the sophistication of the payroll system, the communications program, and so forth. Our experiences with the ongoing costs of administering the flexible benefit plan indicate that we have no more than before we implemented the program. For example, benefits administration per 1000 employees is the same. In 1981 the costs associated with flexible benefits, such as the annual enrollment program changes in payroll computer systems, were a minor cost per employee. Our evaluation of the ongoing costs indicate that they are more than offset by employee goodwill and satisfaction."[4] Reports such as this from companies with flexible benefit plans show that the difficulties of implementation can be surmounted and that both companies and employees gain from benefit flexibility.

An educational effort that informs employees about benefit selection is an important aspect of program development. Information about the child care benefit can help all employees understand why child care is included in the plan and provide data on employee problems with child care, the cost of care, and local resources. It can also help parents weigh the relative benefits of, for instance, amounts of medical coverage against amounts of child care assistance. Inclusion of this kind of child care information in benefits documentation helps clarify issues and bring the reality of child care problems to the attention of all employees.

Companies report that an unexpected outcome of the educational process required for implementation of a flexible benefit plan is better communication between employees and management. This enhanced communication can have a broad-based effect and helps improve the overall tone of employee management relationships.

Flexible benefits are becoming more feasible as rapidly increasing technology simplifies the administration of such systems. They are an important future trend that can maximize the value of benefit dollars, contain benefit costs, and address the individual situations of employees.

Endnotes:

1. Personal communication, Don Hasbargen, Hewitt Associates (January 1983).
2. R. Derren, "Flexible Benefits II: Planning and Implementing Flexible Benefits Plans," *Pension World* (October 1981), pp. 23-26.
3. Hewitt Associates, "Child Care Assistance: Issues for Employer Consideration," (Lincolnshire, Illinois: Hewitt Associates, 1982). Available from Hewitt Associates, General Offices, 100 Half Day Road, Lincolnshire, Illinois 60015.
4. Personal communications with Berwyn Fragner (January 1983).

Chapter 12

CHILD CARE CENTERS

Child care centers are the most familiar of all child care programs. Center staff take care of children in a group setting, the number of children varying from relatively small programs serving 15–20 children to large facilities serving as many as 300 children. The average age of the children served is about 2 to 5 years old; however, centers can also care for infants and toddlers as young as 4 to 6 weeks old and for school-age children who come before and after school and during holidays. Some centers provide additional services such as transportation (usually to get school age children to and from school), care for children who become ill during the day, educational seminars for parents, counseling and referral for family members, and preventive health care services such as screening, hearing tests, and immunizations.

Selecting a Program

Centers are generally open on weekdays for 8 to 12 hours during the day, although some are open extended hours, (in the early mornings, evenings, and on weekends and holidays) for parents who work varied shifts. Some centers have more educationally oriented classroom activities than do others; most offer a range of activities including math, science, art, music, dance, outdoor play, language, and dramatic play.

All states require that child care centers be licensed. The specific licensing requirements vary by state, but they generally include regulations about the amounts of indoor and outdoor space, safety and health factors, group size, staff-to-child ratios, the number and qualifications of teachers and curriculum.

Centers can be operated either as for-profit or not-for-profit organizations. They are run by public and private schools, non-profit community agencies, churches, individuals, and by for-profit child care companies.

The families who use child care centers and other kinds of child care services represent a cross section of the population, including dual-career, single-parent and low-income families. In the past, many child care centers serving low income children were established with government funding through economic opportunity and educational programs, primarily through Title XX of the Social Security Act, which in 1981 was incorporated into the Social Services Block Grant. Some full day Head Start programs provide similar child care services. Even with these programs, in most communities there simply is not enough child care for all of the children who need care, regardless of whether the service is subsidized by public funds or paid for directly by parents.

Children of full-time workers spend approximately ten hours in the center each day (allowing for parents' commuting time). Because these hours comprise the largest part of the day, the center program must be carefully designed to meet many needs including social, emotional, physical, and intellectual development. Responsibility for the whole child is one of the differences between full-day child care and half-day enrichment programs, sometimes called "nursery school" programs. Half-day programs tend to concentrate on educational, cognitive stimulation. Full-day programs can be equally educational but, because they care for the child for longer periods of time, they are also responsible for other daily routine activities such as napping, meals, and health care. Distinctions that used to be made between "nursery schools" or half-day programs and "child care centers" or full-day programs have become less salient; many nursery schools have extended their hours to serve working parents, and most centers have incorporated educational components into their programs. Discussion in this chapter refers to all full-day programs that care for children in a group setting, whether they are called child care centers, Head Start, preschools, or nursery schools.

The National Employer Supported Child Care Project identified 211 employer-supported child care centers in operation in this country in 1981–1982. These included programs enrolling between 6 and 400 children. Most cared for preschoolers, but over half also cared for infants and toddlers under two and 40% also provided care for school-age children. The programs were split almost evenly between those that served only employee children and those that also accepted community children.

Official Airline Guides, Oakbrook, Ill.
OAG, a company of the Dunn and Bradstreet Corporation with approximately 700 employees, opened its onsite center in January of 1981. The center is licensed to serve 66 children from 6 weeks to 5 years old. The company remodeled an existing space, contributed start-up costs, and donates food, nursing and janitorial services. Parent fees (from $44 per week for preschoolers to $66 for infants) support the rest of the cost of the program. Approximately 10% of the employees using the center have been men and about 10% have been single parents. The center had not yet completed the 3-year period allocated for testing the program, but according to the Senior Vice President, indications in 1982 were that it had been highly successful and had made good business sense for the company.

Shawnee Mission Medical Center, Shawnee Mission, Kan.
Established in 1979, the center serves a total of about 400 children between the hours of 6:30 a.m. and midnight. Children from 6 weeks to 12 years attend. The program emphasizes educational and social development and includes a kindergarten class for 5-year-olds. The hospital (which employs about 1,600 people) donated the building, equipment, and labor to start the program and supplements weekly parent fees of $50 for infants, $45 for preschoolers, and $5 for school-age children. The hospital reported that the program has been highly successful in terms of nurse recruitment and retention and has gathered positive publicity for the hospital.

General Life Insurance Company, Bloomfield, Conn.
In 1975 Connecticut General renovated an existing offsite building and leased it to Living and Learning Centers, Inc., a for-profit child care chain later acquired by Kinder-Care Learning Centers, Inc. for a child care center. The program serves 70 children from 3 months to 8 years old, about half of whom are the children of company employees. Connecticut General provides a discount for employees who use the service. Positive response from employees and the community sparked a decision to construct a new 4,500–square-foot center with capacity for 100 children from both employee and community families. The greatest demand for care has been from parents with children under 2, since there are very few facilities that offer care for young children in the area.

Boise Valley Sunset Nursing Home, Boise, Id.
In 1978 the nursing home opened an on-site center for the children of employees, volunteers, and residents. The center, licensed for 15 children, is open Monday through Friday from 6 a.m. to 6 p.m. to serve preschool and school-age children, from 2½ to 9 years old. The program is run as part of the nursing home, which has about 200 employees. The nursing home contributed start-up costs and gives ongoing support. Parents pay $5 per day for preschool children. The child care program has been successful in decreasing turnover and absenteeism and in obtaining positive publicity for the nursing home. The PR generated by

the center has helped support a community image of the home as a "caring place." Some residents help out with the children and this intergenerational aspect of the program is viewed very positively by the company.

Opp and Micholas Mills, Opp, Ala.
The textile company, which employs 1,100 people, runs a kindergarten program licensed for 37 children across the street from the plant. This 50-year-old program is such an established part of the company that the Personnel Director reported, "It has become an accepted institution and no one *ever* talks about getting rid of it; the cost is absorbed by the company willingly."

Children's Hospital, Los Angeles, Calif.
The nursing department of the hospital has established an all-night center for the children of night-shift employees. About 6 children per night, from infants to 10-year olds, sleep at the center while their parents work (from 11 p.m. to 7 a.m.). The hospital pays the full cost, so that the program is free to employees.

Hoffman-La Roche, Inc., Nutley, N.J.
The center, in a renovated house near the work site, is licensed for forty-six 2½ to 7-year-old children. It is open from 6:45 a.m. to 6 p.m. five days a week. Begun in 1977, the program has stringent requirements for teaching staff, and a number of supplemental services, including necessary health screening, speech therapy, parent education and information, and referral for parents whose children are not in the program. Since the center is run as a department of the company, the staff are hired as permanent company employees, with full company benefits. About 98% of the children using the center have been children of employees, and about 45% of the employee-parents have been male. The company, a large manufacturer of pharmaceuticals, plans to renovate additional space to expand the program.

Baptist Medical Center, Little Rock, Ark.
The hospital, which employs about 2,500 people, started its current center in 1974. Prior to that, there had been a small center at the old hospital for over 20 years. The center, licensed for 117 children from the age of 6 weeks, is open from 6 a.m. to midnight every day. During the summer, hours are coordinated to provide care for school-age children before and after a summer recreation program run by a local church. The program has an isolation room for sick children and cares for some sick children as a regular part of the program "if a statement from the doctor indicates that the child is not contagious—for example, ear infections or coughs." The hospital funded the entire development of the center and supports about 50% of the ongoing program costs. Program expansion is planned to accomodate many of the nearly 100 employees who are on the waiting list for the program.

Program Advantages and Disadvantages

Advantages	*Disadvantages*	*Solutions*
Good recruitment tool: most effective when the center is exclusively for employees; is of high quality and cares for children of all ages; particularly effective in attracting women back to work after maternity leave.	Difficulty predicting utilization.	Careful advance planning, taking into account employees' child care demand (needs and preferences) as well as available community child care supply. Start-up by gradually opening classrooms or sections; open programs in September or January, peak months for child care enrollment; involve parents in program planning.
Creates positive publicity, image, and morale: highly visible evidence that the company cares about people; may be especially useful for companies that make family-oriented products.	High cost relative to other options.	Evaluate cost over the long term; set parent fees to cover part of the operating costs; plan for maximum utilization.
Decreased absenteeism and tardiness: helps parents control time lost at work due to child care problems.	Requires administrative involvement.	Minimize company administration by contracting for service, setting-up separate organization.
Reduces employee stress: parents report peace of mind, reduced anxiety, and increased concentration on the job.		
Tax-deductible: capital expenditures and operating costs are deductible.		

Program Development Decisions

The major topics to be considered in the development of an employer-supported child care center program are (1) the legal structure and program auspices, (2) the amount and types of company support available, (3) the ages of children to be served, and (4) the range of services to be offered.

Legal Structure and Program Auspices

Companies have several choices about the legal status and management of center programs. The company can maintain ownership and management of its own center, it can develop the program as a separate non-profit agency, or it can develop a contractual relationship with a child care management firm. The arrangement chosen depends on the amount of responsibility and control desired, tax considerations, and contracting options available in the community. The types of arrangements that have been used by companies are outlined as follows.

1. *The center as a department of the company.* Many work-site child care centers are run as a separate department of the company or as part of an existing department. This arrangement gives the company the most direct control over the policies of the program and simplifies subsidy arrangements. For example, the Mary Grace Hutcheson Child Development Center of Forney Engineering Company in Carrollton, Texas is operated as a department of the company.

2. *The center as separate profit-making subsidiary of the company.* Under this arrangement, the company maintains close control but the tax consequences differ from those it would obtain if the program were within a department of the company. The A.P. Beutal II Child Care Center of Intermedics, Inc. in Freeport, Texas is an example of a center that was developed using this arrangement. The Intermedics center is a wholly owned, for-profit subsidiary of the company. The company is able to absorb their substantial subsidy to the center by writing it off as a tax loss. At the same time, this child care program has contributed substantially to a reduction in employee turnover and absenteeism.

3. *The center as a separate non-profit corporation.* Centers that use this arrangement develop boards of directors composed of parents and company representatives. The center must qualify for an IRS Code Sec. 501(c)(3) non-profit status. In order to qualify, the program must accept children from the community as well as children of employees. Decisions are made on an individual basis as to whether the policies of the program qualify it for tax-exempt status; generally, however, program enrollment criteria must not favor the children of employees over children from the community. An example of a program that is a separate non-profit corporation is the Child Education Center that serves California Institute of Technology and the Jet Propulsion Laboratories in Pasadena, California.

Another way to attain non-profit status is through a voluntary employees' beneficiary association organized pursuant to Code Sec. 501(c)(9), providing child care benefits to members of the voluntary association.[1] Under this arrangement no more than 10% of the children served in the child care program can be from the community. These arrangements give the program a separate status, may cut down on the company's administrative responsibility, and often promote positive feelings from employee participation.

Non-profit status also means that the program may be eligible for some of the resources available to non-profit organizations such as public child nutrition funds, United Way funds, foundation grants, and charitable contributions. These arrangements are particularly attractive to businesses that could not offer much support for the program themselves. An example of a center that was developed and run by parent employees is the Goddard Child Development Center of the Goddard Space Flight Center in Greenbelt, Maryland.

4. *The center as a separate non-profit agency established in consortium with other businesses.* Partners in the endeavor might include other businesses or non-profit agencies such as colleges or public agencies. The contribution from each business is much smaller than would be required to finance individual programs, yet the businesses can generally experience many of the same benefits as those available in operating their own private center. This may be an especially viable option when each employer has a small number of parent employees who need the service. It is particularly appropriate for small businesses wanting center care for their employees. An example of this kind of arrangement is the Garden City Downtown Day Care Center in Missoula, Montana. (See Chapter 16 for further examples).

5. *The center managed by a child care management firm.* Such management firms might include proprietary child care chains, non-profit child care management firms, or operators of local child care centers. The center can still be at the work site, in another company facility, or at a site operated by the contracting organization. Under this arrangement the child care firm carries primary responsibility for the program, including liability. Risks, such as underutilization and slow start-up, would have less direct impact on the company. In exchange, however, the company relinquishes the direct control of the policies of the program, although company input on policies can be significant. The amount of company influence may directly relate to the amount of support given to the program. As with other models, the company can give many kinds of support in addition to direct financial contributions. An example of a child care management firm that manages child care centers for business is Kinder-Care Learning Centers, which operates several, including one in the Florida Medical Center in Fort Lauderdale and one in Walt Disney World in Buena Vista, Florida.

Amount and Type of Company Support

Each company also has options about the amount and types of support to be given to the program. Companies can support the cost of starting up programs and/or their ongoing operation. Unless outside management firms are willing to provide the total cost of start-up, companies will generally find it necessary to provide some start-up support. This assistance can take the form of administrative time, financial contributions, loans, or in-kind service contributions, such as renovation of the facility or janitorial services.

Both the start-up and ongoing support can be designed to match the resources available from the company with program needs. For example, a company may find it difficult to donate operating funds for a company-owned-and-managed child care center, but it could allot maintenance services and space for a center run by an outside management firm.

The amount of support should be carefully designated in terms of the overall budget so that the targeted employee populations can afford the program. Many employees cannot afford to use a center that is totally supported through parent tuition fees. If parents cannot afford the full cost, then the cost to parents must be lowered or the center will not be fully utilized. Cost reductions can be achieved through a number of different methods: (1) the reduction of program overhead by in-kind contributions such as maintenance, food preparation, or rent-free space; (2) direct financial contributions, either in the form of a scholarship fund or as a general contribution to the program; (3) assistance in the solicitation of funds from public agencies, corporate foundations, or voluntary fund-raising organizations such as United Way; and (4) assistance in budget and program design to maximize resource utilization.

The amount and types of support will usually have a direct impact on the benefits the company receives from the program. Companies that find the greatest return from their programs in terms of reduced turnover, absenteeism, positive PR and recruitment capability are generally those that provide higher levels of support to their child care centers. A company program that makes good child care more affordable helps parent employees solve many basic child care problems.

Companies should plan their support with long-term, as well as short-term goals in mind. Short-term economies may leave the child care program operating a poorer quality service, which in the long run can rob the company of benefits from the program.

Ages of Children Served

A center program is most beneficial to the company when it is designed to serve the children of all employees who need the service. This often means serving the full age range of children from infancy through school age. In some places, it may be easier to design a program than only serves preschool children (2 to 5 years old) since licensing requirements often make this an easier group to serve. However, child care centers that serve only preschoolers often find that parents use different services for each of their children and change programs as children grow older.

Many employers attempt to serve as many employees with children as possible. The National Employer Supported Child Care Project found a total of 211 employer-supported centers, 131 of which served infants and toddlers, 198 served preschoolers, and 85 served school-age children. Of these, 54 centers served children from infancy through school age.

If the center cannot serve employees with children under 2 or over 6, companies may decide to gather data on the services used by parents and their satisfaction with them as compared with that of employees using the company center. This kind of information forms the basis for long-term decision making about the range of child care services needed by employees.

Support Services Offered

An important aspect of quality programming is the range of supplemental services offered for families and children. Companies that are concerned about the additional costs of such services will want to evaluate the benefits in terms of employees' desire for them and increased work force productivity. Companies in the National Employer Supported Child Care Project survey reported that their centers provided a number of supplemental services including meals (116 centers), parent discussion groups (66 centers), counseling for children (32 centers), counseling for parents (53 centers), dental services (11 centers), medical services (50 centers) and transportation (14 centers). Support services include the following:

1. *Preventive health care:* Child care programs can provide preventive testing, screening, and immunizations; help arrange for health care; and make appropriate referrals for parents and children needing medical advice. Such services can significantly reduce the amount of time parents miss from work due to their children's illnesses.

2. *Care for sick children:* Approaches to providing care for sick children are discussed in detail in Chapter 5. Such services can be part of a center program.
3. *Transportation for children:* School-age children may need transportation between child care and school if early morning or late afternoon care is offered. Sometimes transportation is provided by the schools or by the after-school program providers. In other communities, where transportation is not generally available, the logistics of getting children to and from several places during the day can be a parent's biggest problem. Some companies provide a minibus or van.
4. *Resource and referral:* Program staff or consultants can give information about local resources and referrals to community services for a range of problems including health, counseling, housing, and legal services. They can also help parents find supplemental (that is, weekend or night-time care) not offered by the company or help parents who are on the center's waiting list find alternative care. This can be tied in with the company's employee assistance program or operated through the child care service.
5. *Educational programs for parents:* The staff can run discussion groups on parenting issues or other topics of interest (for example, discipline, child development, and sibling relationships) or invite guest speakers.
6. *Links to community programs:* Existing programs in the community can help the center to augment classroom activities. Some examples are foster grandparent groups, teacher internships, training programs in local high schools and colleges, and special interest groups dealing with the arts, music, dance, computers, and math.

Issues

The special issues related to providing care in an employer-supported child care center are equity, utilization, and liability.

Equity. Although management often fears that employees who are not parents will perceive the child care benefit as inequitable, this has not proved to be the case among companies with established programs. Of the 35 companies in the National Employer Supported Child Care Projects who were concerned that equity might be a problem *prior* to starting the program, only four considered it to have become an issue. Interviews with company personnel revealed four major reasons for child care programs not being perceived as inequitable by employees:

1. Nonparent-employees realize that they themselves benefit when parent-employees—their co-workers—are more dependable and productive.
2. The company that supports child care shows its concern for and support of its workers and is perceived as more caring and humane by all workers.
3. Workers not currently using the benefit can look forward to using it or can recall having themselves needed child care services in the past.
4. Employees realize that many benefits and services are given or used differentially—that is, some workers use the health plan more, others use more dental care, and so on.

Utilization. Proper planning can reduce the likelihood of fluctuating utilization. The following ideas are helpful in adjusting programs to utilization patterns and maximizing their cost effectiveness:

1. Mount an educational campaign so that employees know about and understand the program (for instance, by helping parents get to know child care staff during lunch-time discussion sessions).
2. Design a program with sufficient flexibility to meet changing needs (for instance, space that can serve different ages or group sizes as the population changes).
3. Involve parents in program planning to ensure that the program is designed to serve the identified needs of parents.
4. Start with a relatively small program and add on as the demand grows.
5. Allow time for parents to assess the program and to make new arrangements before expecting full utilization.
6. Recruit children from neighboring employers or the community when necessary for full utilization.
7. Add new services when the need is demonstrated. For instance, when Boulder Memorial Hospital in Colorado opened a program serving preschoolers in conjunction with a local church and school, parents raised the issues of extending hours to cover the night shift and adding infant care. Administrators figured out how many children were needed to make each service feasible. The parents were then told that the program would expand, as soon as they organized the required number of parents needing these kinds of care.

*Liability.** Companies sometimes worry about their liability should a child be injured in the program. It is encouraging to know that well-run child care programs have extremely low accident rates. Nonetheless, the prudent employer will wish to evaluate potential areas of liability and develop a strong program to reduce the risk of injury to children, staff, parents, visitors, and property. Important injury prevention methods include a thorough safety program, emergency preparedness, written authorizations from parents for emergency medical treatment, first aid training and equipment, and adherence to licensing standards. Reasonable cost insurance is available from professional child care associations and private brokers to provide appropriate protection. General liability insurance covers attorney fees as well as recompense to the injured person. Low-cost medical insurance allows an injured child to be treated effectively at no cost to the parent. Property insurance covers fire and other damage to center-owned property. (Unattached outdoor play equipment may need special coverage.) Vehicle insurance covers accidents in parent, staff, and center-owned cars and vans. Officers' and directors' liability insurance covers those individuals when acting in their official capacities. Bonding of employees protects the program against employee theft. A company can distance itself from liability by establishing a separate corporation to operate the child care program or by contracting with an outside company to provide the service. The service contract should include an indemnification provision under which the outside company agrees to be financially responsible for injuries that occur. It is also wise to be sure that the outside company carries adequate insurance. More information on liability is available from the following Child Care Law Center publications: "Liability Insurance" and "Property and Vehicle Insurance," both of which are listed in Appendix F.

Companies that provide child care centers, subsidies, or services for employees should be sure that their program qualifies as a Dependent Care Assistance Program under Internal Revenue Section 129. If not, the fair market value of the employer-provided child care most likely is taxable to the employee and the company is required to withhold payroll taxes.

This summary is provided as a brief description of selected liability concerns. Employers should consult their own attorneys for assistance in identifying and resolving their individual liability issues.

---

*This section on liability was written by Kathleen Murray, attorney at law, Child Care Law Center.

Starting a Child Care Center

The mix of factors in each employer-supported child care center is unique. Parent needs, community needs and resources, and company cultures and resources all make each program different from all others. Each program is designed to be effective in its own setting. The variations in employer-supported programs reflect the unique requirements, assets, and liabilities of the company's situation. Following are some guidelines showing how all of these factors fit together in effective employer-supported programs. Also included is a discussion of the major variables that need consideration when developing a center program.

Goals and Objectives

Goals define the overall philosophy and intent of the program, and guide the staff in defining program policies. Goals are set in terms of:

1. The number and types of employees to be served (for example, those who have children of certain ages, lower-income families, or particular groups of the staff).
2. The children to be served (for example, their age and whether community children will be eligible).
3. Program characteristics (for instance, staff/child ratios, group sizes, caregiver qualifications, and curriculum).
4. Corporate benefits to be achieved (for example, developing a highly visible model program as a public relations tool, providing a recruitment and retention incentive, or improving labor-management relations).
5. Parent needs and preferences.
6. Range of services offered (for example, night-time care, care for sick children, care for school-age children during summers and school holidays, transportation, or meals provided).

Quality Indicators

Defining "quality" in child care is a complicated task because there are so many different perspectives on the meaning of quality. Issues include long- and short-term effects on the individual child, meeting the needs of parents, understanding the concerns of the child care director and staff, and the issues involved in setting minimum standards through licensing or regulation.

Richard Roupp and Jeffrey Travers discuss the necessary balance between quality and cost as follows:[2]

> *The concern of the parent is finding care that is convenient, affordable, and appropriate to the perceived needs of the child. Parents influence the quality of care received by their children primarily by their choice of a facility and secondarily by direct and indirect participation in the operation of the facility (e.g., serving on governing boards, working as volunteers, exchanging information and suggestions with caregivers).*
>
> *The concern of the provider is to offer services that meet the (varying) needs of clients, children and families on an economically viable basis (i.e., at a cost that can be covered by parent fees and/or government subsidies). The provider can influence quality of care in many ways: by personal interaction with children and parents; by choice of program or "curriculum," equipment, and staff; by seeking government support for special services, such as food and health subsidies; or by training staff.*
>
> *The policymaker at the local, state, or federal level is concerned with the quantity and mix of child care services available to families within his or her purview, as well as with setting a lower bound on quality of care, below which facilities may not operate.*

The National Day Care Study completed in 1979 by Abt Associates was the most comprehensive study of child care programs for 3- to 5-year-olds to date.[3] The study found three important variables associated with high-quality center care. First, the *ratio of caregivers to children in each group* is extremely important for children. The Abt study recommended a staff/child ratio of 1:8 for a group of sixteen 3- to 5-year-olds. (Note: Ratios for quality infant care require a higher ratio, with more adults.) Second, caregivers should have *specific child-related education or training*, not just formal education. Thus, some amount of education about child development or early childhood education or training in an educational setting represents a more relevant qualification for caregivers than having an AA, BA, or other degree in non-child-related subjects. Examples of appropriate caregiver qualifications are a Child Development Associate (CDA) Credential or a Bachelor's or other advanced degree in early childhood education or child development. Third, the *overall size of each group of children* should be kept relatively small. The study recommended a maximum group size of sixteen children for 3- to 5-year-olds and a smaller group size of 8 to 12 for younger children.

Parent criteria for quality programs often include staff they can communicate well with, an interesting and safe environment, a program of age-appropriate activities for their child, and adequate numbers of experienced staff. Most important is that the program be one that the child enjoys and is comfortable in.

Many employers who have decided on center programs realize that high-quality programs best serve the interests of parents, children, and the company. Concern with quality has been a recurring theme in program discussion and reports of employer-supported programs. Quite a few company representatives have spoken of their desire to develop high-quality "model" programs that will attract publicity and be observed and copied by future program designers.

The staff of the National Employer Supported Child Care Project noted a particular concern for quality among employer-supported child care programs. One indicator of this concern was that many of the programs defined their objectives as being "developmental" that is, concerned with the educational and social development of the child, not just caretaking. Directors of employer-supported programs set high standards for themselves and their staffs. They often recruit and keep staff with the highest qualifications of education and experience by paying salaries that are more competitive than the usual minimal rates paid in community child care programs. Some employer-supported programs also offer more fringe benefits than community programs because they want to keep their teachers for the long term.

Another indicator of quality is that parents are actively involved in so many employer-supported programs. The availability and consistency of contact between parents and staff forges mutual understanding that benefits children. When parents and staff are both employees of the same company, they have a mutual stake in the program, and everyone benefits.

Licensing

Most states require that employer-supported centers be licensed using the same procedures required for other child care centers. Licensing requirements vary from state to state, generally including requirements about the physical aspects of the buildings and grounds, group size, staff/child ratios, program administration, personnel qualifications, health and safety regulations, record keeping, and emergency procedures.

Many states require a minimum of 35 square feet of usable indoor activity space and about 75 square feet of outdoor space per child in the center. Additional indoor space will be required for other activities (kitchens, bathrooms, offices, halls, and so forth), and will amount to about one-third more indoor space.

Most states require programs to be located on the ground floor of buildings.

Companies should contact the office responsible for licensing (often in the State Department of Human Resources or Social Services) for exact requirements in each state. These offices generally sponsor orientation meetings for all potential child care providers; licensing staff explain the regulations and procedures for application. After the company has submitted initial papers, a licensing worker will be assigned to work with center staff and inspect the facility for compliance. Licensing workers are very knowledgeable about local conditions and can be helpful to employers who are learning about child care. They will also explain the requirements of other agencies who are involved in the licensing process; these may include the fire department, health department, building and safety departments, and planning or zoning authorities.

*Staff**

Decisions about what staff to hire and how to compensate them can have a more profound effect on the success of the program than any other decision a company makes. The staffing largely determines the quality of the program, according to the National Day Care Study[4]. Major staffing considerations are: (1) the number of staff members to hire, (2) training and education, and (3) compensation. The following are recommendations for high-quality programs.

Number of staff to hire. Maintain a higher teacher-child ratio than the minimums required by state licensing regulations. Most state licensing regulations indicate only the minimum number of staff members required for child safety and are not an acceptable standard for high-quality programming. In establishing proper teacher-child ratios, planners should consider the ratios recommended for quality programs in addition to the minimums required by state regulations.

Training and education. Hire staff with specific training or courses in child development or early childhood education (for example, child development associate training) rather than those with unrelated college degrees. The National Day Care Study and other research indicates that members of the staff with child-related training regularly engage in more facilitative, comforting, and teaching interactions with children.

---

*This section on staff was co-authored by Marcie Whitebook and Sandra Burud.

Compensation. Compensate staff well, appropriate to their level of responsibility and training; do not base salaries on going salary rates for the industry. Child care staff members often have college training. Their jobs also entail significant responsibility for the safety and development of a group of small children. The skills of a well-trained child care worker are technical, including expertise in various aspects of health care, curriculum, and child development theory. Despite their considerable education, training, and amount of responsibility, average compensation packages for child care employees are quite low. Child care workers are among the lowest 5 percent of wage earners in the country, receiving few if any benefits.[5] The reason for low staff salaries is that the overhead costs of child care centers have to be as low as possible in order for parents to afford them, while salaries usually account for 70%–90% of a center's budget. Salaries thus are the major area in which substantial overhead savings can be achieved.

The tendency toward low salaries in the general child care market, however, results in high turnover among staff members and contributes to poor-quality programs. Turnover of staff members at most child care centers ranges from 15%–30% per year, far exceeding the 10% average for most human service workers. A 1980 study of child care staff in San Francisco, corroborated by other research, has shown that poor compensation was the major cause of dissatisfaction, turnover, and stress on the job.[6] Companies wanting good-quality programs find that adequate compensation of staff is a key factor in success.

To establish a compensation package that will attract and maintain a high-quality staff, consider the following:[7]

1. Pay child care workers commensurate with other company employees with similar education and training.
2. If no equivalent positions exist, compensate child care staff at a higher than average level for child care workers in the community. Publicly funded child care programs in each community are usually examples of programs with better-than-average salaries.
3. Give child care staff, whatever their pay rate, the same benefits given other company employees. In a field with limited benefits, offering health coverage, sick leave, paid holidays, vacations, or retirement benefits can be a significant addition to the total compensation package.
4. Establish a regular system of salary increases. While this may be customary practice within other industries, it is not usual in child care and will therefore attract highly qualified personnel to employer-supported programs.

5. Supplement parent fees with company contributions to finance adequate salaries and benefits. Both financial and in-kind contributions can supplement the regular budget and allow for higher salaries than possible from parent tuition fees alone. Direct government monies are unlikely in this area. However, some employer-supported child care programs serving low-income children from the community have attracted Title XX funds. Tax savings, participation in the federally funded child care food program, and use of community services are other sources of funding. Companies can also give their support to community fund-raising drives to obtain grants for the program.

Policy Development

Each center will need policies governing program operation, educational programming, and personnel. The development of policies regarding center operation generally requires input from a broad range of people, including parent-employees. Parent input will be particularly valuable in decisions about issues such as hours of operation, program requirements, and restrictions regarding ages of children allowed, care for sick children, and sibling groups. A parent handbook written by the center director and staff to communicate these policies clearly will establish a basis for communication. Policies about issues of concern to parents such as fee payment, tuition assistance, parent participation, waiting list, withdrawal of a child from the program, and exclusion of a child from the program (for example, a child showing certain symptoms of illness) should be covered in the parent handbook.

The center staff will generally want to play a large role in the development of educational policy. Once policies have been developed by the director and staff, they should be communicated as clearly as possible to parents both in written form and in discussions. Policies concerning personnel, such as pay scales, benefits, raises, sick leave, vacations, contracts, basis for dismissal, and evaluation, should be available to staff members in written form. Having these policies clearly written out provides a better basis for understanding between the staff and the board and/or the staff and the company.

Company-owned-and-operated centers generally do not have distinct policy-making boards, and policy is set by the director in consultation with company management, staff, and parents. In a non-profit center program, policies are set by the center's board of directors, working with the director and staff. The board is established when applying for non-profit incorporation. (Information on the board will be submitted along with other information on the new corporation, including articles of incorporation and bylaws.) Center boards may comprise representatives of all interested groups, including parents and company administrators.

Physical Environment

The company may renovate a space on or near the work site for the child care center, or it may decide to build a new facility. The design of the space is contingent on the educational goals and philosophy of the program, as well as on the ages and number of children to be served. A design process that includes input from the center director, staff, and parent-employees, as well as company management, will result in a functional environment. Drawing on the expertise of a child care director early in the planning process can prevent many potential problems from developing in a new facility. Participation of parent-employees in the planning of the facility and program contributes greatly to their later confidence in and use of the program.

Companies undertaking substantial renovation or construction may want to hire an architect experienced in designing environments for children. A number of publications can help guide companies through the step-by-step process of developing a new child care facility,[8] as well as programmatic planning and administration.[9]

Spaces are needed for indoor and outdoor play, napping, diaper-changing, toileting, eating, food preparation, storage, teacher preparation, and administration. Good environments have the following attributes:

1. They are safe for children.
2. They are easy to clean and disinfect.
3. They are sufficiently flexible that teachers can rearrange the space to fit different activities.
4. They are visible so that teachers can observe all children.
5. They are comfortable and pleasant for both teachers and children.
6. They have centrally located bathrooms with easy access.
7. They allow for group and individual activities.

8. They have an easily accessible and easily visible outdoor play space.
9. They are convenient for teachers and include ample storage.
10. They include varied textured and colored surfaces.
11. They are well-lighted and heated or cooled in summer.
12. They are stocked with a variety of sturdy learning materials.

Enrollment

Most centers do not start with a full roster of children. Many parents need time to observe a new program before they feel confident enough to change their existing child care arrangements. The length of time needed to reach full utilization varies, as experienced by the companies participating in the National Employer Supported Child Care Project study: 76 companies reported that their centers achieved full enrollment in less than one year, for 42 it took between one and two years, and for 16 others it took over two years. After full enrollment was achieved almost all of the centers were able to maintain it, and most now have a constant waiting list for their programs. Center directors can take advantage of the lag time between opening and full enrollment to get the daily operations of the program on an even keel, to hire and train additional staff, to develop relationships with company management and employees, and to do the necessary publicity about the program. A phased-in approach may be most advantageous, especially when the plan is for a large program. The center can start with one group or room and open others as enrollment grows.

Opening the center to children from the community can help keep enrollment higher, if only until it is fully utilized by employees, and it can also create positive relationships between the company and the community. Centers can minimize the lag time between opening and full enrollment by opening at strategic times of the year, such as September and January, when many parents make new child care arrangements.

Parent Participation

Parent participation is critical in maintaining a program that matches employee needs and preferences. A good match will ultimately bring the company a good return on its investment.

Parents serve as an effective quality control mechanism and mutual support system. The most common method of accommodating parent participation in centers is to form parent advisory committees. Parents may meet regularly to participate in all phases of the program from fund raising to classroom activities or at infrequent intervals to discuss more limited concerns. In both cases the limited time available to working parents will require efficient planning of their participation.

Employer-supported centers have been very successful both in terms of benefits reported by the companies and those reported by parent-employees using them. Parent satisfaction is one very important indicator of the success of child care programs in meeting family needs. A sample of parents using employer-supported centers surveyed by the National Employer Supported Child Care Project reported very high satisfaction with their child care. See Appendix A for a full description of this study.

Health Care

The health care program of the center can include many of the functions discussed in Chapter 16 on care for sick children, including:[10]

1. Preventive care, including maintaining doctor's reports on all children, assuring that all necessary innoculations have been given, practicing preventive sanitary measures in the center, training staff to detect potential health problems, referring children for treatment, and planning appropriate safety and emergency procedures.
2. Referrals and follow-up of necessary treatment for children in the community.
3. Education about good health practices, including diagnosis, treatment, and prevention, for children, parents, and staff.

Costs

Although there is a great commonality of items on a center's budget, there is probably no "typical" budget for a child care center. The amounts vary in relation to the number of children served, the staff/child ratio, the hours of operation, physical plant overhead, and the services offered. The following examples of operating budgets are presented to give a basis for comparison.

Budget 1. Basic 1982 annual operating budget of Hollywood Presbyterian Medical Center Child Care Center in Los Angeles, California, serving 32 preschoolers.[11]

Management Cost (director)	$20,498
Technical/specialist cost (3 teachers)	41,141
Total salaries	$61,639
Supplies	$ 520
Equipment	420
Subscriptions/dues	100
Travel/meetings	520
Miscellaneous (petty cash)	360
Total supplies	$ 1,920
Interdepartmental transfer (includes dietary)	$12,984
Maintenance/laundry	1,500
Engineering	500
Total services	$15,084
Total operating budget	$78,653

Budget 2. Estimated 1980 operating budget for Stride Rite Children's Center in Boston, Massachusetts, serving 50 children.[12]

RECEIPTS:	
Company support	$ 42,800
School lunch program	20,000
Negotiated contract with Dept. of Public Welfare*	65,600
Payment from employee participants	16,000
Total receipts	$144,400
EXPENDITURES:	
Salaries	$ 90,000
Payroll taxes (FICA)	6,000
Federal and state unemployment taxes	2,900
Food costs	22,500
Rent+	6,000
Heat and air conditioning+	1,000
Telephone+	1,000
Electricity+	1,500
Daily Cleaning+	2,000
Office services(accounting, secretarial, and supplies)+	2,500
Repairs+	600
Annual cleaning	1,000
Insurance	1,700
Legal	100
Travel and field trips	1,000
Staff training	100
Misc. and equipment	1,000
Depreciation	6,000
Supplies	2,500
Substitutes (teachers)	1,000
Total Expenditures	$150,400

*Based on serving community children.
+Services purchased from Stride Rite Corporation.

Budget 3. Sample annual operating budget for a center serving 45 children (not an actual program budget) in 1981.[13]

PERSONNEL:	*% of Time*	*Annual Salary*	*Total*
Director/head teacher	100%	$14,000	$ 14,000
Secretary/bookkeeper	50	8,000	4,000
Teachers (2)	100	12,000	24,000
Aides* (1)	100	8,000	8,000
(2)	50	7,000	7,000
Cook/maintenance person	100	7,000	7,000
Subtotal			$ 64,000
Fringe Benefits @ 15%			9,600
Substitutes @ $3.20/hr. × 8 wks.			1,050
Total			$ 74,650
OCCUPANCY:			
Rent @ $800/month × 12 months (2,000 square feet @ $4.80/sq. ft)			9,600
Heat			2,300
Electricity			1,700
Telephone			500
Total			$ 14,100
EQUIPMENT:			
Educational			800
Kitchen			500
Housekeeping			200
Office			300
Total			$ 1,800
SUPPLIES:			
Educational			1,200
Housekeeping			500
Office			500
Total			$ 2,200
FOOD:			
1 meal and 2 snacks ($1.60 × 40 × 240 days):			$ 15,400
OTHER EXPENSES:			
Advertising			400
Licensing fees			50
Insurance (liability @ $10/child/year)			450
Subscription/membership			50
Audit			900
			$ 1,850

DEBT:	
Annual payment on $20,000	
start-up loan	$ 5,000
Total expenses	$115,000
INCOME:	
Parent fees (assuming 85% enrollment)	
(45 × 85% × $60/wk. × 50 wks.)	114,750
Fundraising/Donations	250
Total Income	$115,000

The child care centers surveyed in the National Employer Supported Child Care Project were supported almost entirely by parent fees and company contributions; only 47 of the companies reported that their center also received funding from other sources. The companies reported different kinds and levels of participation in getting the centers started: 15 companies reported that they made loans to program organizers for start-up, 29 companies made donations of less than $50,000, 9 companies made donations of more than $50,000, and 81 companies reported that they gave in-kind services to assist in start-up. Companies also reported different levels of ongoing support. Seventeen reported that they gave less than $1,000 per child per year and 23 gave over $1,000 per year; 112 reported that they continued to donate in-kind services.

The companies also varied in the fees paid by parents for child care. Parent fees usually provide the balance of income to the child care program after the company subsidy. Since it generally costs more to provide care for infants and toddlers than for preschoolers (more staff is required), costs per child for infant care usually exceed those for preschoolers. Care for school-age children is provided for fewer hours per day and, therefore, usually costs less than care for either infants or preschoolers. Of the 131 companies reporting fees for infants and toddlers in the National Employer Supported Child Care Project study, 13 reported fees of $25 per week or less, 70 reported fees of between $26–$45 per week, and 47 had fees of over $45 per week. Of the 164 companies reporting fees for preschool-age children, 20 reported fees of $25 per week or less, 106 reported fees of between $26 and $45 per week, and 38 reported fees of over $45 per week. Of the 76 companies reporting fees for school-age children, 13 reported fees of $10 per week or less, 31 reported fees of between $11 and $30 per week, and 32 reported fees of over $30 per week.

Endnotes

1. For further description, see Commerce Clearinghouse, Inc., *Tax Incentives for Employer-Sponsored Day Care Programs,* Tax Angles and Tax Savings Series (Chicago: Commerce Clearing House, Inc., March 1982).
2. R. Roupp and J. Travers, "Janus Faces Day Care: Perspectives on Quality and Cost," in *Day Care: Scientific and Social Policy Issues,* eds. E. Zigler & E. Gordon (Boston, Mass.: Auburn House, 1982), p. 78.
3. R. Roupp, *Children at the Center: Final Report of the National Day Care Study,* Executive Summary (Cambridge, Mass.: Abt Associates, 1979), pp. 2–3.
4. *Ibid.*, p. 14.
5. *Ibid.*, p. 21.
6. M. Whitebook, C. Howes, P. Darrah, and J. Friedman, "Who's Minding the Child Care Workers? A Look at Staff Burn-Out," *Children Today* January–February, 1982.
7. For information on compensatory packages and technical assistance relating to personnel contact the Child Care Employees Project, P.O. Box 5603, Berkeley, California 94705, (415) 653-9889.
8. For instance, see G. T. Moore, *et al., Recommendations for Child Care Centers* (Milwaukee: University of Wisconsin, 1979); U. Cohen, G. T. Moore, and T. McGinty, *Case Studies of Child Play Areas and Child Support Facilities* (Milwaukee: University of Wisconsin, Center for Architecture & Urban Planning Research, 1978); U. Cohen, A. H. Hill, *et al., Recommendations for Child Play Areas* (Milwaukee: University of Wisconsin, Center for Architecture & Urban Planning Research, 1979).
9. For example, see Day Care Council of America, Inc., *How to Start a Day Care Center* (Washington , D.C.: Day Care Council of America, Inc., 1981); R. Roup, *Children at the Center,* Executive Summary, (Cambridge, Mass.: Abt Associates, 1979); P. Click, *Administration of Schools for Young Children,* 2nd ed. (Albany, New York: Delmar Publishers Inc., 1981).
10. J. Richmond and J. Janis, "Health Care Services for Children in Day Care," in *Day Care: Scientific and Social Policy Issues,* eds. E. Zigler and E. Gordon (Boston, Mass.: Auburn House, 1982), pp. 445–456.
11. From a personal communication from Laura Escobido, Director.
12. C. Baden and D. Friedman, eds., *New Management Initiatives for Working Parents* (Boston, Mass.: Wheelock College, 1981), p. 46.
13. Day Care Council of America, Inc., *How to Start a Day Care Center* (Washington, D.C.: Day Care Council of America, Inc., 1981), pp. 26–27.

Chapter 13

FAMILY DAY CARE PROGRAMS

Many children are cared for in the home of a neighbor, relative, or friend while their parents are at work. Such people who care for children in their homes on a regular basis are referred to as "family day care providers." According to the recent National Day Care Home Study, over 5 million children in this country are being cared for in nearly 2 million family day care homes.[1]

The Case for Care in Family Day Care Homes

Parents find family day care through neighbors or friends, advertisements, community child care agencies, or information and referral agencies. According to the National Day Care Home Study, there are three major types of family day care homes. *Regulated homes,* which are licensed or registered with a state regulatory agency, account for 6 percent of family day care. *Sponsored homes,* consisting of regulated providers who "operate as part of day care systems or networks of homes under the sponsorship of an umbrella agency," account for almost 3 percent of all providers and about 42 percent of regulated providers. *Non-regulated homes,* which are neither licensed nor registered by the state, account for 94 percent of all family day care in the United States.[2]

The differences between family day care and care in a child care center are often misunderstood. One major difference is size; family day care serves a small group of children and is usually provided by one adult. In licensed homes, the adult can usually care for no more than six children, including up to two infants. Some states license "group" family day care homes with two adults and up to 12 children. Another difference is the type of facility used. The home of the provider is used for family day care, whereas child care centers are single-purpose facilities used exclusively for the care of children.

Both types of care can be educational for children of all ages and can offer a stimulating environment. However, they have somewhat different advantages. Since family day care is small and home-based, children often have more opportunity for individual attention. There may be less need for the restrictive rules that larger institutions often require, the program can be less formal, and flexibility to meet individual needs is often easier to achieve.

Companies may decide to set up a family day care program rather than a center because their employees prefer child care in a home setting, because the geographical spread of employees makes selection of a single site for care impossible, or because family day care has a shorter start-up time and a more easily changed enrollment capacity.

Parents may prefer family day care for a number of reasons. Many believe that it is better for the care of infants, for preschoolers who need the consistency of one caregiver, for children who require special attention (such as handicapped children), for children who function better in smaller groups, or for school-age children who need transportation to and from school and the ability to attend after-school activities. Family day care may also be preferred by some parents because it is easier to find close to home, because all siblings in a family can be cared for in one place, because it helps the child to make neighborhood friends, or because the hours are often not as rigid when the parent has to work late or unusual shifts. Mildly ill children can be cared for in accordance with the licensing regulations governing family day care. Infants and toddlers often need family day care because most centers do not accept children under 2½ years old; and older children may need it because there are so few day centers or other programs that accept school-age children, particularly before school.

Employer contributions to the development of family day care homes can serve three purposes:

1. Increasing the *amount of care* that is available in the community.
2. *Improving the care* that is available so that it is more accessible and of better quality.
3. *Supplementing center programs* and increase their flexibility for serving certain age groups or geographical locations.

Currently, there are only a few employer-supported family day care programs. In fact, only five of the companies surveyed by the National Employer Supported Child Care Project reported that their *primary* child care service was providing family day care; four other companies also supported family day care programs to supplement their primary child care service. It is likely that the numbers will increase as employers become more familiar with this option and its special advantages. The following examples illustrate the variety of effective employer approaches to family day care.

Pall Corporation, Long Island, N. Y.

The company donated money to the Harbor Day Care Center to sponsor a family day care satellite system for infants and toddlers. Six providers were trained to care for children from infancy to 2 years and 9 months. They received many support services, including vacation pay, sick pay, student nurse visits, and help in making appropriate referrals for other services for parents and children. The program is open to the community as well as to company employees.

Children's Hospital; Merritt Hospital; Providence Hospital; Peralta Hospital Oakland, Calif.

Children's Home Society of California developed a family day care network to serve employees of all four hospitals. Currently about twenty children are served through the network.

Dart Industries, Los Angeles, Calif.

The company gave a grant to UCLA Child Care Services and the Santa Monica Child Care Information Service (a child care information and referral agency) to carry out a year-long project developing a support system to recruit and train family day care providers and educate parents about family day care. The project, *Family Day Care: WESTS,* increased the number and quality of providers available to families in the area and represents a good model for indirect employer support of this important and little-known type of child care.

Illinois Masonic Medical Center, Chicago, Ill.

The hospital sponsors a network of seven family day care homes in addition to its child care center (for children 2½ to 5 years old). The homes serve a total of 14 infants and toddlers from 3 months to 2½ years old.

Program Advantages and Disadvantages

Advantages	*Disadvantages*	*Solutions*
Low cost: Start-up costs are low. On-going costs depend on degree of company subsidy.	Low company visibility.	Mount a publicity campaign within the company and in the community.
Short start-up period: An in-house program can be started more quickly than a center. Contracting with existing child care agencies cuts start-up time even further.	Instability.	Provide back-up for providers when they are ill or need time off.
Flexibility: Capacity is easily altered and homes can be adapted to changing hours or opening homes in new locations.	Caregiver recruitment difficulties.	Increase job appeal by corporate contributions and support services.
Parent choices: Homes with different educational philosophies and caregiver styles can allow parental choice.	Scheduling difficulties.	Develop an adequate number of homes to serve employees on all shifts.
	Variability of quality.	Devise monitoring and inservice training procedures for care providers.
		Consider a satellite system linking the family day care providers to child care centers.

Program Development Decisions

In a 1981 conference on employer-supported child care, June Sale, Director of UCLA Child Care Services, presented four models for employer support of family day care[3] which fall on a continuum from close company control and high involvement to relatively little:

1. The employer hires the family day care providers who then care only for children with parents employed by the company.
2. The employees receive vouchers to pay the family day care provider they select.
3. The employer organizes a network of local providers and provides support services, and parents pay the provider directly.
4. The employer supports a community-oriented program that includes recruitment of new providers, a variety of supports for providers and parents, no limitation on who can enroll, and individual follow-up with company employees.

Employers wishing to use family day care can use one of two service arrangements: a network of homes or satellite homes.

Family Day Care Networks. The company can set up a family day care "network" where individual providers use each other as a support group, share services and equipment, and provide mutual backup in cases of emergency. Family day care networks typically offer a number of services to providers, including client referral, training opportunities, business skills, substitute caregivers, medical back-up, toy libraries, equipment borrowing, financial assistance for the cost of low-income children through Title XX of the Social Services Block Grant, subsidized food programs through the U.S. Department of Agriculture, group purchasing, and insurance coverage.

The company may use existing family day care homes or networks rather than starting new ones. It may be possible to contract with existing networks to serve employees' children or to replicate some aspects of the network in an employer program. Networks may be willing to add providers to serve employees' children in return for financial and in-kind services from the company.

Companies can also refer employee parents to existing family day care homes. The company can keep a roster of local family day care homes, and it can provide information and help parents find the home that best meets their needs. Assisting parents to find existing family day care providers may be very helpful in many cases, but it will not be enough if the homes lack available space, if they are in inconvenient locations, or if their hours do not accommodate the parents' workshifts. Companies can help remedy these problems by arranging with local providers to accommodate the necessary schedules by reserving a few spaces for the children of employees, or by recruiting new family day care providers for unserved locations. Offering these providers additional back-up or in-kind services helps keep the quality of care high.

Satellite Family Day Care Homes. A company can use family day care homes as satellites to a center program. Family day care may be an appropriate choice for children of any age, although it is often thought to have special advantages for very young or school-age children. A company with a child care center that serves only preschool children may decide to add family day care satellite homes to care for infants and/or school-age children. These homes can be located near the center, in specific outlying neighborhoods, or near local schools. Providers may receive the salary and benefits of center staff or be paid directly by parents. As satellite homes they can receive many advantages such as referrals, training, support, and access to toys and resources.

In addition to providing care for infants and school-age children, these homes are also used for the following purposes:

1. Care of moderately ill children who can not be cared for at the center.
2. Accommodation of families waiting for an opening at the center (thereby preserving the recruitment value of the child care program).
3. Accommodation of families who prefer small-group care for older preschool children.
4. Filling of special scheduling needs when it is not cost-effective to keep the center open, such as on night shifts or weekends.
5. Flexibility during times of the year when extra care is needed, such as summer vacation for school-age children, Christmas vacation, or other school holidays.
6. Expansion of the program to accommodate user demand beyond the center's capacity.
7. Meeting emergency care needs when employees cannot use their existing care arrangement for a short time (for example, when the regular caregiver is on vacation or has a medical emergency).
8. Providing care for children of employees who work in branch offices, when commuting with children to a central site is not feasible.

Starting a Program

Family day care services can be run as an in-house program or purchased under contract from a community child care agency. The central functions of either the contracted agency or the in-house staff are:

1. Identification of family day care providers.
2. Recruitment of new providers where necessary.
3. Informing parents about child care selection.
4. Administering appropriate support services, such as equipment and toy loans, training seminars, or group purchasing.

In-House Programs. If the coordinator is in-house, family day care may be combined with other kinds of services, such as parent education or information and referral. For instance, a coordinator might begin by providing referrals to parents and then establish a small family day care project when parent needs are identified. Experience with family day care might also bring other child care problems to the surface—especially needs for a preschool center or after-school care. The advantages of having an in-house coordinator are that the company retains flexibility in adapting its child care services to its own employees' needs, in monitoring and evaluating the service, and in giving individual attention to employees.

When hiring an in-house program coordinator, the company will want to look for specific family day care experience in addition to management skills and the ability to educate parents and train providers about various aspects of child care.

Contracting Agencies. Agencies that can contract to provide family day care include community child care agencies, social service groups, and associations of family day care providers. An agency may help the company determine the extent of need for family day care, locate providers, set up the service, provide information for employees about the program, and evaluate the program's continuing effectiveness. The advantages of contracting with an agency to provide family day care are that the agency will have specific knowledge of the other child care resources in the community, will have already developed expertise in providing family day care, and will assume responsibility for daily operations of the program. An employer who wants to contract for family day care services should look for the following qualities in a potential contracting agency:

1. Experience with family day care.
2. Experience in administering child care programs, rather than only direct teaching or child care program experience.
3. A tie-in with the community child care service agencies, through coalitions or advocacy groups.

Licensing and Registration. Most states require that family day care providers be licensed or registered. Licensing regulations usually require that the home have adequate facilities for indoor and outdoor activities, set caregiver-to-child ratios and maximum group size for children of different ages, and stipulate that the provider be checked for prior criminal offenses. States that do not not license family day care simply register providers without issuing a license. In registration systems, caregivers certify that they meet state standards and are spot-checked on a random basis for compliance. Most registration systems also follow up on parents' complaints; however, there is minimal monitoring and caregiver support. Employers should investigate the regulatory requirements in their state by calling the state or county department of human resources or social services, and they should be sure that providers supported by their programs meet state standards.

Operating Policies. Policies must be set regarding issues such as tuition rates, records, contract approval, placement of children, grievances, and the role of the program coordinator. Additional policies regarding geographical distribution of providers and optimum size of the provider pool may also be necessary, based on program goals and parent need. Eligibility policies are important, such as whether to allow employees who are not regular users of the service to use it in emergencies.

Provider Recruitment. Programs that recruit new family day care providers help expand the total amount of available child care. However, since it is often difficult to find qualified new providers, some employer-supported programs may restrict their recruiting and concentrate on finding the best of the existing providers. The company can then refer employees to this group of providers. For many providers such an arrangement would be attractive because they, as small business people, can benefit through association with an employer, either by client referrals or through other supportive services. Other providers (for instance, those who have as many children as they can accept) may not want to lose their independence by association with a company. One key incentive in recruiting new or existing family day care providers to work with company program are the support services it offers. A full range of support services designed specifically for local family day care providers enhances recruitment and helps to assure quality child care.

Quality Criteria for Providers. The system for selecting providers should include a review of the providers' credentials and/or experience, the home setting, and the educational program offered to children. Establishing criteria can assure high-quality child care both in the initial selection and ongoing monitoring of the family day care providers. In the initial selection of providers, companies may find that most providers have little formal training in child care. Including only providers who need and maintain compliance with state regulatory requirements will help the company assure that minimum standards are met. The company may wish to set higher standards for its providers than the minimal ones required under state licensing regulations. If providers are not currently licensed, the company may help by financing the cost of the licensing process.

Support Services. Decisions about support services and their method of delivery can have a significant impact on whether the program works smoothly and on the ultimate benefit to the company and parents. Potential support services include training in early childhood education and child development; employee benefits for providers, including vacation and sick pay; substitute caregivers; medical back-up; toy and equipment loans; revolving loan funding to purchase equipment and make building improvements; insurance; group purchasing (giving providers access to lower rates); access to government food programs; legal counseling; and in-kind services such as maintenance and business management expertise. Support services can improve the quality and stability of care and increase the satisfaction of parents using the program.

Support services can help overcome some of the potential disadvantages of family day care. For instance, family day care may be less stable than center care because it depends on the availability of one person. When that person is ill or on vacation, parents have to find other arrangements. If back-up caregivers are made available, care is more stable. Family day care often varies in quality; offering services such as training and equipment loans can make the quality of the providers more uniform. With all of these support services, the cost of care to parents can still be kept low. Other programs such as no-interest loans to providers, State Social Services Block Grant funds, and federal food programs (available for low-income children) may also be available.

Adequate provision of employee benefits can be an important tool in the retention of competent providers. Family day care providers generally do not receive any employee benefits. The minimal salaries they receive are often not enough to maintain an adequate standard of living and many are forced to seek other work. Employee benefits can augment their salaries and increase the number of caregivers available to parents.

Training. Training providers is an especially important part of the operation of a family day care program. The range of education and experience among providers is very broad. Each brings strengths to the program, but there will be areas in which providers need and appreciate extra training. A full training program, includes:

1. Pre-service training on the organizational structure and policies of the program and an overview of how to deliver quality child care services.
2. In-service training workshops on topics such as discipline, age-appropriate activities, communication with parents, record keeping and bookkeeping, early childhood education, child development, management, tax advantages to providers, and early warning signs of health problems (for example, illnesses, learning disabilities, or hearing problems).
3. Access to resource courses offered in the community.

The National Day Care Home Study[5] found that training programs (ranging from two-day workshops to comprehensive programs) had strong positive effects on the way providers interacted with the children. It is in the company's best interest to provide a full training program for providers in order to attract and retain the best providers as well as to help ensure high-quality services for children.

Community Development. Family day care can also be part of a broad approach to community development. The family day care model developed by ASIAN, INC. in San Francisco, California had several aims.[6] First, it wanted to help the economic development of the community by training people to run their own small businesses. Second, it wanted to contribute to the revitalization of the neighborhood by rehabilitating existing housing. And third, it wanted to create more family day care in an area where finding appropriate facilities was a major disincentive to the development of needed child care programs. The ASIAN INC. approach involved a number of supports for providers, including a comprehensive training program. Some providers were offered apartments in a building restored by the agency. The providers who moved into the building cared for children and offered relief, support, and help to each other. The program has received funding from a number of sources, including hospitals in the area.

Costs. Since the cost of family day care is generally set by individual providers, it varies enormously. One employer-supported family day care program reported that the average cost for children under two was $65–$75 per week, while costs in community family day care programs ranged from $55 to $100 per week. Another program reported that the company subsidized the cost of care, with parents paying $45 per week and the company providing another $30 per week to cover the balance of the program cost.

One of the most important program policy decisions is whether or not to offer a small guaranteed fee to providers to assure their availability for employee children. Policies about how providers are paid and who collects the tuition from parents must also be set. Providers hired as employees of the company (with fees collected by the company) will be on the company payroll. Non-employee providers receive their salaries from parents in the fees that they themselves collect.

Expenses for the provider include food, household purchases, educational equipment, furnishings, first-aid materials, medicines, maintenance and repair services, insurance, salaries, rent or mortgage payments, heat, electricity, telephone, and transportation.[7] As the National Day Care Home Study concludes:[8]

From the parents' perspective, family day care may appear a costly endeavor . . . .From the provider's perspective, however, family day care is not a lucrative profession. The average weekly wage for providing care is $50.27 to $62.09 after payments are made for food, supplies and insurance.

Liability*

Companies affiliated with family day care homes may be concerned about their liability should a child be injured during care. To reduce the risk of injury, companies can encourage or require attention to safety, first-aid training of caregivers, and emergency preparedness, including written authorization for medical treatment from parents. Perhaps the single most effective method a company can employ to reduce its *own* liability is a carefully drawn written contract that delineates the relationship between company and provider. The contract should contain a provision by which the provider agrees to indemnify the company and accept financial responsibility for any injury that occurs. To insure compliance, the contract should also contain a provision by which the provider agrees to obtain a specified amount and type of insurance. The company can easily verify that the insurance has actually been purchased. A carefully drafted contract can also help to delineate the relationship between the company and the homes as "independent contractor" rather than "employer-employee." If the family day care provider is characterized as an employee, the employer is responsible for withholding wages and paying social security and other payroll taxes. To avoid employee status, the family day care provider must be a true independent contractor who retains control of his or her own business and meets the numerous other statutory and caselaw test of an independent contractor.

Companies that provide child care subsidies or services for employees should insure that their program qualifies as a Dependent Care Assistance Program under Internal Revenue Section 129. If not, the fair market value of the employer-provided child care most likely is taxable to the employee and the company must withhold payroll taxes.

This summary is provided as a brief description of selected liability concerns. Employers should consult their own attorneys for assistance in identifying and resolving their individual liability issues.

---

*This section on liability was written by Kathleen Murray, attorney at law, Child Care Law Center.

Endnotes

1. S. Fosberg, *Family Day Care in the United States: Summary of Findings* 1, Final Report of National Day Care Home Study, U.S. Department of Health and Human Services (Cambridge, Mass.: Abt Associates, 1981), p. 3.
2. P. Divine-Hawkins, *Family Day Care in the United States: Executive Summary,* Final Report of the National Day Care Home Study, DHHS Publication No. 80–30287 (Washington D.C.: U.S. Department of Health and Human Services, 1981), pp. 2–7.
3. M. Snider and J. Becker, "Parents at Work, Your Assets for the Eighties," A Conference for San Francisco Employers (October 29. 1981), p. 10.
4. Fosberg, *Family Day Care in the United States: Summary of Findings,* p. 5.
5. *Ibid.,* p. 82.
6. P. Fong, *The Child Care Job and Economic Development Project, A Model for Job Creation in Small Business Child Care Service Enterprise,* 4 vols., Summary Report (San Francisco: ASIAN, INC. 1981).
7. B. Squibb, *Family Day Care: How to Provide It in Your Home* (Harvard, Mass.: Harvard Common Press, 1976), pp. 85–87.
8. Fosberg, *Family Day Care in the United States: Summary of Findings,* p. 103.

Chapter 14

DIRECT SERVICES FOR SCHOOL-AGE CHILDREN

Child care programs serve children of all ages, from infancy into the teenage years. This chapter addresses the special needs of school-age children. This group is addressed separately here both because older children present unique logistical problems and because there is a particularly acute shortage of school-age child care. Children old enough to attend school need care during mornings, afternoons, holidays, and vacations to supplement their regular school programs. Parent employees want to be sure that their children are safe and well cared for during all of the hours of the working day, not just those hours when schools are normally open. But most communities today do not have enough care to provide for all of their school-age children.

Through the 1960s and 1970s most of the nation's attention was directed to the care of the preschool child. Now, with the increasing number of dual-income career and single-parent households in America, the need for school-age child care is fast becoming recognized.

Indicators of the need can be observed at work sites all over the country. Managers are noticing that employee absenteeism and requests for schedule changes tend to increase when school is out during snow days, teacher workshops, and scheduled holidays. As summer approaches, parents become even more frantic over child care arrangements. Tardiness is particularly likely to occur during before-school hours, and concern for the safety of chil-

---

NOTE: This chapter was written by Ellen Gannett, School-Age Child Care Project, Wellesley College Center for Research on Women, Wellesley, Massachusetts.

dren who are on their own until the end of the work day contributes to what is known as the "3:00 syndrome." Parents who check on a child's safe arrival home from school often find themselves mediating arguments between siblings or supervising their behavior over the telephone.

In 1979 it was reported that approximately two million school-age children between the ages of seven and thirteen were without supervision before and after school.[1] This figure does not include the 5- and 6-year-olds in similar situations, nor does it indicate the increasing number of children who are probably caring for themselves now. These "latchkey children," so-called because they often wear house keys around their necks, are caring for themselves at home, in school playgrounds, or on the street for several hours each day. The Children's Defense Fund writes in their 1982 *Data Book*, "What is happening to these children while their parents are on the jobs? The most accurate answer is that, as a nation, we do not know."[2]

According to Thomas and Lynette Long of Catholic University, who in 1981 conducted a small study (with 53 latchkey children and 32 adult-supervised children), "Children who were left alone routinely during after-school hours experienced more fear. Forty percent could neither go outside nor invite friends over while their parents were absent. Isolation for latchkey children became especially pronounced during vacation and holiday periods."[3] This research seems to indicate that, for many children, being alone is a scary, lonely experience. A recent statewide study in Minnesota and Virginia found that fully a quarter of working parents relied on self or sibling care for their school-age children.[4]

Selecting a Program

School-age child care programs include those that care for children before and after school and during holidays and vacations. Some are located in the public schools and are run by community agencies, by parents, or by the schools themselves. Others are based in youth agencies such as Y's, girls' or boys' clubs, or campfire groups. Still others are located in and run by community institutions such as religious organizations, community centers, or local day care centers.

Some communities offer home-based, family day care for their school-age children, such as the Satellite Family Care Program in Reston, Virginia. In Reston the home providers are carefully selected, trained, and supervised by the center's program director. Homes are selected close to neighborhood schools. Each provider cares for five children, all of whom live in or near the same neighborhood. During a typical afternoon under the supervision of the caregiver, the children go outside to play, attend lessons, go to their own homes for a quick visit, and return to the provider's home for snacks and a planned activity.

Another program offers a different solution, giving reassurance by telephone to children who are at home alone. "Chatters" in Houston, Texas offers families a telephone reassurance service for an annual fee of $30. Parents enroll their child in this service, which is based in a day care center close to the child's home. The child routinely checks in with a telephone counselor, chats briefly about his or her day, and periodically calls if he or she feels lonely or afraid. In the event of an emergency, the counselor is available to come to the child's home. A call-waiting and call-forwarding system allows other children's calls to be directed to that counselor while at the child's home. A training component is built into the service, for both child and parent. The child learns emergency, burglary, fire, storm, and other emergency procedures. Late or overnight emergency care is then coordinated by "Chatters," which acts as a resource and referral service for the families by connecting them to Houston's social service agencies.

Local businesses can support programs like "Chatters" either by funding the salary of a telephone counselor or by subsidizing the cost of the service for their employees.

There are many program models for school-age care and possible combinations of care. It is important to note that no one model is mutually exclusive of another; communities often put together various elements of several models to fit their individual needs.

Most communities find that school-age child care is a lower-cost service than preschool or infant/toddler child care because (1) programs are commonly located in no or low-cost community facilities; (2) fewer hours of care are needed per day; and (3) the staff/child ratio is lower. These reduced payroll and rental costs make such care very attractive to those employers who choose to support it.

Program Examples

The National Employer Supported Child Care Project survey found that employers are supporting school-age child care by backing community programs, by developing summer camps, and by caring for school-age children (as well as younger children) in child care centers on or near the work site. Eighty-six of the companies that have their own child care centers reported that they care for school children age 6 and over. The number of school-age children enrolled in these programs varied, with 15 programs serving fewer than 11 children, 42 serving between 11 and 50, and 8 serving more than 50. Twenty-four of the programs reported that the oldest child was under nine, while 41 served children as old as 9–12 years of age and another 4 served children over 12. About as many programs were located at the work site as were not. Roughly two-thirds of the programs were open year-round; another third were only open during the summer. About two-thirds reported that they were open more than 8 hours per day, while the other third were open 8 hours or less. Eighteen programs reported that they provide transportation. Examples of successful programs supported by companies are presented below. Each program profile lists advantages and limitations of the particular model from the point of view of the employer as a care contributor, of the employee as a parent, and of the child as a program participant.

An Off-Site Child Care Center That Extends Its Program

In 1971 Control Data Corporation in Minneapolis, Minnesota cooperated with a local department store and the Federal Reserve Bank to fund the Northside Child Development Center. The consortium was later joined by Northwestern Bell, Northern States Power Company, Farmers and Mechanics Savings and Loan, Lutheran Brotherhood, and the Pillsbury Company. The companies originally contributed the local match money for federal funding, but today they no longer provide direct financial support to the center.

The center started with 20 infants and 80 preschoolers. It now serves an additional 26 school-age children up to age 13. For $7.25 per day the children receive breakfast before school, are transported to their school, and return to the center at 3:00 p.m. Their parents pick them up at the end of the day.[5]

Advantages

1. It is a familiar program for "graduates" of the preschool.
2. The center is an already operating and licensed facility.
3. The program adds revenue to the day care center.
4. Services are open and available year-round.[6]

Limitations:

1. Unless the company's employees are geographically concen-

trated in one area, this model can serve only a small proportion of families who happen to live near the child care center.
2. Space in an existing preschool child care center may be inappropriate for older children. Centers are often ill-equipped and improperly staffed to meet the developmental needs of school-age children.
3. Even if transportation were provided by the company, parents often prefer that their children remain in their own neighborhoods and not be transported long distances after school.
4. The school-age component may not have exclusive use of a classroom and may have to share space with the preschoolers.
5. Locating in an existing preschool center may make communication difficult between the child's school teachers and the child care personnel, thereby allowing for little or no knowledge of the child's day at school.

A Company-Run Summer Camp

In 1970 Fel-Pro Industries, a Skokie, Illinois manufacturer of chemical and automotive gaskets, purchased 220 acres of rural property 40 miles from the factory. Initially intended as a recreation area, it was developed by Fel-Pro with the addition of a swimming pool, ball fields, and barbeque pits for the employees. At the time the recreation area was purchased, the company was also investigating the possibility of an on-site day care center. Surveys indicated low interest, however, and the company decided that a day care center would not be cost-efficient.

Instead, the company chose to use the grounds as a summer camp for children from 6 to 15 years old. The chilren come to work with their parents in the morning; four buses provide transportation between the factory and the camp; and the children return home with their parents at the end of the day. Now in operation since 1973, the camp serves over 300 children for nine weeks during the summer. It has a 24-member staff with training and experience in camp crafts, nature programs, and sports. Costs to the company average $80,000 per summer; parents pay $10 per week. According to Daniel Kornblut, Director of Triple R, 35%-40% of the approximately 1500 employees' children use the summer camp.

Advantages

1. Serves a demonstrated need for supervision and age-appropriate activities over the long summer vacation.

2. The company's commitment is short-term and easily manageable for nine weeks per year.
3. The camp utilizes existing company facilities.
4. Transportation arrangements are simple.
5. The company addresses one specific type of child care need and focuses its energy in that area.
6. Lends itself to cooperative ventures with other groups.

Limitations

1. A summer camp fulfills employees' child care needs for only nine weeks per year. Before-school, after-school, holiday, and vacation care is still an unmet need.
2. A summer camp could be considered a costly investment for the employer, given that it operates for such a short period of time each year.
3. Access to full recreation facilities may be unavailable for many companies, thereby making a camp environment difficult to achieve.

Collaboration among Employers, Public Schools, and Parents

The Ayrlawn School Age and Kindergarten Program was initiated in 1975 by a group of National Institute of Health employees in cooperation with the Ayrlawn Elementary School, both of Bethesda, Maryland. The year before, the same parent board founded the NIH Preschool Development Program, a private non-profit center located on the NIH grounds. The preschool program receives free space, utilities, and custodial services at the work site, but the school-age program receives no financial support or direct subsidization from NIH. Instead, the program initially rented space from the Montgomery County Public Schools in an operating elementary school with surplus classroom space, thereby adopting a leasing concept known as "joint occupancy." The lease fee was relatively low and charged according to the licensed capacity of the program. In this case it was tied directly to the child care revenues of $39 per week.[7]

The program primarily serves NIH families. (NIH empoyees' children were allowed to transfer to the Ayrlawn Elementary School if they needed child care.) This school-age child care program also enrolled children from the local community. Beginning with 35 children in grades K–6, the Ayrlawn program now serves 147 children and uses eight classrooms. In fact, the program has grown so dramatically over the past seven years that no operating school in the county has the capacity to house it.

In 1981 the Ayrlawn School closed and transferred its student population to other local elementary schools. The school-age child care program remained at the original location but under different contractual terms. It now sub-leases space from the YMCA, which took over the Ayrlawn School facility. The Montgomery County Public School System remains a supportive partner in the program, even though it is no longer housed in an operating school facility. Public school transportation from neighboring elementary schools is provided free of charge, thereby allowing full community access to the program.

Advantages:

1. A public school, an employer, and a community agency act as partners in the delivery of services.
2. The parent-administered program encourages high quality because parents have a stake in creating policies and procedures that directly affect them and their children.
3. Space in a school allows access to gyms, lunchrooms, and playgrounds in addition to classrooms—an ideal situation for school-age children.
4. Free transportation may be provided by the school.

Limitations:

1. Most parents with work and family responsibilities find it difficult to keep up with ongoing administrative tasks imposed by a program that depends heavily on volunteer effort.
2. Programs in public schools are subject to the priorities set by the local school board.

Corporate Foundation Support for a Community Program

The Kid's After-School Recreation and Enrichment program in Sioux Falls, South Dakota (KARE-4) was established under a grant from the Gannett Foundation as a result of a three-year study completed by the United Way and various social service agencies in Sioux Falls. Their surveys indicated that a high percentage of latchkey children would utilize existing recreation and enrichment programs in the city *if* transportation were available.

The Sioux Falls Argus *Leader*, a newspaper subsidiary of the Gannett Company Inc., submitted a joint-agency proposal to the Community Priorities Program (CPP) of the Gannett Foundation. Four community agencies under the umbrella of KARE-4 (Boy's Club, Girl's Club, YMCA, and YWCA) were awarded a $40,000-grant to lease private vans and city busses and pay for the salary of a project coordinator. A trial period was completed in March of 1982; full-time operation began in the fall of 1982.

The grant funds the KARE-4 Project for.one year. Additional funding comes from agency contributions and parent fees, which range from $5 to $50 per month. Support from local employers has been solicited, highlighted by the distribution of letters, newsletters, and personal visits to the work site.

The primary goal of the project is to expand the scope and use of the existing programs. With the added transportation, the number of children served is expected to increase from 60 per day to about 500 per day.

Advantages:

1. Costly duplication of services is eliminated by using existing community agencies and programs.
2. For a company that chooses not to start or run a program on its own, this model contributes substantial support with few administrative problems or responsibilities.
3. This model results in community agencies working cooperatively rather than competitively in the delivery of services.

School-Age Child Care as a Community Development Project

In the early 1970s Northwestern National Bank of Minneapolis, Minnesota initiated a financial counseling service in South Minneapolis as a community development project. By 1975 marketing studies showed that the service was being used poorly, and the bank reluctantly decided to discontinue it. Officers of the bank still felt an obligation to the community, however, and they decided to assess the need for other services in the community. An informal needs assessment suggested a need for school-age day care. Neighborhood leaders, community representatives, and members of the clergy agreed that many children in the neighborhood were unsupervised after school hours.

With Federal Community Development Block Grant Funds, the Bank initiated the Northwestern Community Center School-Age Child Care Program in collaboration with the Minneapolis Community Education Department and the Powderhorn Development Corporation, a neighborhood commercial development group. A fire-damaged dry cleaning shop was renovated as the site.

During the planning stages, the bank was involved on several levels. Officers helped with the design of the building and program and assisted in the coordination between the community and those who would be accountable for the administration of the program. Because, as Janet Dudrow, the bank's social policy and programs administrator, said, "We knew we shouldn't directly be in the day care business," the bank's continuing involvement in the program has been primarily that of liaison and financial underwriting.

Changes in the Minneapolis public schools in the 1982 school year resulted in the availability of a large community room in the nearby Wilder Elementary School. The Northwestern Latch Key moved to that space in September of 1982, thereby allowing the program to expand its enrollment from 25 to 35, to offer a wider range of activities, and to reduce costs. (Space is provided as an in-kind contribution by the Minneapolis Public Schools.) While subsidization by the bank used to be about 75%, it is now about 20%, in the form of a contribution to a sliding-scale fee-assistance fund. Additional revenue comes from the USDA lunch program and parent fees.

Advantages:

1. Offering financial support is a better use of the bank's expertise than running the program itself.
2. The actual needs of a community can be identified and a program designed to meet them, using essential contributions from each of the partners.
3. Everyone benefits from collaboration between schools, community agencies, and business.

Limitations:

1. During the start-up phase, intensive involvement in renovation, building design, and program development may be required.
2. Financial support is ongoing and covers operating expenses—a long-term commitment.
3. This model is a "community development project" and does not directly assist the child care needs of the company employees.

Issues

Employer Roles. Given all the options available, with their corresponding advantages and limitations, the question that must be addressed is, "What is an appropriate role for the employer who supports school-age child care?" Preschoolers can accompany their parents to work, but school-age children are in their neighborhood schools for most of the day and cannot be easily transported to the work place for child care. Unless a company's employees are geographically concentrated, it may make little sense to support an on-site center. The logistical problems of transporting children from several school districts to a central work location may be complex and programs can be very costly. (Summer camps and child care during school vacations are exceptions.)

*Liability.** School-age child care programs involve the same liability issues as child care centers. Sometimes there is special concern about the risks of transporting children from a school site to an after-school program, and indeed, transporting children on a regular basis does involve a significant degree of risk. Careful precaution should be taken to insure the safety of the children, including attention to driver qualifications, use of safety belts, and vehicle maintenance. Adequate insurance is clearly mandated; although available it may be somewhat difficult to find. More information is available from the Child Care Law Center publication, "Property and Vehicle Insurance," listed as a resource in Appendix F.

Companies that provide school-age child care, child care subsidies, or services to employees should be sure that their program qualifies as a Dependent Care Assistance Program under Internal Revenue Section 129. If not, the fair market value of the employer-provided child care most likely is taxable to the employee and the company must withhold payroll taxes.

This summary is provided as a brief description of selected liability concerns. Employers should consult their own attorneys for assistance in identifying and resolving their individual liability issues.

Program Advantages and Disadvantages

Advantages	*Disadvantages*	*Solutions*
Relatively inexpensive, it provides maximum return on the employee dollar. Fills a pressing and widespread need.	Geographic spread of children.	Support community programs in areas of need; provide transportation if necessary.
Simplicity of program development; can be added to existing programs with relative ease.	Staff scheduling problems.	Incorporate program into an existing center; plan and hire competent staff, including part-time staff members.
Positive PR and community relations.	Presumed difficulty of program.	Use a combined approach, supporting community programs and helping parents find and use care.

*This section was written by Kathleen Murray, Attorney At Law, Child Care Law Center.

Endnotes

1. U.S. Senate Committee on Labor and Human Resources, *Child Care Act of 1979*, 96th Congress, 1st session (Washington, D.C.: U.S. Government Printing Office, 1979).
2. Children's Defense Fund, *Employed Parents and Their Children: A Data Book* (Washington, D. C.: Children's Defense Fund, 1982), p. 9.
3. T. Long and L. Long, *Latchkey Children: The Child's View of Self Care*, ERIC, ED 211 119 (1982), 29 pps. (Available from ERIC Document Reproduction Services, P.O. Box 190, Arlington, Virginia 22210.)
4. Applied Management Sciences, *School-Age Day Care Study*, Final Report of National Day Care Home Study, DHHS (Washington, D.C.: U.S. Department of Health and Human Services, Administration for Children, Youth and Families, 1983).
5. D. E. Friedman, *On the Fringe of Benefits: Day Care and the Corporation* (New York, N.Y.: Center for Public Resources), p. 44. (Available from the Center for Public Resources, 680 Fifth Avenue, New York, NY 10019.)
6. R. Baden, A. Genser, J. A. Levine, and M. Seligson, *School-Age Child Care: An Action Manual* (Boston, Mass.: Auburn House Publishing Company, 1982), pp. 43-44.
7. R. Posilkin, "Day Care Programs Are Optimal Joint Tenants," *Phi Delta Kappan* (December 1980), p. 285.

Chapter 15

CHILD CARE FOR SICK CHILDREN

Child care for sick children addresses one of the most difficult problems for working parents. Children of course are subject to varying degrees of illness, including days when the parent wants to remain home with the child, days when symptoms are moderate and someone else could care for the child at home, and days when the child is only mildly ill but the regular caregiver will not accept him or her. For most parents, there simply are not enough child care alternatives to fit these different situations. Either the child is well enough to be admitted to the regular child care program or the parent has to stay at home. Employers know what a problem this can be when employees have to reschedule care at the last minute, leave work unexpectedly, or stay at home for an extended period with a child who is convalescing.

This chapter describes selected child care arrangements for sick children in addition to those programs presently supported by employers, with the objective of illustrating the full range of possibilities for employer support in developing temporary child care options for parents when their children are sick.

Selecting a Program

Employers can provide direct services including care in the home, care at the child's regular center, and care in a separate program at another site. They can also help parents deal with

---

NOTE: This chapter was co-authored by Noa Mohlabane and Jacquelyn McCroskey.

their children's illnesses by providing indirect supportive services.

A number of different approaches to the problem of caring for sick children are being developed around the country. Of the companies participating in the National Employer Supported Child Care Project, five reported that they currently support child care programs for sick children; one of these supports a community program and four provide care in the company's child care center. Other employer-supported centers have extensive preventive health care programs or care for children who suddenly become ill during the day until their parents can pick them up. Employers also have given financial support to community programs that provide home health services, that provide care for sick children in the child's home, or that sponsor special centers and family day care homes to care for children with particular kinds of illnesses.

Direct Services

Model 1: In-Home Care. Companies can support the development of a home health service that will coordinate the hiring, training, and scheduling of home health care workers who go into the child's home to provide care. Such programs usually require that the child has already been seen by a doctor. The home health worker carries out the doctor's and the parents' instructions and can provide activities for the child. Workers are assigned by a telephone dispatcher and, whenever possible, the same worker cares for a given child for the duration of the illness.

In order to maintain staff stability and to ensure the availability of these workers, many programs pay them a set salary rather than an hourly wage. These employees can take on other responsibilities when they are not needed to provide sick child care (for instance, visiting and helping at local child care centers that the children attend).

The advantages of this type of program are:

1. The child does not have to leave the home.
2. The child remains in a familiar and restful environment conducive to recovery.
3. The contagion factor is minimized.
4. The child receives individual care.

The disadvantages are:

1. The amount of care needed fluctuates with somewhat unpredictable high and low seasons of demand. Adjustments may be difficult in this type of program.

2. This type of care is costly because one caregiver is generally required for each child, except when siblings are sick together at home.
3. The program may not be fully utilized by parents because of anxiety about leaving the child with an unfamiliar person.
4. Children may be anxious about being left with an unfamiliar adult.
5. The job can be isolating for the child care worker.
6. The environment in which the worker has to care for the child is unfamiliar, unpredictable, and sometimes unpleasant.
7. In the event of an emergency, the worker is alone, unless close back-up support is available.

The Berkeley Sick Child Care Program, Berkeley, California provides care for sick children by combining in-home care and center care. Parents who need care leave a telephone message on a tape. A trained dispatcher (from 7:00–10:00 p.m. and from 7:00–9:00 a.m.) asks for details such as the child's age, the doctor's diagnosis, the time care is needed, the address, and the telephone number, and then assigns a worker.

The worker arrives about half an hour before the parent has to leave, allowing time for the parent to give verbal instructions and to fill out an information sheet. The worker brings along appropriate play materials, administers prescribed medication, follows instructions left by the parent, and writes a daily report for the parent's information. The same worker can return to care for the child for the duration of the illness. The parents pay for the care on a sliding scale ranging from no fee to $3.50 per hour. The program is staffed by workers who have raised their own families and who are experienced in providing in-home care or practical nursing and by workers entering the field of child development. All home health workers participate in ongoing training, including first aid and child development. Administrative functions of the program include coordinating and training, maintaining ongoing communication for support and problem solving, and record keeping.

Model 2: Care at the Child's Regular Center. Companies can support development of a sick care program as a part of planning for a new child care center or as a component to be built into an existing child care facility. One alternative is to support the development of a "sick bay" or "get well room" at the center where children can stay during bouts of minor illnesses. The other option is to develop provisions that allow the child with a minor illness to remain in his or her regular room with the regular staff. Both of these options have been tried, as evidenced by the following program examples, and have functioned successfully. They require the following elements:

1. Medical consultation to establish safe and reasonable guidelines.
2. Staff and parent training workshops.
3. Environmental design to minimize stress and overstimulation, providing a cozy, restful environment that is easy to sanitize.
4. Adequate staffing to provide individualized care when required.
5. Development of detailed preventive health care practices and procedures.
6. Development of reliable and effective record keeping for communication between parents and staff.

The advantages of this type of program are:

1. Care is immediately available.
2. This type of program is more likely to be utilized by parents because both the parents and the children are already familiar with the program and trust the staff.
3. The workers are familiar with the child.
4. The physical environment can be specifically set up to accommodate children with minor illnesses.
5. Backup support is readily available in the event of an emergency.

The disadvantages of this type of program are:

1. Licensing regulations in some states are either unclear or prohibit care for sick children.
2. Many child care facilities do not have the space or adequate staffing to provide on-site care.
3. Programs may be reluctant to try this type of care because of anxiety regarding contagion. However, medical research indicates that, with proper precautions, there is no significant increase in either incidence or severity of illness.[1]

An example of the "sick bay" or "get well room" program is *the San Juan Batista Child Development Center in San Jose, California,* which serves 250 children ranging in age from 2 months to 12 years. Child care for sick children is provided in a specially designed unit at the center. It is staffed by assistants who have had prior experience with children in a medical or health-related setting and who participate in a special training course after they are hired. Supervision is provided by a LVN, an RN, and a Public Health Nurse; the program has a medical orientation. The guidelines, procedures, and listing of danger symptoms are elaborate. Educating parents about ongoing health care and detailed daily communication during a child's illness are stressed. Children with different types of symptoms are separated. The staff-child ratio is one adult to five children. Parents pay for this service on a sliding scale.

The Fairfax-San Anselmo Children's Center, Fairfax, California, which has provided care for sick children since 1974, is another example. They began by providing the care in a family day care home, but since 1981, they have cared for sick children at the child care center. The center serves just over 100 children ranging from infants to school-age children. It is located in a former public school with one of the classrooms used as the "get well" room. This room has a capacity of 6 children per day, and use averages 3 or 4 children per day. It is funded by a foundation grant that pays for staffing. The room is staffed by regular child care workers with specialized training. There is an arrangement with local pediatricians for telephone consultations when needed, and the staff is visited weekly by a local public health nurse. Care at the local hospital is also available in case of an emergency. The room is a warm and friendly place designed for quiet play. The policy guidelines for the room are purposely kept simple and are printed on one page for easy reference. The parents give the staff information about the child's evening and morning symptoms, and a log of the day's events is kept by the workers and reported in turn to parents. Children who become ill during the day are taken to the "get well room." The parent is notified but is not required to pick the child up immediately if symptoms are not severe. When there are no sick children, the staff work in one of the other rooms, or the "get well" room is used for small-group activities.

An example of care in the child's regular classroom is *the Frank Porter Graham Child Development Center in Chapel Hill, North Carolina*, which has operated as a part of a research project at the University of North Carolina at Chapel Hill for more than ten years. From the onset their policy has been to allow children to attend the center and stay in their regular classroom when they have minor illnesses. Children with measles and chicken pox are excluded from the center, although there has not been a case of measles in ten years thanks to immunizations. The children are cared for by regular child care workers, but there is a full-time pediatrician and a family nurse practitioner nearby who are available to examine the children if necessary.

The reasoning behind the policy of keeping children with minor illnesses in the classroom is that children are contagious prior to the appearance of symptoms and it therefore is of little protection of others to exclude them once symptoms have appeared. The care provided in this familiar setting by familiar adults also aids in the children's recuperation. The research from this program shows that there is no significant increase in either the incidence or the severity of illness among the children in the program. They have also found that the children regulate their own levels of activity. Nor has it created a problem for the staff in the room caring for the hild. Hygienic practices such as hand-washing are stressed.

Model 3: Care in Other Locations. Another way to provide care for sick children is to establish a family day care satellite home connected to a child care center. The family day care home is designed and reserved specifically for the care of children with minor illnesses from one particular center. This home is preferably in close proximity to the center. Children can be taken to the home from the center when symptoms appear. When no children are ill, the family day care provider can go to the center to work, or well children can visit the home to get acquainted.

An example is *the Fairfax-San Anselmo Children's Center in Fairfax, California,* which offered sick child care in this manner for seven years. A licensed provider was engaged to serve up to six sick children from the center in her home. Parents called her directly, either the evening before or in the morning before 9:00 a.m. On days when there were no sick children she worked in the center. If a child became ill during the day, the parent was called and the family day provider took the child home with her. If she was already in her home caring for a child and another child became ill at the center, a staff person took the child to the provider's house. A public health nurse consulted with her once a week. The director of this program feels that one satellite family day care home can serve a mixed-age-range center of 100 to 150 children.

Opening a separate facility to care for sick children is another option that comes to mind when planning child care for sick children. This course appears to be the least beneficial for children and parents, with the following major problems:

1. A restful environment must be created (that is, stress minimized) to enhance the child's recovery. Caring for a child in an unfamiliar environment with unfamiliar staff and unfamiliar children potentially increases stress and anxiety rather than minimizing it.
2. The children at each center may develop a common set of

germs. This occurs even when children are kept in separate rooms, because of shared space, staff, and equipment and through siblings. Serving sick children in a regional child care center creates possibilities for cross-contagion, exposing children to new germs when they are least able to combat them.

3. Parents may be reluctant to entrust their sick child to an unfamilar center.

Indirect Services

In addition to providing services for children, companies can also contribute to the development of other kinds of services or policies designed to ease the strain on parents when their children are sick.

They can help parents adapt their work schedule to care for their children when they are sick by offering "family leave" time, which can be used during the illness of family members, or by allowing parents to make up work missed or to work at home during children's illnesses.

Companies can also offer in-kind and/or financial support to community service groups that provide care for sick children or that are working to develop sick care options in the community. For example, centers' staff generally do not have the expertise or time to review health policies, many of which are unclear or outdated. Financial support can be provided for medical consultation to revise and clarify health policies in community child care centers. Employer support can also be used to train family day care providers or center staff in preventive health care procedures, recognition of symptoms, care of children with minor illnesses, and first aid practices.

Issues

Fluctuating Demand. The amount of care needed for sick children is neither constant nor predictable. There are high and low seasons of demand, and the pattern of demand varies regionally. Programs must adjust to needs that change from day to day and season to season, plan for the best utilization of facility and staff when there is little demand for care of sick children. One approach is to build other functions into the care program, so that the staff and facility are used even when all of the children are healthy. Activities can include developing preventive health care practices or educating parents, staff, and children about health care.

Policies. Every child care program has health policy guidelines that stipulate when children will or will not be allowed to participate in the program. Programs providing care for sick children must consider factors such as the medical consultation available, staffing, facilities, and the nature and severity of illnesses in the community when developing their guidelines. Child care programs serving sick children also need detailed guidelines outlining procedures for recognizing symptoms, responding to emergencies, and providing proper care for children with minor illnesses. These policies can be developed in consultation with doctors and other health professionals.

Medical Consultations. Child care programs for sick children need medical consultation ranging from procedural advice, training of staff and parents, and occasional phone consultations, to more major investments of time in direct medical services. The cost of medical consultation can be reduced by using existing community resources, including public health departments, medical schools and training hospitals, visiting nurses associations, and groups of retired doctors and nurses.

Anxiety. Administrators, staff, and parents often experience substantial anxiety about the health risks of a program for sick children. Two issues causing major concern are *contagion* and whether such a program will *enhance a child's recovery.* High-quality programs have demonstrated that, with the proper precautions, risks can be avoided.[2] To combat natural anxieties, three components must be built into a program for sick children: (1) medical consultation, (2) staff and parent education, and (3) parent-staff communication.

Often the risk of contagion involves upper respiratory viral infections such as the common cold and influenza. These illnesses are airborne, and evidence indicates that their victims are contagious prior to the appearance of any symptoms. By the time adults are aware that a child is sick, other children and adults have already been exposed and the benefits of excluding or isolating the child are minimal. Good ventilation may be more beneficial in preventing airborne viral infections than isolating victims after symptoms have appeared.

Other contagion risks involve bacterial infections, hepatitis, and parasites. All are spread through direct contact. The most effective way to avoid contagion is to follow good hygienic procedures, particularly in hand washing, diapering and food preparation.[3]

The severity of disease can be reduced and complications avoided when there is good communication between parents and staff and when the staff is well trained to handle parental requests and doctor's orders. Facilities and policies that allow the child to rest properly and get appropriate nutrition are also key to success.

Liability*

A company that operates a facility for sick children should be aware of the liability issues common to all child care programs. In addition, there may be special risks involved in caring for sick children. Since child care for sick children is a relatively new phenomenon, little specific guidance is available. However, it is likely that such programs will be held to a higher standard than child care programs for well children. Consequently, they should be developed and operated under competent medical supervision. Special liability insurance might also be considered.

Companies that provide child care subsidies or services to employees should insure that their program qualifies as a Dependent Care Assistance Program under Internal Revenue Section 129. If not, the fair-market value of the employer-provided child care most likely is taxable to the employee and the company must withhold payroll taxes.

This summary is provided as a brief description of selected liability concerns. Employers should consult their own attorneys for assistance in identifying and resolving their individual liability issues.

Program Advantages and Disadvantages

Advantages	*Disadvantages*	*Solutions*
Reduces absenteeism: The number of days missed due to children's illnesses can be reduced. Parent-employee illnesses can also be reduced when preventative health care programs are offered.	High per-child cost. Programs can be complex. Demand fluctuates.	Justify by comparing child care cost to absenteeism cost. Use ideas from model programs and establish joint programs with other companies. Combine care for sick children with other child care services to make the staff multifunctional. Support development of community sick child facility.

*This section was written by Kathleen Murray, attorney at law, Child Care Law Center.

Conclusion

One of the most significant problems encountered by the working parent is locating affordable, dependable care for a sick child. This is particularly true of parents with young children who frequently contract minor illnesses. This chapter has given a brief overview of the issues to be considered and has offered a number of viable program alternatives that can be used singly or in combination with others.

Many companies already recognize the impact of this current unmet need for care. Two surveys of working parents showed that over 80% expressed need for programs for sick children.[4] Clearly provision of such options can have a significant impact on the morale and absentee rate of parent employees.

There are many misconceptions about caring for ill children which often result in reluctance on the part of companies to become involved. In fact, however, the risks are avoidable with carefully thought-out, well-executed programs, and the advantages can be tremendous.

Endnotes

1. F. A. Loda, W. P. Glezen, and W. A. Clyde Jr., "Respiratory Disease in Group Day Care," *Pediatrics* 49 (3) (March 1972), pp. 428–437.
2. A. D. Peters, "Health Support in Day Care," in *Day Care: Resources for Decisions*, ed. E. Grotberg (Washington, D.C.: Office of Planning and Research Evaluation, 1971), p. 323.
3. *Ibid.*
4. M. E. Kiester, *Health*, Part III of *Programs for Infants and Young Children* (Washington, D.C.: Appalachian National Commission, 1970).

Chapter 16

SPONSORSHIP VARIATIONS

Child care programs discussed in this book are sponsored under a variety of arrangements. Let us consider these variations from various perspectives, as follows: (1) a single employer, (2) consortia (groups of employers), (3) employee groups such as unions, and (4) the three major types of companies sponsoring child care programs.

Single-Company Sponsors

Most child care programs are sponsored by single companies. Many employers prefer this arrangement because it offers them the greatest degree of control over the program and because, with fewer parties involved, it is simple to administer. If it serves only one company's employees, then the program will also have greater recruitment and retention value than if other companies have access to it as well. A company receives other benefits when in full control of the program, such as setting the hours and days of operation to match work schedules and special work shifts, establishing the level of quality and supplemental services that its parent employees want, and tailoring the program to the specific needs of its employee group. Also, when changes in the needs of its employees occur, the program can be more easily changed—for example, when there is greater need for infant care among its employees, that part of the program can be expanded without debate.

Some types of programs lend themselves more readily to single-company support. Work site centers are the most obvious example. Information and referral systems, on the other hand, are often most effective when sponsored by a number of companies, because duplication of effort is avoided in gathering information.

Of the companies included in the National Employer Supported Child Care Project, 234 reported that they were the sole sponsor of their child care program. These companies offer different service options, including on-site or near-site centers, reimbursement programs, family day care homes, and in-house information and referral programs.

Consortia Sponsored Programs

Under the consortium approach to child care, several businesses jointly support a child care program. Expenses and administrative responsibility are shared, and each company receives the benefits of child care. Such support often makes each business more visible as an active contributor toward community development. It also gives companies a forum for working together and promoting goodwill. A multiple funding and enrollment base means that more comprehensive programs are possible than a single company's needs and resources may warrant.

Some consortia are initiated, established, and administered by representatives of individual companies. Others fall under a looser definition of consortia, involving an already existing community child care program supported with start-up and/or operating funds from several businesses. A company has a less demanding role in the administration of the program under this arrangement, but it also has less control.

The benefits of sharing resources and responsibilities may be particularly appealing to companies having a small number of employees with children, those located in industrial parks or downtown areas near similar businesses, or those taking a cautious first step into providing child care services. The consortium approach works well when many different groups of people see the same need for child care. Child care professionals and company representatives can work together to develop programs that meet local needs, whether the emphasis is on meeting the needs of the community as a whole or of the employees in a particular location.

Of the companies in the National Employer Supported Child Care Project, 125 reported that another company was involved in supporting the child care service. These programs include a wide spectrum of cooperative arrangements between companies, ranging from informal to highly structured agreements. The following examples of shared sponsorship or consortia approaches to the development of child care centers illustrate the range of possibilities for employer involvement.

Downtown Day Care Center, St. Louis, Mo.

Started in 1978 when a number of downtown businesses joined together to form a non-profit child care consortium, the center serves 60 children from 2 years old through kindergarten age, five days a week from 7 a.m. to 6 p.m. An average 30%–40% of the children served have parents employed by the companies supporting the program. About 25% of the employees who have used the center have been men. The companies, which preferred to remain anonymous, have continued to support the program with financial and in-kind contributions.

Garden City Downtown Day Care Center, Missoula, Mont.

This non-profit program, begun in 1978, serves children in the downtown area. The City of Missoula donated money for the renovation of a building and local businesses donated money for equipment and supplies. Representatives of some of the businesses continue to serve on the board of directors of the centers. The center is licensed for 38 preschool children; it reached full enrollment about 4 months after it opened. About 20% of the children in the center have parents employed by the contributing companies. (The contributors were the City of Missoula, Banker's Clearinghouse, the *Missoulian*, Montana Power Company, First Federal Savings and Loan, and Champion Products).

The Broadcasters' Child Development Center, Washington, D.C.

The Broadcasters' Center was established in 1980 as a project of the D.C. Chapter of the National Academy of Television Arts and Sciences after start-up donations were made by local stations. The Academy continues support of the center even though it is now a legally separate organization. The center is licensed for 60 children from 3 months to 5 years. About 25% of the children have parents employed by the supporting companies. (The contributors were the Academy, WJLA, WDVM, WRC/NBC T.V., WMAI Radio, and WTTG.)

The Renaissance II Child Care Center, Pittsburgh, Pa.

The Renaissance II Child Care Center, opened in 1981, is funded in part by a consortium of local businesses. The Louise Child Care Center, which operates the Renaissance II Child Care Center, is a multi-service agency with extensive experience in training, research, and the provision of quality child care. It was initially approached by the Corporate Medical Director of Alcoa to investigate the possibility of developing a downtown program. The executive director of the center coordinated development of the program, involving the United Way and donations from five local corporate foundations. (The contributors were Alcoa, Pittsburgh Plate Glass, Heinz, Bell Telephone, and Koppers.)

The Renilda Hilkemeyer Child Care Center, Houston, Tex.

The program serves the children of employees of the seven hospitals of the Texas Medical Center. The child care center, a part of the medical center, recently expanded its program so that it is licensed to serve 323 children 24 hours a day, seven days a week. Parent fees pay a portion of the cost of the program and the 7 hospitals' contributions cover the operating deficit. The cost is split among the hospitals, based on a prorated percentage of employee usage. The program, first established in 1968, has more than tripled in size since its beginnings. The center serves children from 6 weeks old through kindergarten age. (The hospitals are Ben Taub General, Methodist, Texas Children's, Texas Institute for Research and Rehabilitation, Hermann, M.D. Anderson, and St. Luke's.)

Employee-Sponsored Programs

For the most part, company child care programs are offered by the employer. However, a small number of child care programs have been established by groups of employees. Union programs are the most distinctive example.

Union involvement in child care services varies from situations in which child care appears on the union bargaining agenda to those in which unions support and run centers. A number of joint efforts by union and management have resulted in high-quality child care programs that meet the needs of parent employees. One current joint effort is co-sponsored by the Service Employees International Union Local 399 and the Kaiser Permanente Health Maintenance Organization in Los Angeles. They established a joint committee to study the child care needs of employees. As a result, Kaiser now employs a child care information and referral coordinator and is studying the possibility of on-site center care.

There are few solely union-sponsored or joint union-management child care programs currently in operation. Only six participated in the National Employer Supported Child Care Project. The following examples illustrate the kinds of roles that unions have played in developing child care programs.

The Hyman Blumberg Child Day Care Center, Baltimore, Md.

The Health and Welfare Fund of the Amalgamated Clothing and Textile Workers' Joint Board (including company and union representatives) oversees the child care center program. Start-up funds for the center were donated by local textile companies, which gave 1% of the gross hourly payroll for several years before the center was opened. Ongoing funds are contributed by the companies, with 2% of the gross hourly payroll going to the union's Health and Welfare Fund, which sponsors the center along with other health and welfare services. The center, opened in 1969, offers a full program for children 2 to 5 years old whose parents are union members. Licensed for 300 children, it is open five days a week from 6 a.m. to 6 p.m. and provides two meals a day, medical and dental screening for children, and opportunities for parent involvement in a PTA. Cost of the program to parents is $15 per week, compared with an average cost of about $45 per week for comparable services in the community. (The other Amalgamated centers are The Chambersburg Day Care Center in Chambersburg, Pa; the Amalgamated Child Day Care and Health Center in Chicago, Ill.; and the Verona Child Day Care Center in Verona, Va.)

Park Village Day Care Center, Cleveland, Ohio

The United Food and Commercial Workers International Union Local 427 and the Service, Hospital, Nursing Home, and Public Employees Union Local 47 in Cleveland sponsored a child care center as part of a housing development in a distressed area of the city. The center is open to members of the unions but primarily serves residents of the housing development. Union support, which includes reduced rent, utilities, and in-kind services, is combined with public funds and parent fees to provide a full-service center serving 41 preschool and school-age children.

Children's Village, Philadelphia, Pa.

The center, licensed for 125 children, was established in 1976 through the Philadelphia Apparel Producer's Association Council of Labor and Industry and the Flash Trimming Company. Funds for the center come to the Council from corporate donations, public funding, and parent fees.

Public Agencies, Industry, and Health Care Organizations as Sponsors

Business/industries and health care organizations have about the same number of programs, each representing 47% of the total sponsored by employers. Public agencies have a relatively small number of programs, with only 4% of the total.

Many patterns appear in a comparison of the programs of these three types of employers by the National Employer Supported Child Care Project. Health care organizations and public agencies more often have on-site centers than other forms of child care. Industries most often support child care in the community; 52 companies have company centers, while 103 support programs in the community. Industry and health care programs both span a broader range of programs, with all types represented. Public agencies are limited primarily to work-site centers, with a few support arrangements with community child care providers. A greater proportion of programs are new in industry than in the other two groups. More rapid growth in the number of industry programs in the last four years (from 9 to 197) accounts for this fact.

The degree and type of support from each type of employer differs. A higher number of industries give financial start-up contributions, but the amount of the financial start-up contribution given by health care organizations is often greater. This statistic probably reflects the tendency of this group to have more on-site centers, which of course have greater start-up expense. The cost to parents of care for infants and preschoolers is lower in health care programs than in industry or public agency programs. However, the cost of school age care is slightly higher in health care programs.

The reasons for instituting programs vary among these types of employers, as do the decision-making processes involved. Health care organizations most often have established their programs for the express purpose of recruiting health care professionals in short supply, such as RNs. This fact is related to the greater number of on-site centers among health care organizations. Reflecting their purpose, these programs are often management-initiated and operated. Public agency programs are more frequently initiated by employees. Industry programs are more of a mixture, although they are management-initiated; the older programs and those in family-owned business are more frequently management-initiated than others. As employees become more verbal about this issue, employees in industry are expected to be more active in initiating programs.

Public Agency Programs

Federal, state, and local agencies have sponsored a number of child care programs for their employees. The 17 public agency child care programs participating in the National Employer Supported Child Care Project study include those sponsored by several different types of agencies, including the Multnomah County Government in Portland, Oregon; the Department of Motor Vehicles in Sacramento, California; the Goddard Space Flight Center in Greenbelt, Maryland; and the Departments of Labor, Health and Human Services, and Education in Washington, D.C.

Public agency programs are often established through the efforts of groups of concerned parent employees. Generally the employee group asks to be allowed to form an on-site center and the agency donates space in which to run the program. Parents generally have to support the full cost of the program through fees.

A common problem with this kind of minimal support arrangement is that many parents cannot afford the high fee level and therefore cannot use the service. Consequently there can be insufficient utilization of the program, increased overhead, and an unstable cash flow which leads to deficits. Cash flow problems notwithstanding, many public agencies have been able to find creative ways to support child care programs by giving inkind donations, services, and space or by helping to orchestrate funding from various private sources. The role of public agencies in the development of some recent programs has been to organnize the implementation of new services and to focus efforts on achieving cooperative public/private programs. Following are some program examples.

The Housing and Urban Development Child Care Center, Washington, D.C.
This center is a private non-profit corporation; HUD gave a loan for start-up expenses and provides space, maintenance, and utilities. Planning for the center began in 1973 and included the HUD Women's Caucus, the Recreation Association, and the American Federation of Government Employees Local 476. The center opened in 1976 and is licensed for 60 preschool and school-age children. Although the parents using the center are principally HUD employees, up to 35% may be employed by other federal or private agencies.

Sandyhook Child Care Center, Fort Hancock, N.J.
The U.S. Department of Commerce has provided start-up and ongoing support for a small child care center established in 1980. The center, serving 15 children from 6 weeks old, is set up as a non-profit corporation. It is the only center in the area that cares for infants.

Empire State Day Care Services, Inc., Albany, N.Y.
This non-profit agency was established in 1979 by the Governor's Office of Employee Relations in response to contract negotiation demands for child care services from several employee unions. The board includes management and union representatives and public leaders. Joint labor-management committees agreed that child care was an important issue for New York State public employees and have allocated a $150,000 funding pool to be used as seed money for new child care programs. Empire State Day Care provides technical assistance to these projects; the assistance is based on experience with Children's Place, an on-site center established in the Empire State Plaza in 1979, which serves 106 children ages 8 weeks through 5 years.

Children's Center of Knoxville, Inc., Knoxville, Tenn.
The center was established in 1976 using start-up funds donated by the Tennessee Valley Authority. The Second Presbyterian Church donates the space and utilities for the program. Licensed to care for 88 infants, toddlers, and preschoolers, the program is open to families from the community as well as to employees of TVA. The program is very popular, with a substantial waiting list.

Industry Programs

Both manufacturing and non-manufacturing companies support child care. Most notable among them are industries with a predominantly female labor force, those who need recruitment inducements, family-owned businesses, and "third-wave industries" such as computer/electronics, information processing, and service industries. Banks and insurance companies are among the leaders in providing child care; both are information/service industries employing large numbers of women.

Pharmaceutical companies are representative of other "third-wave industries" with child care programs. For example, Hoffman LaRoche, Inc. and Merck, Inc. (both of New Jersey) each has a child care center.

Although the above types of companies are among the recent leaders in new programs, child care is rapidly appearing in all types of companies. Others with child care include, for example, the food, transportation, printing, entertainment, and utility industries. And there are still child care programs in the textile industry, where they began. The following examples display the variety in both type of companies and type of programs.

Maui Pineapple Company Ltd., Kahulai, Maui, Hawaii

The company established an on-site center in 1981 for 50 preschool children. It contributed toward both the start-up and ongoing operation of the program, which was established to attract younger workers into a highly stable workforce.

Timesavers, Sunnyvale, Calif.

Timesavers, a temporary employment service, reimburses employees for a percentage of child care costs. The care must be licensed in order to qualify for a reimbursement.

Merck Company, Inc., Rahway, N.J.

Merck, a pharmaceutical company, renovated space for an employee child care center. Established in 1980, The Employees Center for Young Children, Inc., is run by a parent orgnization and is legally separate from Merck, which contributes to its ongoing operation with in-kind donations.

Society National Bank and Ameri Trust Bank, Cleveland, Ohio

These companies support an information and referral service through a community agency, the Center for Human Resources. They pay for the services as they are provided.

Forney Engineering, Carrollton, Tex.

This family-owned high-technology company established its on-site center, which serves 70 preschoolers, in 1973. The center's start-up costs were entirely paid for by the company, and it receives ongoing company support for operating costs.

National Semiconductor, Santa Clara, Calif.

This electronics company has been providing on-site information and referral since 1980. The information is given by a company employee at the work site.

Health Care Organization Programs

The health care industry has led the way in the provision of employer-supported child care services, and health care continues to be the single industry with the greatest number of employer-supported child care programs. There are several reasons why hospitals are especially likely to value child care. They need recruitment incentives to attract nurses and other highly trained health care professionals in short supply. Their work forces generally have a high degree of child care usage. They also have special scheduling needs, using workers on night and evening shifts and on weekends and holidays. The fact that they are part of a service industry may also predispose hospital administrators to appreciate the rationale and benefits of child care.

On-site programs are the most frequently used form of child care among health care organizations, because centers exclusively for employees offer unique recruiting advantages. Company centers also give hospitals the control they need to set the hours of the program to match their schedules and to design the program to maximize effective recruiting. For example, the program can include infant care to attract workers back to work soon after childbirth.

The hospital child care programs studied by the National Employer Supported Child Care Project support these patterns. Almost half of the companies with child care were hospitals. Hospitals more frequently had child care centers than any other type of service; 152 had centers, while only 43 offered other service types (including 5 family day care programs, 7 reimbursement programs, 17 child care information and referral services, and 14 supported community child care programs).

The differences between hospitals and other company sponsors of child care centers in this survey reflect the common patterns among hospital center programs. For instance, the hospitals are least likely to involve another company in supporting programs; only 25 of 125 companies reporting that another company was involved were hospitals). This statistic probably reflects the fact that hospitals have work forces of an adequate size to support their own centers. Hospital centers are also more likely to be open more hours during the day and more days of the week than are centers run by other kinds of companies: 51 hospital centers (as opposed to 3 other centers) were open more than fourteen hours per day, and 46 of the hospital centers (as opposed to 4 of the other centers) were open seven days per week. Round-the-clock schedules at hospitals make these longer service hours necessary.

Methodist Hospital of Southern California, Arcadia, Calif.

The hospital's on-site center is one of the oldest in operation. Established in 1958 to recruit and retain RNs, it has recently been expanded to serve infants as well as preschoolers. The hospital gives substantial contributions to the program covering approximately half of the operating costs. Only employees of the hospital are eligible to use the center.

Kaiser Permanente, Los Angeles, Calif.

This group of health care facilities has an information coordinator on staff who is compiling a directory of licensed child care centers in the area. The coordinator's position was created as a result of a union/management team formed to study the issue of child care. An additional task for the coordinator is to study assistance needed by employees in addition to child care information and referrals and to make appropriate recommendations to decision makers.

Retirement Center of Wright County, Buffalo, Minn.

This retirement center uses an externally owned and managed center for employees' children. Thirty-one infants and preschoolers are served in this center, which is located at the work site. A unique aspect of the program is that the children interact with the residents of the retirement center, which gives both an experience often missed in our mobile society. Furthermore, the retirement center staff have noticed that the older residents seem to do better with the children near.

Visiting Nurse Association, Burlington, Vt.

The association opened its own child care center for 35 infants and toddlers. It donated space and in-kind services toward the start up of the program, which was established in 1975.

* * *

The sponsorship of child care programs clearly varies as much as the type of service. The most suitable sponsorship arrangement in an individual instance is determined by characteristics of the group initiating the service—its goals, desire for control and involvement, and the type of company involved.

Part Five

CONCLUSION

Chapter 17

AN IDEA WHOSE TIME HAS COME

As economic and social trends continue to stimulate changes in the labor force, growing numbers of corporations are recognizing the need for a redefinition of certain policies and practices. Current "personnel" policies were established for a predominantly male work force, in the context of a society with distinctly separate male/female roles. But these roles are now evolving and merging, and the world of work and that of the family are no longer distinctly differentiated by sex. A productivity drain from the mismatch of old policies and new lifestyles has induced many companies to reconceptualize some of their human relations policies.

Early Programs: What Has Been Done

One area in which new company policies are developing is the provision of child-care-related services for working parents. The pressing need for child care is an outgrowth of the increase in two-income couples and working mothers with young children and the decrease in the traditional suppliers of care (because they, too, have migrated into the paid labor force).

A variety of different employer-related child care services have been developed, the choice of type depending on the particular circumstances of the company and its workers. Some companies offer flexible personnel policies that can reduce the need for child care, such as flextime, job sharing, permanent part time employment, work at home, and family leave. Others give child care assistance indirectly through informational, educational, or financial assistance programs. Still others extend their corporate giving to include community child care providers, and some provide direct child care services—often in a company child care center, less often in family day care homes.

As of June 1982, 415 organizations with child care services were identified across the country. The growth in activity from 105 child care centers in 1978 represents a four-fold increase. Even more dramatic is the 20-fold increase during the same period in the number of programs in business and industry, from 9 in 1978 to 197 in 1982.

The National Employer Supported Child Care Project, which identified these programs, studied their characteristics and their impact on the companies. Roughly half of these programs replicated an already established type of employer-supported program: the on-site center. Others used innovative new concepts in employer-supported child care, creating and refining new prototypes. One quarter of the companies used programs such as child care information and referral, family day care networks, reimbursements, or educational programs for parents; the remaining quarter gave corporate contributions to child care programs in the community. Although the concept of corporate giving is not a new one, many of these companies added a new variation, making contributions to programs used by their employees. They also sometimes made the contribution in a nonfinancial form such as technical expertise or in-kind services. Corporate contributions were the most common form of child care support among business and industry, possibly reflecting the desire to remain at a distance from the ongoing administrative responsibilities of programs. However, as most of these programs are new, this choice may reflect a trend toward "phased-in" approaches in which companies begin with modest forms of support, using them as stepping stones and need indicators while moving toward more extensive or direct services.

The dynamic nature of the field is revealed throughout these trends, but several current patterns can be identified. Programs were predictably found in predominantly female-employee industries. Nonetheless, companies discovered that usage by male employees was substantial. Although child care benefits may be created for the female worker, who is still perceived as primarily responsible for children, the fact of its use by men attests to its practicality for all parent workers.

The types of companies having child care services are clustered in the service, information, and technology industries—for example, banking, insurance, computers, health care, and the media. Philosophically many of the newer companies, such as those in the computer industry, are characterized by experimentation. And because they are so new, they often do not have entrenched corporate policies. Older industries such as banking, insurance, and health care, in a different perspective, need a high proportion of female workers. It is understandable that industries such as these would be among the leaders in establishing child care services, even though for different reasons. The current geographical dispersion of programs may reflect the proliferation of child care in high-growth areas with California, Minnesota, and Texas having the most programs.

Health care was the first industry to provide child care, with roughly as many programs as in all other industries combined. It uses on-site centers more often than other forms of care by a margin of 3 to 1. There are a number of possible explanations for this predominance. The intent of hospitals to use programs as recruitment tools and their need to accommodate hospital work shifts, and their familiarity with the delivery of human services may make hospitals less reluctant to provide direct child care services.

Child care services are not limited to companies where a high *percentage* of workers need child care; some find the provision of child care expedient for a small portion of their workers. For example, some use it to retain a small group of specially trained technical workers who otherwise would be out of the workforce for extended maternity leaves.

The size of the companies providing child-care-related services varies. Some of the new types of employer-supported child care, such as information and referral and reimbursements, are adaptable to small, medium-size, and large companies. In our survey, the companies with child care programs ranged from a work force of under ten to over 5000 at the location where child care was offered, with most companies having between 1,000 and 5,000 employees.

The findings of the study also revealed child care as being exceptional among employee services and benefits in the tangible returns it brings to a company. Not all companies had measured its effects. Of those that were aware of its effects, however, many reported that child care helped them to reduce the costs of turnover, absenteeism, and tardiness; to improve company visibility and corporate image; and to enhance worker morale and motivation and thereby improve overall company productivity. Companies reported far-reaching effects in both the short and the long term. In fact, some reported saving enough from these changes to fully recover the expense of the services. Overall, they overwhelmingly reported the effort to be well worthwhile.

A Scenario for Action: What You Can Do

The information compiled by the National Employer Supported Child Care Project for this book was gathered to aid companies considering the establishment of child care services. It includes a report on what other companies have done and how effective they find their programs to be from a business standpoint. Based on the actual experiences of these 415 companies, the how-to materials in the book also outline a course of action.

When a company considers child care, it needs a rationale for involvement, a guide to the important information to consider, knowledge of alternative approaches, and a process for gathering and synthesizing pertinent data for decision making. The rationale lies in the sweeping changes in the labor force coupled with those in the supply of child care, the effect of these changes on corporate productivity, and the potential for child care services to serve corporate goals.

Pertinent information to consider is the nature of the gaps between child care supply and demand in a particular work force and community, as well as the possible impact of that gap on the company. Information on the demand for care can be gathered directly from employees or indirectly—for example, through child care referral service records. The supply of care available can be ascertained by a company study or by consulting existing community agencies. The potential effect of a gap between supply and demand on company productivity can be estimated using materials in this book.

If management perceives a need for child care assistance from the company, a critical consideration for selecting a child care service is the company's goals and resources. These affect both the decision about whether to institute child care service and how to design it. Companies have different preferences about the amount of support given, whether it is a one-time contribution to assist with startup or an ongoing subsidy for operating costs, and whether the contribution is made in a financial or nonfinancial form such as donated technical assistance. They also vary in terms of how involved they want to be in the ongoing management of the program—that is, whether to run it in house, contract with a management firm, or use other arrangements.

In summary, the needs of the parents, the supply of care already available, and the resources and preferences of the company regarding ongoing management relationships narrow the initial range of program alternatives. Companies can then consider the cost, feasibility, and potential management value of these remaining alternatives and select the most appropriate one.

When a program decision has been made and implementation begun, the design of the program can be finalized and adapted to any changes in parent needs that have occurred during the study process. The key action steps mentioned above and discussed in greater detail in Chapter 5 therefore are as follows:

1. Determine needs.
2. Consider alternatives.
3. Estimate costs and benefits
4. Identify resources.
5. Select program.

Strategies for the Future

Growth Predictions

The continued expansion of employer-supported child care services is predicted by many companies, business groups, social policy makers, public officials, and social scientists. A number of trends noted in the National Employer Supported Child Care Project support this prediction. Consciousness of child care needs is building and filtering throughout the private sector. More and more company administrators are becoming cognizant of the changing demographics of the work force and the need for child care. Most companies have yet to identify the problem in their own workforce, however, because workers tend not to reveal child care difficulties. This phenomenon is the result of decades of conditioning workers not to complain about personal problems or let them interfere with work. Employers are becoming aware, however, that they can help with child care, partly as a result of media attention to the topic. The growing number of programs also increases the likelihood that parents will hear of this new trend and encourages them to communicate their need for child care, particularly when they are convinced of a genuine interest on the part of the company.

Employer-supported child care is becoming more adaptable to the wide variety of employer situations in that there are now a number of ways that companies can support it. Companies that in the past have hesitated to initiate a child care service because their only option seemed to be a work site center now are aware that they can start with less costly services and build upon them as they become convinced of the need. This variety of options also means that there are appropriate courses of action for companies of various sizes in addition to on-site centers, which are best suited to midsize companies or work sites. Various options also make it possible for child care program decisions to be made at different levels of the company. For example, company-wide policy decisions can be made at the corporate level, but modest programs (such as one-time contributions) can be instituted on a local level, often without corporate approval.

The types of employers who find child care useful are expanding. Most of the programs in 1978 were supported by a single industry; health care alone accounted for 71% of the total. By 1982, however, that group represented less than half of the companies with child care, and those in business/industry had grown from 9% to 47% of the total. These newer programs represented a wide range of industries including banking, insurance, manufacturing, retail, entertainment, publishing, utilities, transportation, and charitable foundations.

The sophistication of information and expertise in the field has matured. New information has been developed as a result of corporate grants for study. Publicly funded projects have helped to develop new model programs and how-to materials and to sponsor training sessions. The increased skill of child care specialists means that more outside resources are available for the essential technical assistance needed in child care program development.

The fact that more programs exist now can increase the growth rate in a snowball effect. In communities where there is at least one program, others tend to follow quickly, because companies can observe demonstrable models and thereby overcome apprehensiveness. In southern California, for example, three programs existed in 1978; but by 1983 there were over 25, and the number continues to rise.

Finally, most of the incoming generation of managers will have working spouses. This change in life style, which breeds familiarity with child care as a necessity of working life, will be experienced first-hand by more managers than ever before. More of these managers will also be women, who will be involved in corporate decision making more than women have been in the past.

The rationale for establishing child care services is expected to evolve. Early programs often resulted from a paternalistic decision-making process hinging on the personal experiences, opinions, and decisions of a single company executive. This type of decision making is often found in family-owned businesses, which were the leaders in industry-sponsored child care programs. An example of a program that was the brainchild of a company executive is the one at the Institute for Scientific Information in Philadelphia. The president of the company had experienced child care when young and later became a single father who had difficulty finding child care for his son. As a result, he vowed to provide child care for his workers when he was in a position to do so. The company centers at Forney Engineering and Zales, both in Dallas, Texas, were also initiated because of the personal experience of company executives, each of whom had visited such programs abroad and decided to replicate them. The small number of programs resulting from this early period is not surprising, considering the relatively few corporate executives likely to have had such experiences.

The current business trend, however, is to make decisions more participatively. Decisions about implementing child care depend more heavily on data-based decision-making processes including documented need, in-depth considerations about the economic feasibility of programs, and the strength of child care as a management tool. This information is deemed necessary to justify a leap into a relatively new realm of employee benefits.

During the next phase in the development of programs, several conditions will promote maximum growth. Hesitancy about whether child care is an appropriate role for companies must diminish and companies will have to alter their corporate posture accordingly. Flexibility in dealing with child care will develop over time with more exposure of the concept, in a manner similar to that of all new benefits. When companies become convinced of the effectiveness of child care as a management tool, the traditional attitudinal questions about its appropriateness as a corporate endeavor will lose much of their impact. New data about the corporate benefits of child care will expedite this process, particularly if more in-house data collection procedures about the effects of programs are established in companies with child care. As these data are accumulated, many forms of child care which now appear to be more costly than most other employee benefits may hold greater appeal.

Companies will need a more accurate picture of the need for child care among their employees. Causative factors will include increased employee awareness and requests for assistance with child care. Management will have to be more tenacious in uncovering disguised need, and good systems for the delivery of services must be developed, including information networks and community services throughout the country. Finally, a process must be utilized to bring all of this information together at the decision-making level.

Once employer-supported child care is firmly established in the business community as a legitimate activity, it will become a vital part of competitive benefit packages. By this time, however, the mechanisms for delivering all kinds of child care services are likely to have become so sophisticated that it will be easier to offer a multi-service child care benefit which is adaptable to the varying needs of employees and communities.

Community-Level Structures for Planning and Delivering Services

As the concept of employer-supported child care spreads, it will be important to plan for an efficient and effective total child care system. Let us take a broader look at employer-related services, including how large multi-site companies can implement child care and how employers can be part of the planning and delivery of services at the community level.

It is important to take a wide view in planning employer-supported services for the ultimate good of both the corporation, which seeks the most efficient use of its resources, and the community, which needs an improved integrated system of services. One major consideration in broader planning is better coordination of services, which presently are fragmented and often segmented by social class. Head Start, for example, is designed for low-income children, whereas preschool centers generally serve those who can afford to pay the full cost of care. In addition to reducing such fragmentation, which results in underserved populations and uneven quality care, increased services are needed in almost all sectors. Quality improvements are also necessary, as is increased accessibility. Information about existing programs needs to be more readily available to families, so that they can make maximum use of them.

Comprehensive information about the supply and demand of care is required by child care planners and corporations. It is important that such information be gathered by an efficient, cohesive process, so that data from the different segments of the community will be parallel and that the resultant picture of need will be an integrated whole. The development of new funding sources is probably the most essential requirement, with the more efficient use of and better coordination of funding resources also critical. Improved coordination could mean better leveraging of funds and accommodation of underserved populations. Community planning efforts can work toward all of these goals.

An example of one such comprehensive planning effort is under way in Portland, Oregon. Operated through Portland State University under a federal grant from the Administration for Children, Youth, and Families, it combines the technical expertise of veteran child care researchers, a community child care agency, public funding, and support from educational institutions and local employers. It is a collaborative effort to profile the supply and demand of child care throughout the entire Portland community, surveying 10,000 employees at 32 area employers, as well as measuring child care usage and preference. A comprehensive resource and referral program in the area will also be linked to employers, with an up-to-date profile of supply and demand by neighborhood. It will identify the kinds of child care in short supply and the neighborhoods in which new resources need to be developed. From data it gathers can also be extracted the needs of a particular employee population; it therefore will serve as a source of data for many companies simultaneously. The project is also measuring the differential effects of various types of child care usage on the work place.

In broad planning processes, consideration should be given to the various groups affected by child care. Representation should be sought from sectors such as economic development groups, businesses, volunteer groups, private funders, public educators, child care providers, support agencies, and other advocates for children, as well as from public policy makers, social planners, families, community agencies, business organizations, and civic, service, and professional groups. Many of these players—particularly those connected with the business community—have never been included in child care planning, but an integrated planning process should include them. Like other aspects of the community environment such as utility services, zoning laws, and housing availability, availability of child care affects business operations. Child care impacts the number of available workers, their productivity level, and the labor costs of doing business. Therefore, business is an important member of the planning team. Using their status within the community, business leaders and business group representatives can often be effective partners in accomplishing changes needed in the child care system. For example, they can advocate legislative changes and be heard as a fresh voice by policy makers, improving the legislative status of children's issues from their present relatively weak position. Business people are also the most effective advisors about new laws to promote employer-related child care services.

Along with the need for community-level planning procedures is a need for development of community-level systems to deliver services. These broader systems are often more in line with employer preferences than are individual programs. They enable companies to share referral information, utilize existing child care programs and expertise, cut overhead costs, impact quality and accessibility, and reduce administrative involvement. An additional advantage of such systems is that they can be in operation and link up with corporate contributors as they develop. Because they rely on many sources, they are more stable and can bear the fluctuations of funding cycles and the decisions of individual funding sources.

Two interesting systems that link corporate dollars with other child care funding in new and comprehensive delivery systems have been created. One administers corporate dollars from *employee benefit* funds as a child care reimbursement; the other receives corporate *charitable* contributions. In both cases a single intermediary agency administers the funds to child care programs in a broad-based manner, improving the overall child care system in the community.

The Child Care Assurance Plan in Orlando, Florida, is administered by Community Coordinated Child Care for Central Florida, Inc. (4C), which is a non-profit community-based agency. The plan manages the placement, enrollment, monitoring, and accounting of child care provider agencies. 4C administers three types of public funds (through Title XX, Food Services, and CETA), employer dollars given as a direct child care reimbursement for employees, and other private funds such as donations from United Way. The plan assesses each parent in terms of the subsidies from these sources for which they qualify. This well-coordinated delivery system continues to track eligibility simultaneously from these sources, and changes in subsidy sources do not interrupt the child's care.

Employer subsidies are administered at a flat percentage of program cost after other possible subsidy sources have been evaluated. Because the agency provides child care referrals to the community at large, companies automatically receive this service as well. In addition the plan makes the employer subsidy payment to the child care provider, handles the billing, and keeps the records of payment for the employer. Employers contribute dollars under the Dependent Care Assistance Plan discussed in Chapter 4, and the employer subsidy is considered a non-taxable employee benefit.

Several aspects of this approach promote the enhancement of quality. First, the quality of each program is monitored and this information is made available to parents and companies. In fact, some of the public dollars are administered differentially on the basis of program quality ratings, and programs rating higher in the quality assessment are paid at a higher rate to provide an incentive. The assessment tool itself also serves an educational function for program operators regarding quality. Secondly, support services are offered to child care providers, including staff training, a toy library, and a number of health-related services such as child immunization clinics, health workshops, and low-cost physical, medical, and special-needs referrals. Together, these various quality supports have proved effective, for the average rating of programs has risen substantially since this system was instituted.

The Corporate Child Development Fund in Austin, Texas exemplifies how corporate charitable dollars can be administered along with other supporting funds to maximize the effectiveness of all funding and to better coordinate community child care services. The Fund, conceptualized by the Levi Strauss Foundation and the Texas Department of Human Resources, is a separate non-profit agency which solicits corporate contributions and awards them in the form of grants to child care programs. It also administers scholarships to local community colleges for the training of skilled workers. It has received operating fund grants from the Texas Department of Human Resources and private foundations, allowing 90% of all other contributions they receive to go as direct grants to programs.

Grants to child care programs most often are given to Title XX programs for low-income children and are generally used to leverage more public dollars. Contributions are also made to other non-profit child care programs for purchasing playground or educational equipment or providing administrators with management training. Such training has an important impact on program quality and also ensures organizational survival.

Programs that receive the grants are selected through a proposal process, with certain geographical areas targeted relative to company priorities. The emphasis is on helping smaller towns and rural areas, inasmuch as they are often more underserved than urban areas and lack access to private funds from which to leverage public dollars. In some cases company employees use the child care programs which receive grants; in others the contributions are seen as a charitable gift from which the company receives a public relations benefit.

The Fund currently assists 28 child care programs serving 1,000 children. It has enabled 700 parents to find and hold jobs and 250 to enroll in job training, by helping establish or expand child care programs and prevent program closures.

A second aspect of the Fund, provision of training scholarships for child care providers, also helps to improve the quality of existing programs. Between 1982 and 1983, 600 scholarships were awarded, totaling $20,000 for staff at 175 different family day care homes and child care centers. Community colleges do the child-development-related training, which is funded by contributions from Target Stores. These training programs are located in areas where Target has stores, so their employees as well as the public can benefit from better-quality programs. On the drawing board are plans to provide cash stipends to pay the credentialing fee for child care staff who want to complete Child Development Associate training. One indicator of the success of this Fund is its support by the business community. Over forty corporations support the Fund, with program grants ranging from $500 to $10,000.

Policies and Services for Multi-site Companies

Instituting company-wide child care services presents a particular challenge to large multi-site companies. Child care needs differ from one employee group to another, as do the existing services in various communities. In addition, one region may have a well-coordinated system of child care delivery that a company can tap into, whereas others do not. For some large companies there are relatively simple single-option solutions such as a company-wide child care reimbursement, but in others it is necessary to establish an integrated though varied approach. For example, if the company had branches where there was an insufficient supply of child care, the same reimbursement as that for an area with an adequate supply would essentially be ineffective and would have to be supplemented by some means to stimulate the development of more care. There are a number of considerations in designing an integrated multi-site system:

1. Will services be instituted all at once? Alternative options are to pilot one or more ideas in specific areas or to use a phased-in approach to test and refine program designs.
2. Will the services be available across the board to all employees or be targeted to specific employee groups or locations? If the company has different management goals at various locations, these can be differentially addressed while still meeting parent needs. For example, different services may be offered if a recruitment incentive is needed at one work site while a way to reduce absenteeism is needed at another.
3. What is the company's posture about operating the program? Does management want to run all or parts of it in house, or do they prefer to use outside management groups?
4. Can the company support child care with both operating funds as well as charitable dollars, or is it limited to one source? If it can do both, the company has greater flexibility.

A fictional high-tech firm, "ABC Company," is used here to

illustrate how a varied approach might work. ABC has offices in Boston, Phoenix, Minneapolis, and "Smalltown" and corporate offices in Los Angeles. The work force is comprised of managers, executives (mostly in the Los Angeles corporate office), and highly skilled technical workers such as computer programmers, assemblers, and clerical staff. ABC Company might form a company policy to support the child care needs of its workers by establishing a variety of child care services at various branches in line with local needs. For example, at the corporate headquarters where the staff is comprised mostly of executives and clerical staff, a sliding-scale child care reimbursement and salary reduction could be offered. Thus, lower-paid personnel would receive help with the cost of child care and the salary reduction arrangement would assist higher-paid employees by lowering their taxable income. The company may in fact offer the salary reduction company-wide, along with other services which benefit lower-income employees as well.

In Minneapolis, where the work force is comprised of relatively highly paid data processing personnel, employees can more readily afford the cost of care. In this hypothetical example, the total picture of child care need is not known, although it is clear that parents have difficulty locating existing sources—particularly of infant and school-age child care. A corporate contribution could be given to the local computerized information and referral service to serve ABC's employees and at the same time further define the child care need.

In Phoenix where care is plentiful but often of poor quality, grants could be given to the existing child care programs in close proximity to the company to improve quality—that is, for the training of caregivers, purchase of equipment, and improvement of the facility.

In Smalltown, ABC's rural assembly plant, there is not enough care. There is also a problem with child-care-related job separations. Here an on-site company center could be established, subsidized by the company or other sources so that the cost to these low-income workers is affordable.

Thus it is possible to create a varied company-wide policy that is flexible, addresses the priorities of the company, and is tailored to the varied needs of its employees. It is also cost-effective because it makes use of existing resources and addresses actual needs.

When a multi-site company wants to link up with community services, it has a number of options. There is no country-wide firm or group which delivers all of the many different kinds of child care. It is usually necessary, therefore, to use different management firms or brokering agencies in different areas to address the total demand for care. Some management firms cover large geographic areas, but most are limited to one type of service—for example, those that operate a chain of child care centers. These firms can be paired with other kinds of firms, such as those providing information and referral, to give a balanced service. It is critical in selecting outside firms and in designing an integrated approach that the *quality* of delivered services be weighed heavily, for quality can vary considerably. It is usually best to seek the advice of an outside early childhood education professional before making a selection.

For some companies, early education professionals can also simplify the ongoing management of a company-wide system. They can assume responsibility for the ongoing monitoring and management of the system, coordinate the firms used in various areas, and evaluate the ongoing effectiveness of the various components. As the composition of each work force and the supply of care fluctuate, services must be provided flexibly to maximize the cost-effectiveness and success of programs. A child care expert can be part of company staff or operate from an outside agency on a consulting basis. In either case, training in child care administration and strong educational background in early childhood education and/or child development are important prerequisites for such a role.

Effects of Employer-Supported Child Care on the Larger Society

A number of sectors of society can be affected by employer involvement in child care. Each has an important role to play. Obviously the child care market itself is affected, but children, families, businesses, and the community are impacted as well.

The Child Care Market

Employer involvement in child care can raise awareness about the need for child care, its relevance, the extent of its use, and difficulties in the existing system. Corporate advocacy can also impact regulations that affect all day care centers. Employers can stimulate improvements in the coordination of child care services by supporting information and referral services, community child care planning, and community delivery systems. They may unify the day care providers in the community in their planning efforts or provoke competition among them if they are competing for employer dollars.

Greater availability of employer-supported child care can mean greater differentiation of care and thereby create yet another segment of child care users. This new group may be differentiated by a number of criteria such as income, industry, or geographical area if employer-supported child care programs occur more frequently in some sectors than others. Employer programs may, for example, serve a disproportionately large number of higher-income parents in those cases where the employees are professional and technical rather than assembly line workers. Community programs may therefore be left with a user group that by itself is unable to support financially care of high quality. If, on the other hand, a large number of employers with employees at various income levels support community child care, thereby increasing the total amount of financial resources available and providing other supports, there will be a positive impact on the care for all children.

The opportunity for parents to choose care according to their own values and preferences can be affected either positively or negatively by employer involvement. Employers who limit reimbursements to a single program, for example, essentially limit parental choice. On the other hand, one that reimburses for a variety of programs including centers, homes, and relatives may give parents more choice than they had before. The additional dollars might even make it possible for parents to use programs they could not afford before.

Reimbursements may indirectly affect long-term supply and demand trends as well. For example, corporate contributions to centers may reduce the market for in-house family day care and in the long run thereby reduce the supply of that care. In some cases these market changes may cause other side effects. If, for example, reimbursements are tied to programs that meet a certain level of quality, they may discourage lesser-quality programs and eliminate them from the supply side. Parents' expectations about the level of quality in child care may be raised if employer involvement gives them experience with quality care or helps educate them about the quality elements of care. Emphasis on some forms of care may also change parent preferences. Parents who use infant care in an employer-supported center, for example, may decide they like it better than other types.

The child care market can play a number of roles in both the stimulation of employer-supported child care and the delivery of services. Child care administrators often act as *spokespeople* about the need for improved care. They are *experts* to whom companies and community planners turn for advice. They have *services* that companies can link up with. These services and the voices of their administrators often *impact policies,* such as child care licensing regulations. Child care professionals are often the *creative thinkers* who devise and refine improvements in the child care system. By contributing to the body of knowledge about children and education, they *support research* and the *development of thought* in the field.

Families

The quality of life of families is affected most by employer involvement in child care. It can mean more time spent together for children and parents if programs reduce overload and fatigue, cut commuting time, or replace piecemeal care. Parents experience peace of mind when the quality, convenience, accessibility, or selection of care is improved. Parents are better able to meet both professional and family goals when conflicts between the two are reduced. And, employer-supported child care can help parents resolve, rather than juggle, their conflicts.

Children are profoundly affected by the kind of care they receive. Their environment has a critical impact on what they learn and how they develop. They need care which addresses their intellectual, emotional, social, and physical development, and their early care experiences have a lasting effect.

Employer-supported child care has great potential to impact children's care environment positively. It can provide a safe place and a caring adult for children who would otherwise be in "self-care" or in the care of a sibling. If care is educational rather than merely custodial (supervisory), it can be expected to produce some of the same results as those noted in studies such as the High Scope Foundation's Perry Preschool Study. This longitudinal study of low-income and minority children who had a high-quality preschool education found the following effects: less special education needed later, increased lifetime earnings, higher achievement test scores, less teenage delinquency, less adult unemployment, fewer high school dropouts, less need for welfare assistance, and reduced crime resulting in imprisonment.[1] The economic benefits of these effects are obvious.

If employer-supported programs are located near or interact closely with the place of work, children often have more opportunity to view the world of work first-hand. This perspective may reestablish the job role models that have disappeared in our industrialized society where children, separated from their parents, have difficulty developing pictures of what their jobs are like. Because employer-supported programs reduce parents' stress, children often also receive more relaxed parental attention at home.

The family can also serve a number of functions regarding child care. They are the *consumers* for whom programs are designed. Parents can be the *initiators* of child care activity among employers, raising management's level of consciousness about the problems they face. They can begin grass roots movements and serve as *organizers*. They are crucial *members of the planning process* in that they are *information sources about need* and barometers of satisfaction with the services that exist. They are also, therefore, as one center director put it, the best *quality control* mechanism for employer-supported programs. Often choosing to be highly active in the programs they use, they are valuable *advisors* and program supports to program staff.

Business

Employer involvement in child care broadens the role of employers, lessening the work/family split which is a part of industrialized society. It reflects an up-to-date management theory, characterized by quality circles and participative management. It also reflects the individualistic character of our technically sophisticated society, providing benefits which have particular appeal to a certain group of employees. Although not the first benefit to do so, employer-supported child care reflects a growing trend away from standardization of benefits, particularly when used within a flexible benefits program. It may spark further developments along these lines, such as benefits for the care of older or incapacitated family members.

A profound impact that such programs may have on business, in addition to the achievement of numerous management goals, is an increased ability to offer equal employment opportunity. With the availability of affordable good-quality child care, women with all kinds of professional aspirations will find it easier to achieve career goals. They are likely to have greater access to promotion-track positions. And minorities, which traditionally use child care at a higher rate, may also have greater access to jobs.

Employers can play a number of roles in the child care arena. As *advocates*, they can promote broad changes in state, local, and federal legal systems; encourage the overall improvement of systems; and stimulate other companies into more active roles. As *liason* they can help parents and community groups connect with needed services—for example, connecting community agencies with resources from business organizations. As *motivators for change* they can, for example, offer matching incentive grants to new child care providers or to encourage other companies to join in child care partnerships with them. They can create mechanisms within their programs to stimulate change, such as giving corporate contributions only to community child care programs which meet certain standards of quality. As *technical experts,* they can assist community planners (contributing business acumen), providers (particularly in business management areas), and families (by informing them of tax credits for child care). Finally as *providers of direct services* they can impact the child care market and serve as a model.

The Community

For the community, the involvement of employers has the potential to improve and stabilize existing services. Of community concern, however, is the capability of a new system of employer-supported child care to further differentiate the services available to the public. In the overall view it is important that there not be a child care "rich," who receive a child care benefit at work, and a child care "poor," who do not work for a company that offers child care or who are not yet employed (such as people in education or training programs). The issue of these unserved populations underscores the fact that employer support is only one part of the societal solution to child care needs.

Of special community concern is the issue of quality in employer-supported child care programs. Communities do not want existing child care problems merely shunted to a different arena. Because level of financing is often the pivotal point in dealing with these problems, adequate corporate subsidies and education by community leaders about the best uses of these resources point the way to the solution.

The Impact of Employer Support on Quality of Child Care

Because the quality of child care is important to families, variability in programs has a widely differential effect on them. Programs of poor quality can be unsafe for children and harmful to their social, emotional, physical, or intellectual development. They can also be inconvenient and are certainly worrisome to parents.

There are several reasons why poor-quality programs survive. Some parents continue to use them because they have no other choice: Either they cannot afford the higher cost of good programs, there are not enough quality programs to go around, or they are unaware how to select a good program. Some programs meet only the state regulations, which are not standards for high quality but rather minimum requirements below which programs are considered dangerous. In some states these regulations are quite lenient, and regulating agencies often have inadequate funds to monitor programs effectively for compliance. The recent thrust toward deregulation threatens to worsen the situation.

Several elements are necessary for quality in child care centers and in family day care homes. It is important that there be an adequate ratio of caregivers to children. The staff should constitute a stable work force and have an early-childhood-related educational background. The groups of children should be relatively small in the interest of individualized care. Also important are adequate amounts of educational equipment, a safe and properly designed facility, sound management, and an educational program appropriate to the age of the children.

Another element of quality is how well the program matches the preferences and needs of parents and the supply and demand of care in the community. Programs must fit the hours that care is needed, be conveniently located, and be well advertised. These requirements hold true for programs supported through many employer child care mechanisms, much as they do for those included in referral services, those which receive reimbursements or corporate contributions, and those which employers offer directly in homes or centers.

Employers can potentially impact the quality of the child care market either positively or negatively. They can perpetuate poor quality by establishing new programs without quality elements or by supporting existing poor-quality programs without requiring quality improvements. The danger of establishing poor-quality new programs is particularly acute where companies try to make programs for low- or moderate-income families completely self supporting through parent fees. Poor quality also can result from company programs established without the expertise and guidance of qualified child care professionals. Effort is required to ensure quality programs, but it is to the company's advantage to make the effort, for only programs of quality are in its best interest. Poor programs, although perhaps less expensive, do not usually accomplish the goals for which they were established. They seldom meet parents' child care needs as well as do high-quality programs, and they can have utilization problems because parents may find other ordinarily unsatisfactory child care arrangements preferable. Poor-quality programs are not likely to have the same impact on turnover, and are less likely to attract positive publicity and support a positive corporate image. They also may do less to reduce parental worries about child care and thus may not have a beneficial impact on worker concentration and energy, and consequently productivity.

On the other hand, good-quality programs are usually quite attractive to parents. They offer an incentive to employees to work for the company. They give parents peace of mind in knowing that their child is well cared for and thus can maximize their energy for work. They usually attract more media attention and present a better corporate image.

There are a variety of ways that employers can promote quality in child care programs. In the child care centers or homes that they provide directly, they can meet the quality criteria discussed in this book. When providing indirect child care services such as information and referral, reimbursements, or corporate contributions, companies also have opportunities for supporting and enhancing quality. Incentives can be offered to strengthen the quality of programs through requirements for appropriate teacher child ratios, group size, and staff educational requirements such as child developmental associate training. These requirements should be met before the program is eligible for referrals, reimbursements, or corporate contributions.

Or companies can require that program coordinators and staff complete orientation training once in the system, such as courses given by local colleges or child care groups. This training can be paid for by corporate dollars through scholarships or operating funds contributions. Another incentive is to have a monitoring and rating system administered by local child care professionals. Those ratings should be passed on to parents, because informed parent choice is a major remedy for quality problems. The ratings can also be used to qualify programs differentially for subsidies. Inasmuch as the reason for the poor quality of some programs is financial, companies can help poor programs improve their quality by giving grants for the purchase of educational materials or equipment, for staff training, for addition of staff, for building repairs, or for management training for administrators.

One general rule of thumb for promoting quality is to use professionals to establish or administer programs. These people have training in early childhood education and child development rather than in other fields such as psychology, elementary education, counseling, or health care. Although the latter fields may appear to be related, background in them usually does not qualify one for teaching or administration in child care and can, indeed, result in ineffectual programs. Early childhood education and child development are disciplines which focus specifically on the young child, whose needs are very different in all-day care than in other settings. Child development training is an example of career preparation suitable for child care staff. Companies should also be sure that these professionals have experience in quality *all-day* care programs, rather than, for example, a *half-day* nursery school.

An additional quality safeguard is that the program maintain an ongoing connection with professionals in the community. Some company programs have a regular consultation arrangement with a local expert in early childhood education to ensure that their program maintains quality standards. This concept is particularly important in in-house programs where company personnel in a supervisory capacity do not have a child-care-related background. Such an arrangement helps them to evaluate the program and its director's performance.

Probably the greatest impact on quality is made by the program's level of financing. This in turn often dictates the staff-child ratio, the facility, group size, and the compensation, and therefore the stability and background of, the staff. Thus, a critical factor in safeguarding quality of employer-supported child care programs is ensuring that they are adequately subsidized by companies (whether in dollars or some other form of support) or other sources to provide the funds above what parents can afford to pay.

To summarize, employer involvement in and of itself is not a guarantee of high quality. Quality must be deliberately planned into new programs and into systems using existing community services. But it is well worth the effort, for both the company and the family have a stake in the outcome. Perpetuation of poor-quality programs will serve everyone poorly in both the short and long run, but all stand to gain from cultivation of quality.

In conclusion, employer involvement in child care is an exciting opportunity. It is highly recommended by companies who have tried it and deeply appreciated by the employees who use it. It is one of the rare programs which benefits such diverse groups as the family, the corporation, and the larger society. It is an innovative area of corporate endeavor offering a challenge from which there are both tangible and intangible returns. At the same time, it supports family life. It is a unique opportunity that brings results in the short term and also has a profound impact on the future.

Endnote

1. L. J. Schweinhart and D. P. Weikart, "Young Children Grow Up: The Effects of the Perry Preschool Program on Youths through Age 15" *Monographs of the High/Scope Educational Research Foundation, No. 7 (1980).*

APPENDICES

Appendix A

THE NATIONAL EMPLOYER SUPPORTED CHILD CARE SURVEY

During 1981–1982 a national survey was conducted by the National Employer Supported Child Care Project among employers providing some form of child care service. The purpose of the study was to gather two kinds of information about the program to form the basis for a manual: descriptive data about how programs are designed and how they function, and data from companies about the effects of a child care program. As there was no current listing of employer-supported programs, the Project conducted an extensive location process, identifying a total of 415 companies that supported child care services for their employees. This group was thought to represent very nearly all the programs in operation at the time.

The Survey

A two-part written survey was mailed to the chief executive officer of each company, one part requesting information about the program and the other asking about its effects on the company. The chief executive officer was asked to assign each part of the survey to the people in the organization best suited to supply the information. For the most part, the information describing the programs came from the child care program directors, and the information about the effects of child care on the company came from company human resource managers. Companies that did not respond to the written survey were contacted by telephone and asked to verify program information and to answer selected questions from the written surveys. Information was gathered on all of the 415 identified programs. Of the total, 47% completed the written survey, 52% participated in the telephone interview, and 1% supplied other written information.

The part of the survey about the corporate benefits of child care (Part B) was completed by fewer companies that the part describing the programs (Part A), primarily because some companies had inadequate data regarding the corporate benefits. Of the total of 258 companies (62%) completing Part B of the survey, 40% completed the written form and 60% participated in the telephone interview. Virtually all of the companies completed Part A of the survey. Chief executive officers of each company were also given an opportunity to comment on the value of the child care program on a response postcard.

Part A asked for a description of the program services, the user population, costs, support arrangements with the company, staffing patterns, levels of staff compensation, and group size. Part B, regarding the corporate benefits of the program, was intended to accomplish three types of informational goals: (1) pinpoint the effects of child care on a large number of employee work behaviors; (2) assess the relative influence of child care as a personnel management tool, compared with other methods the companies used; and (3) identify companies with the most complete statistical information about the extent and value of the effects of child care.

Findings

Major findings from the studies are described in Chapter 2, which gives data about the corporate benefits of child care in tables and in case study format and describes program characteristics. Program examples, typical program design, and findings particular to the different types of child care are in the sections describing each program type in Part Four. Additional data tables are included in this appendix. (Note: An additional research document by project staff, designed for policy makers and researchers, will report and analyze more program descriptive data and compare the program characteristics further. Only data pertinent to those designing programs are contained in this manual.)

Methodology

Special attention is given here to the part of the survey that gathered data about the corporate benefits of child care (Part B).

The results are presented in Chapter 2. This part of the survey contained a variety of questions regarding corporate benefits. Some questions required that the company report statistical information from company records, such as questions asking for overall company turnover rates and the turnover rates of child care program users. Other questions allowed for reporting subjective impressions about the effects of the child care programs—for example, "Would you say that the child care service has had an effect on any of the following aspects of company operation?" This question referred to some 22 items such as turnover, absenteeism, tardiness, publicity, and morale. Possible responses were "positive effect, no effect, negative effect, or unknown," allowing for a distinction among nonpositive responses between companies that felt there was no effect, companies with inadequate data to measure the effect, and companies that did not respond at all.

A second type of question (which allowed subjective impressions) asked companies to compare the effect of child care in reducing turnover and absenteeism, recruiting workers, and enhancing public relations with results achieved by other methods used by the company to achieve the same goals. Companies were not asked what other methods they used. Other questions allowed for estimates or calculated figures—for example, "How many times has your company received publicity from the child care service?" Companies were not asked to specify whether such reported figures were estimates or actual statistics.

Interpretation

The responses to Survey B may not be representative of the total population of employer-supported child care programs, because certain types of programs responded to this portion of the survey more frequently than others. More employers with direct service programs (company child care centers, company family day care homes, and company school-age child care programs) responded about the benefits of their child care programs. Fewer indirect programs (information and referral services, child care reimbursements, informational programs for parents, and employer support of community child care programs) responded regarding the benefits of their child care programs. Seventy percent of the companies responding to the corporate benefits section of the survey had direct programs, whereas 30 percent of the respondents had indirect programs. The numbers of direct and indirect programs in the study in the total group studied, however, were approximately equal. This difference in response rate may be due to the difficulty in observing the effects of indirect programs, a fact confirmed by many respondents during the telephone interviews.

It is not known whether respondents differed from non-respondents in any other ways that would bias the study results. A high overall response rate and follow-up telephone interviews, however, helped to reduce any potential bias.

The survey relied on information already available in company records and on the one-time response to a written or telephone survey. It did not gather information over time, and did not control for other relevant variables. As a result, causal conclusions cannot be drawn about the effects of child care.

Other Reported Data

The following reports of a small group of companies provide more detailed data about the extent and value of child care's impact.

Turnover

- 18 companies had data that allowed them to compare the turnover rates of child care program users with the rates of the total workforce.
- 17 of the 18 companies reporting found lower turnover rates for employees who used the child care service than for the total workforce.
- The average turnover rate for all employees at these companies was 44%. The average turnover rate for employees using the child care service was 19%, a difference of 25 percentage points.

The companies reporting these data were divided almost evenly between those in the business-industry category and those in health care organizations (10 health care organizations and 8 from businesses).

Recruitment

- In 10 companies estimating the annual recruitment value of child care, $16,400 was the estimated annual recruitment savings. All but one of these ten companies were health care organizations. The average figure is based on the number of recruits in the company's top two job categories targeted for recruitment and on the company's reported cost for recruiting a worker in each category. Because only two job categories were included, total recruitment savings may have actually been higher.

- Companies also reported that their child care service has helped to recruit workers into the following job categories:
  - Secretaries
  - Computer programmers
  - Key punch operators
  - Bank tellers
  - Cannery laborers
  - Textile workers
  - Managers
  - Accountants/auditors
  - High-tech assembly workers
  - Registered nurses
  - Licensed vocational nurses
  - Licensed practical nurses
  - Physical therapists
  - Laboratory technicians
  - Medical technologists
  - Radiology technicians
  - Pharmacists

Publicity

9 companies estimated the average annual value of child care in terms of the publicity it brought the company. Child care was estimated to be worth $13,000 annually to each company. About half (4) of the nine companies reporting this data were from the business-industry category; the balance (5) were health care organizations.

Overall Cost-Benefit Comparison

95% of the 147 companies that compared the overall costs and benefits of child care said that the benefits of child care outweigh the costs. In drawing this conclusion they considered only measurable benefits.

TURNOVER

Positive responses by type of program:

*Program Type**	*No. Positive Responses*	*No. Programs Responding*	*% Positive for Prog. Type*
Direct	73	113	65%
Indirect	43	65	66
Total	116	178	65%

*Direct = company centers and family day care homes.
Indirect = reimbursement, information and referral, parent education, and support of community programs.

Positive responses by age of program:

Program Age	*No. Positive Responses*	*No. Programs Responding*	*% Positive for Age Group*
Less than 1 year	14	24	58%
1-5 years	51	82	62
Over 5 years	49	66	74
Age unknown	2	6	33
Total	116	178	65%

Positive responses by type of industry:

	1	2	3	4	A	B	A + B	1/A
Industry Type	*Positive Effect*	*No Effect*	*Negative Effect*	*Unknown Effect*	*Total Respondents 1-4*	*No Response*	*Total Programs*	*% Positive of Total Industry Type*
Business/ industry	35	8	0	14	57	140	197	61%
Health care organization	75	15	0	23	113	82	195	66
Public agency/ union	6	1	0	1	8	15	23	75
Total	116	24	0	38	178	237	415	65%

ABSENTEEISM

Positive responses by type of program:

*Program Type**	*No. Positive Responses*	*No. Programs Responding*	*% Positive for Prog. Type*
Direct	61	113	54%
Indirect	33	65	51
Total	94	178	53%

*Direct = company centers and family day care homes.
Indirect = reimbursement, information and referral, parent education, and support of community programs.

Positive responses by age of program:

Program Age	*No. Positive Responses*	*No. Programs Responding*	*% Positive for Age Group*
Less than 1 year	11	24	46%
1-5 years	47	82	57
Over 5 years	33	66	50
Age unknown	3	6	50
Total	94	178	53%

Positive responses by type of industry:

	1	2	3	4	A	B	A + B	1/A
Industry Type	*Positive Effect*	*No Effect*	*Negative Effect*	*Unknown Effect*	*Total Respon-dents 1–4*	*No Response*	*Total Programs*	*% Positive of Total Industry Type*
Business/industry	29	13	0	15	57	140	197	51%
Health care organization	61	19	0	33	113	82	195	54
Public agency/union	4	0	0	4	8	15	23	50
Total	94	32	0	52	178	237	415	53%

RECRUITMENT

Positive responses by type of program:

*Program Type**	*No. Positive Responses*	*No. Programs Responding*	*% Positive for Prog. Type*
Direct	93	113	82%
Indirect	57	64	89
Total	150	177	85%

*Direct = company centers and family day care homes.
Indirect = reimbursement, information and referral, parent education, and support of community programs.

Positive responses by age of program:

Program Age	*No. Positive Responses*	*No. Programs Responding*	*% Positive for Age Group*
Less than 1 year	18	24	75%
1-5 years	72	82	88
Over 5 years	54	64	84
Age unknown	6	7	86
Total	150	177	85%

Positive responses by type of industry:

	1	2	3	4	A	B	A + B	1/A
Industry Type	*Positive Effect*	*No Effect*	*Negative Effect*	*Unknown Effect*	*Total Respon-dents 1-4*	*No Response*	*Total Programs*	*% Positive of Total Industry Type*
Business/industry	50	5	0	1	56	141	197	89%
Health care organization	94	10	0	9	113	82	195	83
Public agency/union	6	1	0	1	8	15	23	75
Total	150	16	0	11	177	238	415	85%

PRODUCTIVITY

Positive responses by type of program:

*Program Type**	*No. Positive Responses*	*No. Programs Responding*	*% Positive for Prog. Type*
Direct	57	110	52%
Indirect	26	59	44
Total	83	169	49%

*Direct = company centers and family day care homes.
Indirect = reimbursement, information and referral, parent education, and support of community programs.

Positive responses by age of program:

Program Age	*No. Positive Responses*	*No. Programs Responding*	*% Positive for Age Group*
Less than 1 year	9	23	39%
1–5 years	39	78	50
Over 5 years	32	62	52
Age unknown	3	6	50
Total	83	169	49%

Positive responses by type of industry:

	1	2	3	4	A	B	A + B	1/A
Industry Type	*Positive Effect*	*No Effect*	*Negative Effect*	*Unknown Effect*	*Total Respon-dents 1–4*	*No Response*	*Total Programs*	*% Positive of Total Industry Type*
Business/industry	27	14	0	13	54	143	197	50%
Health care organization	53	20	0	34	107	88	195	50
Public agency/union	3	1	0	4	8	15	23	38
Total	83	35	0	51	169	246	415	49%

PUBLIC RELATIONS

Positive responses by type of program:

*Program Type**	*No. Positive Responses*	*No. Programs Responding*	*% Positive for Prog. Type*
Direct	98	114	85%
Indirect	55	65	85
Total	153	179	85%

*Direct = company centers and family day care homes.
Indirect = reimbursement, information and referral, parent education, and support of community programs.

Positive responses by age of program:

Program Age	*No. Positive Responses*	*No. Programs Responding*	*% Positive for Age Group*
Less than 1 year	23	26	88%
1–5 years	69	81	85
Over 5 years	55	66	83
Age unknown	6	6	100
Total	153	179	85%

Positive responses by type of industry:

	1	2	3	4	A	B	A + B	1/A
Industry Type	*Positive Effect*	*No Effect*	*Negative Effect*	*Unknown Effect*	*Total Respondents 1–4*	*No Response*	*Total Programs*	*% Positive of Total Industry Type*
Business/industry	52	7	0	1	60	137	197	87%
Health care organization	93	11	0	7	111	84	195	84
Public agency/union	8	0	0	0	8	15	23	100
Total	153	18	0	8	179	236	415	85%

MORALE

Positive responses by type of program:

*Program Type**	*No. Positive Responses*	*No. Programs Responding*	*% Positive for Prog. Type*
Direct	102	115	89%
Indirect	61	66	92
Total	163	181	90%

*Direct = company centers and family day care homes.
Indirect = reimbursement, information and referral, parent education, and support of community programs.

Positive responses by age of program:

Program Age	*No. Positive Responses*	*No. Programs Responding*	*% Positive for Age Group*
Less than 1 year	22	26	85%
1–5 years	77	81	95
Over 5 years	58	67	87
Age unknown	6	7	86
Total	163	181	90%

Positive responses by type of industry:

	1	2	3	4	A	B	A + B	1/A
Industry Type	*Positive Effect*	*No Effect*	*Negative Effect*	*Unknown Effect*	*Total Respon-dents 1–4*	*No Response*	*Total Programs*	*% Positive of Total Industry Type*
Business/ industry	56	2	0	1	59	138	197	95%
Health care organization	100	4	2	8	114	81	195	88
Public agency/ union	7	0	0	1	8	15	23	88
Total	163	6	2	10	181	234	415	90%

QUALITY OF SERVICES

Positive responses by type of program:

*Program Type**	*No. Positive Responses*	*No. Programs Responding*	*% Positive for Prog. Type*
Direct	39	106	37%
Indirect	22	57	39
Total	61	163	37%

*Direct = company centers and family day care homes.
Indirect = reimbursement, information and referral, parent education, and support of community programs.

Positive responses by age of program:

Program Age	*No. Positive Responses*	*No. Programs Responding*	*% Positive for Age Group*
Less than 1 year	6	22	27%
1–5 years	26	78	33
Over 5 years	26	57	46
Age unknown	3	6	50
Total	61	163	37%

Positive responses by type of industry:

	1	2	3	4	A	B	A + B	1/A
Industry Type	*Positive Effect*	*No Effect*	*Negative Effect*	*Unknown Effect*	*Total Respondents 1–4*	*No Response*	*Total Programs*	*% Positive of Total Industry Type*
Business/industry	19	21	0	11	51	146	197	37%
Health care organization	41	24	0	40	105	90	195	39
Public agency/union	1	3	0	3	7	16	23	14
Total	61	48	0	54	163	252	415	37%

QUALITY/WORKFORCE

Positive responses by type of program:

*Program Type**	*No. Positive Responses*	*No. Programs Responding*	*% Positive for Prog. Type*
Direct	50	114	44%
Indirect	24	64	38
Total	74	178	42%

*Direct = company centers and family day care homes.
Indirect = reimbursement, information and referral, parent education, and support of community programs.

Positive responses by age of program:

Program Age	*No. Positive Responses*	*No. Programs Responding*	*% Positive for Age Group*
Less than 1 year	9	24	38%
1–5 years	35	81	43
Over 5 years	28	67	42
Age unknown	2	6	33
Total	74	178	42%

Positive responses by type of industry:

	1	2	3	4	A	B	A + B	1/A
Industry Type	*Positive Effect*	*No Effect*	*Negative Effect*	*Unknown Effect*	*Total Respon-dents 1–4*	*No Response*	*Total Programs*	*% Positive of Total Industry Type*
Business/ industry	24	19	0	14	57	140	197	42%
Health care organization	49	27	1	36	113	82	195	43
Public agency/ union	1	3	0	4	8	15	23	13
Total	74	49	1	54	178	237	415	42%

TARDINESS

Positive responses by type of program:

*Program Type**	*No. Positive Responses*	*No. Programs Responding*	*% Positive for Prog. Type*
Direct	41	112	37%
Indirect	28	63	44
Total	69	175	39%

*Direct = company centers and family day care homes.
Indirect = reimbursement, information and referral, parent education, and support of community programs.

Positive responses by age of program:

Program Age	*No. Positive Responses*	*No. Programs Responding*	*% Positive for Age Group*
Less than 1 year	10	24	42%
1-5 years	30	81	37
Over 5 years	28	64	44
Age unknown	1	6	17
Total	69	175	39%

Positive responses by type of industry:

	1	2	3	4	A	B	A + B	1/A
Industry Type	*Positive Effect*	*No Effect*	*Negative Effect*	*Unknown Effect*	*Total Respon-dents 1–4*	*No Response*	*Total Programs*	*% Positive of Total Industry Type*
Business/industry	25	15	0	16	56	141	197	45%
Health care organization	40	35	0	36	111	84	195	36
Public agency/union	4	0	0	4	8	15	23	50
Total	69	50	0	56	175	240	415	39%

EQUAL EMPLOYMENT OPPORTUNITY

Positive responses by type of program:

*Program Type**	*No. Positive Responses*	*No. Programs Responding*	*% Positive for Prog. Type*
Direct	48	109	44%
Indirect	20	62	32
Total	68	171	40%

*Direct = company centers and family day care homes.
Indirect = reimbursement, information and referral, parent education, and support of community programs.

Positive responses by age of program:

Program Age	*No. Positive Responses*	*No. Programs Responding*	*% Positive for Age Group*
Less than 1 year	8	22	36%
1-5 years	31	81	38
Over 5 years	27	62	44
Age unknown	2	6	33
Total	68	171	40%

Positive responses by type of industry:

	1	2	3	4	A	B	A + B	1/A
Industry Type	*Positive Effect*	*No Effect*	*Negative Effect*	*Unknown Effect*	*Total Respon-dents 1-4*	*No Response*	*Total Programs*	*% Positive of Total Industry Type*
Business/industry	19	28	0	8	55	142	197	35%
Health care organization	44	42	1	21	108	87	195	41
Public agency/union	5	2	0	1	8	15	23	63
Total	68	72	1	30	171	244	415	40%

SCHEDULING FLEXIBILTY

Positive responses by type of program:

*Program Type**	*No. Positive Responses*	*No. Programs Responding*	*% Positive for Prog. Type*
Direct	55	110	50%
Indirect	31	62	50
Total	86	172	50%

*Direct = company centers and family day care homes.
Indirect = reimbursement, information and referral, parent education, and support of community programs.

Positive responses by age of program:

Program Age	*No. Positive Responses*	*No. Programs Responding*	*% Positive for Age Group*
Less than 1 year	11	23	48%
1-5 years	41	81	51
Over 5 years	31	62	50
Age unknown	3	6	50
Total	86	172	50%

Positive responses by type of industry:

	1	2	3	4	A	B	A + B	1/A
Industry Type	*Positive Effect*	*No Effect*	*Negative Effect*	*Unknown Effect*	*Total Respon-dents 1–4*	*No Response*	*Total Programs*	*% Positive of Total Industry Type*
Business/industry	26	20	0	8	54	143	197	48%
Health care organization	55	30	4	21	110	85	195	50
Public agency/union	5	0	0	3	8	15	23	63
Total	86	50	4	32	172	243	415	50%

Companies That Reported the Effects of Child Care

Employee Behavior	*Number of Companies That Reported Effects*					*% Positive of Total Responses*	*Numbers of Companies That Did Not Report Effects*	*Total Number of Companies Surveyed*
	Positive	*No Effect*	*Negative*	*Unknown Effect*	*Total*			
Turnover	116	24	0	38	178	65	237	415
Absenteeism	94	32	0	52	178	53	237	415
Recruitment	150	16	0	11	177	85	238	415
Productivity	83	35	0	51	169	49	246	415
Public relations	153	18	0	8	179	85	236	415
Employee morale	163	6	2	10	181	90	234	415
Quality of products or service	61	48	0	54	163	37	252	415
Ability to attract new/returning workers	139	22	0	15	176	79	239	415
Quality of workforce	74	49	1	54	178	42	237	415
Equal employment opportunity	68	72	1	30	171	40	244	415
Tardiness	69	50	0	56	175	39	240	415
Scheduling flexibility	86	50	4	32	172	50	243	415
Employee work satisfaction	147	13	1	17	178	83	237	415
Employee commitment	126	18	1	28	173	73	242	415
Employee motivation	108	24	1	39	172	63	243	415
Publicity	143	22	0	13	178	80	237	415

Parent-Employee Perceptions of Employer-Supported Centers

As part of the National Employer Supported Child Care Project, some parent employees were asked to rate their feelings about their company's child care center. Parents from 19 centers completed questionnaires; the directors of these 11 hospital centers and 8 industry centers administered the questionnaires and tabulated the results. The responses of the 691 company employees who answered the questions indicate that parents who use employer-supported child care centers have very positive feelings about the programs.

Methodology. Child care program directors were offered the opportunity to use a parent questionnaire developed by the National Employer Supported Child Care Project. Nineteen center directors completed the process and returned copies of the results to the Project. Of these, 16 programs were used only by employees and 3 were also used by some community children. The 691 parents whose responses are reported here were all company employees. The median response rate for all centers was 64%. The respondents were primarily female; only 8% were male. Eighteen percent were single parents. The responses covered 842 children, with 22% of respondents having more than one child. The children's ages ranged from less than 6 months to over 6 years old; about 11% were under one year old, another 15% were between one and two years, 52% between two and five (average preschool age), 14% were between five and six, and 8% were over six.

This part of the survey was an exploratory assessment of parents' reactions to employer-supported child care programs. The parents were not selected randomly and they may not represent the full range of opinion among parents using employer-supported centers. Nevertheless, this information is more comprehensive than any that has been available previously on users of employer-supported services. These data point up two important facts: First, *parent users of employer supported services are happy with their child care arrangements;* and second, *parents say that their child care services affect their job performance positively in a number of ways.*

Satisfaction with Child Care. There has been quite some debate among researchers as to what "satisfaction" really means. Parents may say they are satisfied with their child care simply because they do not know that they have any alternatives, because the alternative services are impossibly expensive or inconvenient, or because they do not want to admit to themselves that the place where their child spends so much time is inadequate.

General questions such as, "Are you or are you not satisfied?" do not reveal all of the many real differences in parental perceptions of child care programs; accordingly, this study asked about specific aspects of the child care service. To allow comparisons with a similar study of a general population of 117 child care users, the questions were the same as those used by Jacquelyn McCroskey in a 1980 study of child care satisfaction, *Working Mothers and Child Care: The Context of Child Care Satisfaction for Working Women with Preschool Children.*

Although the two samples were not randomly selected and were queried at different points in time, it is significant that the users of employer-supported centers were much more satisfied than the other group of parents. These parents reported higher general levels of satisfaction and also higher satisfaction with the individual aspects of child care convenience, dependability, price, staff competence, physical facility, quality of teaching, love and understanding shown the children, and opportunities for socialization with other children. In addition, more parents said that they did not worry about leaving their children during the day, and that their spouse and child liked the program. The relative percentages of parents in both groups who were most highly satisfied in each category are indicated in the table below.

Comparison of Satisfaction with Child Care: Employer-Supported Center Users Compared with Other Child Care Users

	Parents Using Employer-Supported Programs	*Other Parents*
1. High overall satisfaction (extremely or very satisfied)	87%	63%
2. Rated overall satisfaction between 76–100% (on a scale 0–100%)	92	45
3. Highly satisfied with convenience	94	59
4. Highly satisfied with dependability	96	82
5. Highly satisfied with price	65	55
6. Highly satisfied with staff competence	87	72
7. Highly satisfied with physical facility	88	82
8. Highly satisfied with teaching	90	42
9. Highly satisfied with love and understanding toward child	81	68
10. Highly satisfied with socialization for children	91	62
11. Rarely or never worry about leaving child at child care program	88	64
12. Child likes progam	97	73
13. Spouse likes program	91	80

Clearly the 691 parent employees with children in employer-supported child care centers are very satisfied with their services. Employer-supported care generally gives parents easier access to convenient, dependable care that is likely to be highly satisfactory to them. Small dissatisfactions are more easily adjusted because parents are more closely associated with the program, and the arrangements reflect parent needs and preferences.

Job Performance Benefits. The parent employees were also asked to say whether the child care program had affected their job performance in a number of ways. The responses of these 691 parents illustrate how significantly child care services can affect parent employee work behaviors:

- *Recruitment:* 38% said that the child care program was a factor in their decision to take their current job.
- *Turnover:* 69% said that it was a factor in their continuing to work at their current job.
- *Performance:* 41% said that their job performance had been affected positively by the child care program.
- *Attitude/morale:* 63% said that they have a more positive attitude toward the company because of the child care.
- *Absenteeism:* 47% said the child care had allowed them to miss less time from work.
- *Scheduling:* 42% said that the program had made it possible for them to work overtime or odd shifts.
- *Promotions:* 11% said that the program had made it possible for them to accept a promotion or change in jobs.
- *Recruitment and public image:* 53% said that they had recommended their employer to others because of the child care.
- *Other:* 10% reported other benefits, such as being nearby in case of an emergency.

Appendix B

FURTHER RESEARCH ON THE CORPORATE BENEFITS OF CHILD CARE

In addition to the National Employer Supported Child Care Project, whose results are the basis for this book, other studies have addressed the effects of employer-supported child care on a company. Although past studies have been few in number, they corroborate the findings of the National Project, further supporting the conclusion that child care is an effective management tool. These studies are described briefly here and are also listed in the Resources List for those who wish to analyze them further.

Studies still in progress as of July 1983 are also discussed. These new studies will add significantly to the current body of knowledge, particularly inasmuch as a number of them are longitudinal studies, collecting data over time.

Past Studies

The Northside Child Development Study. In 1971–1973 a study was conducted regarding the effects of child care on the working behavior of employee parents who used an employer-supported child care program, the Northside Child Development Center in Minneapolis.[1,2] This center was established in 1971 and provided comprehensive care for children from infancy through school age. Seven businesses supported the center, but employees from only one of the companies (Control Data) were selected for the study, which was conducted by a research team from the University of Minnesota Graduate School of Business Administration.

The results of the study indicated that employees using the employer-supported center had significantly lower turnover and absenteeism rates than the two control groups: eligible employees not using the center, and other employees. These two control groups were matched with the group using the center on several variables, including job tenure and job function.

The day care participants had average monthly turnover rates of 1.77 and absenteeism of 4.40, compared with turnover rates of 6.30 and absentee rates of 6.02 for non-participating parents, and 5.50 and 5.00 for other employees. These differences are statistically significant for both groups in comparison with the rates of program participants.[3] Not only were the participants' rates lower than the other two groups, but the absentee rates of participants themselves decreased annually during the study. In 1972 there was a decline in their absenteeism of 21.4% since they had enrolled in the program. In 1973 there was a decline of 22.5% from pre-enrollment rates, with average monthly absenteeism rates 2.25 percentage points lower after enrollment.[4] Although child care was thought to be a primary factor, other relevant variables could not be controlled in this pre-post test of absenteeism, and there may have been factors in addition to child care that contributed to this drop in absenteeism.[5]

The Kathryn Senn Perry Study. A study in 1978 conducted by Kathryn Senn Perry at the University of Wisconsin identified and studied the employer-supported child care centers in operation at that time, including military as well as civilian centers.[6] A total of 105 civilian centers were found to be currently in operation. A written survey of these programs was conducted and responses were received from 42 hospitals, 5 industries, 6 labor unions, and 5 government agencies (a response rate of 55%). Respondents were asked to indicate areas such as turnover in which they had noted changes as a direct result of child care. For those not indicating a change, there was no distinction between respondents who felt there was no effect and those who were unable to observe whether there was an effect or not. A substantial number of companies reported that child care had an impact in the work place. The findings are summarized in the table below:

Changes	*Percentage of Companies Noting Change**
Lower job turnover	57%
Lower absenteeism	72
More positive attitude toward employer	65
More positive attitude: work experience	55
Increase: attracting new employees	88
Increase: attracting minority employees	21
Improvement: community relations	36
Publicity: articles on day care	60

*Only civilian companies are reported.

Studies in Progress

Bank Street College's Work and Family Life Study in New York (a cross-national research project) is comparing the effect of family life changes on work place productivity. In this project "researchers will concentrate initially on one work site to obtain baseline measurements on family and work life, including productivity. The employer at this site will permit workers (both fathers and mothers) to make changes that the workers believe will improve their lives but not diminish their productivity."[7] Data will be studied at regular intervals to determine how the workers' changes affected their productivity in the work place and their family life. Parallel research will be conducted in West Germany by the state-funded Deutschesjugend Institut, and discussions are underway about cooperative research in Great Britain and other countries.

Austin Families, a non-profit agency in Austin, Texas has two studies in progress regarding the corporate benefits of child care. One is the Hospital Child Care Project in Austin, Texas which provides child care for four participating hospitals. Funded by the U.S. Department of Health and Human Services, Administration for Children, Youth, and Families, the project will include an evaluation of the work behavior of participants—that is, turnover, absenteeism, and employee attitudes. Longitudinal data will be collected from parents, before entering the program, periodically during the program, and at the end of the evaluation period. Control groups are expected to consist of parents on a waiting list or another group of matched eligible nonparticipating parents.

The second evaluation by Austin Families will be focus on participants in the Austin Independent School District Child Care Voucher Program. This program pays for approximately half of the child care cost of bus drivers and other transportation employees. Information on work behaviors, safety records of drivers, stress, and the financial impact of the program is being collected over time. This information will allow comparison of participants' behavior before and after receiving child care vouchers, with eligible but non-participating parents, with non-parents, and with aggregate data.

The Administration for Children, Youth, and Families has also recently funded several other studies on the corporate benefits of child care. The Portland State University, for example, is conducting a survey of Portland area employers and their employees to examine the relationship between workers' day care situations and workplace behaviors such as absenteeism, turnover, and morale. In addition, a comprehensive resource and referral program operating in the Portland area (4-C's) will be linked to the employers and to the geographic profiles developed of supply and demand on a neighborhood level. A pilot study has already been completed which links child care arrangements with changes in absenteeism.

In another instance, Foundation for Human Service Studies, Inc., is conducting an experimental study to determine the costs and related effects of employer-supported child care systems on employee absenteeism, turnover, performance,and job satisfaction. The study will be carried out in five different geographical areas with a cross-section of profit and not-for-profit organizations providing on-site care, off-site care, or referral services.

These new studies may be able to demonstrate even greater benefits to business from child care because they will be examining child care's import in previously unmeasured areas. It may also be expected that the effects of child care on the company will expand as the number of employees with child care needs increases.

Endnotes

1. Northside Child Development Center, *Northside Child Development Center: 1973 Annual Report* (Minneapolis: Northside Child Development Center, 1973).
2. G. Milkovich and L. Gomez, "Day Care and Selected Employee Work Behaviors," *Academy of Management Journal* (1976), pp. 111–115.
3. *Ibid.*, p. 113.
4. *Ibid.*
5. *Ibid.*, p. 114.
6. K. S. Perry, "Survey and Analysis of Employer Day Care in the United States," (Ph.D. dissertation, University of Wisconsin, 1978).

Appendix C

METHODS FOR COMPARING COSTS AND BENEFITS OF CHILD CARE

There is a choice in the type of analysis used to compare costs and benefits of child care. In the various types of analysis, many of the same elements are included. The elements necessary for the comparison of costs and benefits are described as follows:[1]

> *In general, only real benefits (those that involve real resources) should be included in the analysis; they may be direct or indirect. Most planners include both direct and indirect benefits in their calculations, although the latter are more difficult to identify and measure. An example of a real and direct benefit is the reduction in training costs that result from lower turnover. An indirect benefit might be the value of unsolicited publicity about the program that enhances the image of the employer in the community.*

Cost Benefit Analysis

After a value is figured or estimated for each of the benefits and costs, the values of all the benefits are added together and the value of all the costs is subtracted. The result is the net cost of the child care program (if costs outweigh benefits) or the net benefit (if benefits outweigh costs). Such a calculation is a *cost-benefit analysis.*

In order to predict whether a program can pay for itself, all costs and benefits should have values placed on them. Many companies will be unable to conduct an ideal cost-benefit analysis because of difficulties in quantifying some of the expected benefits. If very few of the benefits can be quantified, the employer may want to consider using an alternative technique such as cost-effectiveness analysis, which is described below.

Benefits and costs that extend beyond one year should be subjected to a discounting procedure, because costs and benefits received tomorrow are worth less than those received today. Child care often involves long periods of time for both the outlay of funds (as in the capital expenditures for facilities) and the receipt of benefits (such as reduced turnover). Discounting is probably necessary, however, only when a relatively complete number of possible costs and benefits are being compared. Determining the appropriate discount rate can be difficult, but employers may decide to use the same rate they use for other similar investments. As a simple example, a discount rate of 20% is roughly equivalent to expecting the investment in an on-site center to pay back within five years. The most widely used discounting procedure is "net present value," which can be calculated by using the following formula:

$$\text{Net Present Value} = \frac{\text{Benefits}_t - \text{Cost}_t}{(1 + r)^t}$$

where t is time[2], measured in years.

The program with a positive net benefit, with the highest net benefit, or with the lowest net cost should be undertaken. The following two examples illustrate this procedure.

Example A

Cost for Year 1 of child care program: $100
Benefits received in Year 1: $110
Discount rate = r = .05

$$\frac{\text{Benefits}_t - \text{Costs}_t}{(1 + r)^t}$$

where t is time measured in years

$$\text{NPV} + -100 + \frac{110}{1.05} = -100 + 104.76 = 4.76$$

Example A is a financially feasible project because it has a positive net benefit.

Example B

10-year time period
Initial cost = $100
First-year cost = $108
Ten-year benefit = $300

$$\text{NPV} = \frac{-108}{(1.05)^1} + \frac{300}{(1.05)^{10}} = -100 + -102.8 + 184 = -18.8$$

In example B, 184 represents $184 of discounted benefits or what the $300 worth of benefits are worth now.

Example B is not a financially feasible project because it has a negative net benefit.[3]

Cost Effectiveness Analysis

Another process can also be used to select the most effective program from among several alternatives. This type of analysis, called cost-effectiveness analysis, differs from cost-benefit analysis in that it tries to separate the costs of a project from its benefits (effectiveness); while costs are measured in numbers and units, benefits are not. For example, a company may want to determine which type of child care service would have the greatest impact on turnover for an annual expenditure of $25,000. Cost-effectiveness analysis would not require determining whether the reductions in turnover would recover the total $25,000 expenditure (which cost-benefit analysis could do), but requires instead determining which of the proposed programs would have the greatest impact on turnover.[4]

> *Cost-effectiveness analysis is a method of comparing programs that do the same thing—i.e., a voucher program and on-site care. It tries to show how a given level of effectiveness can be achieved at minimum cost or to show how the maximum effectiveness can be achieved at some given level of costs. But CE analysis will not tell you if the program yields positive net benefits—whether it pays for the employer to provide child care assistance. CB analysis, on the other hand, will tell you this, but it does require more quantification of benefits. In practice, the distinction between CB analysis and CE analysis will be largely a matter of degree, since the ideal forms of either technique are seldom used. Cost-effectiveness analysis is most beneficial as a decision-making tool when choosing between mutually exclusive products that are trying to achieve the same specific objectives—e.g., recruiting employees for specific shifts.*

A number of additional factors should be taken into consideration when the value of savings in an individual area such as turnover are being determined. The effect that one area (such as turnover) has on another should be considered; this is called the "interdependence of benefits." For example, if turnover is reduced, the company may also save money on unemployment insurance. The time preference of benefits should also be considered—that is, the time that the benefit is introduced may determine the extent of its effect. The child care program may have a greater recruitment value, for example, if it is begun in the summer rather than in the fall, or if established this year rather than another year. The certainty of the projected costs and benefits should be considered, as well as whether there is a small or large amount of variability in the possible costs and benefits.

Additional Considerations

After each of the individual values for the separate costs and benefits have been determined and a total net cost or total net benefit has been figured, there are several additional considerations that affect the overall value of the child care program. The state of the economic times will have an effect on how the total net cost or the total net savings of a child care program are viewed. Benefits accrued in difficult economic times are sometimes more valuable than the same benefits in less difficult times, depending on the industry, region, and other factors. The certainty with which any risks associated with the program (such as liability) can be avoided should also be considered. It is also important to consider whether the possible outcomes of the child care service will be moderate or not. The degree of control the company has over possible outcomes and the degree to which positive outcomes can be enhanced should be examined. Conflicting use for or restrictions on a given amount of capital should be considered. Additionally, the opportunity costs associated with program investments should be considered: What is the value of the resources' best alternative use?

Figure A-C-1 Estimation Model for Turnover Costs[5]

Activity	*Nonexempt Cost*	*Exempt Cost*	*Total*
1. Employment advertising	$ 25,000	$ 30,000	$ 55,000
2. Agency and search fees	5,737	25,000	30,737
3. Internal referrals	10,800	3,979	14,779
4. Applicant expenses	500	9,318	9,818
5. Relocation expenses	3,000	79,132	82,132
6. Employment staff compensation	10,200	25,000	35,200
7. Other employment office expenses	1,150	1,150	2,300
8. Recruiters' expenses	3,000	500	3,500
9. Direct hiring costs (sum of 1–8)	$ 59,387	$174,079	$ 233,466
10. Number of hires	278	84	362
11. Direct costs per hire (9 ÷ 10)	$ 214	$ 2,072	$ 645*
12. Indirect costs per hire (from Figure 2)	3,705	6,180	
13. Total costs per hire (11 + 12)	$ 3,919	$ 8,252	$ 4,840†
14. Number of replacement hires (turnover)	200	54	254
15. Total turnover costs (13 × 14)	$783,800	$445,608	$1,229,408
16. Target percent reduction	25%	25%	25%
17. Potential savings (15 × 16)	$195,950	$111,402	$ 307,352

*Calculated by dividing total direct hiring costs (line 9) by the total number of hires (line 10).
†Calculated by dividing the total turnover costs (on line 15) by the total number of replacement hires (on line 14).

Figure A-C-2 Breakdown of Indirect Turnover Costs[5]

	Nonexempt Cost	*Exempt Cost*
18. *Cost of management time per hire*—estimated dollar cost of management time spent orienting new employees (average hourly rate × hours spent per hire).	$ 98	$ 293
19. *Cost of lead employees' time per hire*—Estimated cost of time spent by lead employees in orienting and training new hires (average hourly rate × hours spent per hire).	407	—
20. *Cost of training per hire*—Estimated total training costs allocated to new hires (total training cost ÷ new hires).	203	—
21. *Cost of learning curve labor productivity losses*—Nonproductive labor costs of new employees from lines 26 & 32 in Figure 3.	$2,997	5,837
22. *Total indirect hiring costs per hire*—The sum of lines 18-21.	$3,705	$6,180

Figure A-C-3 Estimation Model for Learning Curve Productivity Losses[5]

Job Classification	*Average Weekly Pay Rate*	*Weeks Learning to 90% Productivity*	*% Effective During Learning Curve*			*Learning Curve Losses per Employee*
			First 1/3	*Second 1/3*	*Third 1/3*	
23. Management	$780	17	20%	32%	86%	7,160
24. Professionals	637	14	27	60	86	3,775
25. Sales	605	15	25	50	80	4,386
26. Weighted average—exempt job classification						$5,887
27. Technicians	445	12	15	55	90	2,492
28. Office and clerical	312	7	42	60	85	823
29. Skilled crafts	452	6	30	61	75	1,211
30. Operating-semiskilled (assembly)	238	4	22	60	90	406
31. Service (janitors and the like)	$247	3	48%	60%	83%	$ 269
32. Weighted average—nonexempt job classifications						$2,997

NOTE: *Direct costs* are defined as those costs normally incurred in the employment function that are easily identifiable and typically directly associated with the recruitment effort. Indirect costs are the less visible ones; most of them, like training and productivity losses, occur after the new employee has been hired (see Figure A-C-2).

Completing the Model

Once you have compiled the necessary data, preferably for a one-year period, complete the model (beginning with Figure A-C-1) as indicated in the following steps. Enter annual costs separately for nonexempt and exempt job classifications and total them in the column to the right. Again, if accurate data are not readily available, complete the model by using informed estimates.

1. *Employment advertising.* Include here all recruitment advertising and related costs.
2. *Agency and search fees.* Include all fees to employment agencies, search firms, and recruitment consultants.
3. *Internal referrals.* Include all costs for bonuses, fees, gifts, and so on, awarded to employees participating in a company-sponsored applicant-referral program.
4. *Applicant expenses.* Include the travel and subsistence costs entailed in bringing an applicant (and spouse) to the place of interview. Also include cost of the spouse's travel, if applicable.
5. *Relocation expenses.* This includes the costs of travel, moving of household effects, subsistence allowances, and all other costs associated with relocation.
6. *Employment staff compensation.* Include all salaries, benefits, and bonuses of the employment staff.
7. *Other employment expenses.* Include all other expenses that can be attributed to the employment function, such as the cost of facilities, telephones, equipment depreciation, office supplies, printing, physical examinations, consultants, and so on.
8. *Recruiters' expenses.* Include here subsistence allowance and all expenses reimbursed by the company for recruitment trips. Don't forget any extra costs in connection with interviewing an applicant, such as tickets to sports and cultural events, wining and dining, and so on.
9. *Direct hiring costs.* The total of items 1 through 8.
10. *Number of hires.* The total number of permanently hired employees during the year.
11. *Direct cost per hire.* Divide direct hiring cost (9) by number of hires (10).
12. *Indirect costs per hire.* These figures are obtained from line 22 in Figure A-C-2.
13. *Total cost per hire.* This is the sum of direct (11) and indirect (12) costs per hire.
14. *Number of replacement hires (turnover).* Enter the number of yearly terminations, not including temporary hires.
15. *Total turnover costs.* Multiply total cost per hire (13) times number of replacement hires (14).
16. *Target percent reduction.* This is to be used in planning turnover reduction for individual companies.
17. *Potential savings.* This is to be used in estimating dollar savings to the company if the planned turnover reduction is achieved. To obtain this figure, multiply target percent reduction (16) by total turnover costs (15).

Figure 3 shows the major job classifications used by the federal government on EEO form 100. This is for your convenience in calculating average rates of pay. Complete this part of the model as follows:

Column 1: Enter the average weekly pay rate, including benefits, for current incumbents in each job classificatin.

Column 2: Enter your best estimates of the number of weeks required for the average new employee to achieve a 90 percent productivity level.

Columns 3-5: Enter the percentage of effectiveness that you feel a typical new employee has reached according to his or her job classification. For a management employee, for example, you may estimate that the learning curve is 24 weeks, with the typical new hire being 25 percent effective during the first third, 60 percent effective during the second third, and 85 percent effective during the final third. The overall time frame and percentage of effectiveness will, of course, vary according to job classification.

Column 6: Enter the productivity losses (in dollars) incurred for the average new hire by using the following calculation:

$$\frac{WW}{3} \times PR\ (1.00 - PE) = LCC$$

where WW = the number of workweeks required to reach a 90 percent effectiveness level; 3 = learning "thirds"; PR = average weekly pay for an incumbent; 1.00 – PE = 100 percent minus the percentage of effectiveness; and LCC = learning curve cost.

Next, calculate the weighted average of exempt job classifications by listing the number of incumbents in each of your job classifications (lines 23–25) and enter this figure on line 26, column 6. Repeat this process for nonexempt classifications (lines 27-31) and enter the result on line 32, column 6.

Five-Company Survey of Turnover Costs

To test the validity of this approach to estimating total turnover costs, five companies with high turnover rates were surveyed. As shown in Figure A–C–4, total average turnover cost for a nonexempt employee was $3,136 and for an exempt employee, $11,094. The combined average per employee cost was $4,596. One significant finding was that for a nonexempt employee, direct turnover costs represented only 15 percent of the total turnover cost. For exempt employees, direct costs represented 30 percent of the total. This fact points up the importance of establishing total turnover costs in organizations so that you can get an accurate focus on the total picture and then take appropriate action. The five companies surveyed, all located in California, were involved in or related to high-technology manufacturing, and had an average employment of 1,298 employees. The ratio of exempt to nonexempt employees varied from company to company. The average company in the survey spent $1,446,600 for employee turnover.

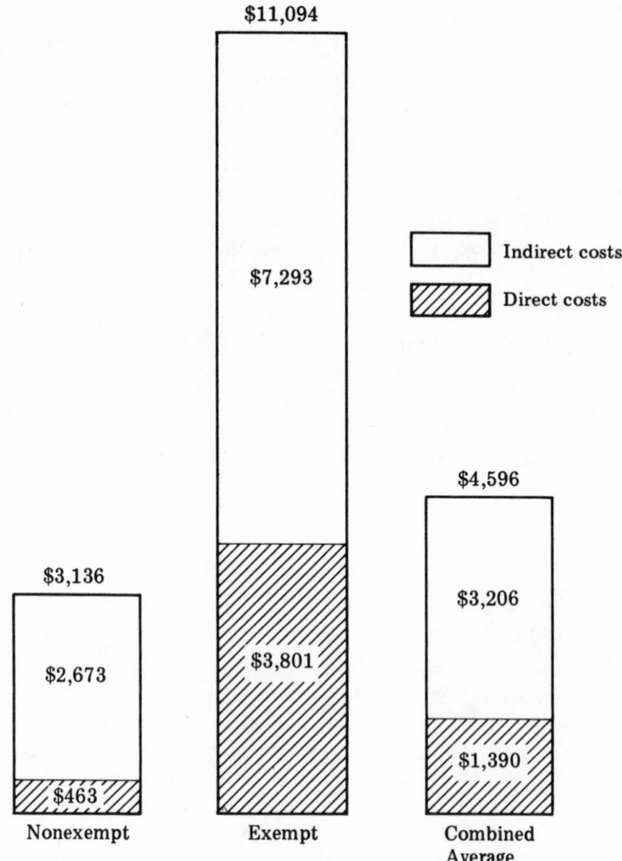

Figure A-C-4 Average Turnover Costs for Surveyed Companies: Mean Turnover Cost per Replacement Hire.

Endnotes

1. Personal communication with Mary Young, Economic Analyst, Austin Families, Austin, Texas (June 3, 1983).
2. P. G. Sassone, and W. A. Schaffer, *Cost-Benefit Analysis: A Handbook* (New York: Academic Press, 1978), pp. 14–17.
3. Personal communication with Mary Young.
4. *Ibid.*
5. T. Hall, "How to Estimate Employee Turnover Costs," *Personnel Journal* (July/August 1981), pp. 43–52.

Appendix D

GUIDELINES AND SAMPLE MATERIALS FOR DATA COLLECTION AND DECISION MAKING

The following materials have been specifically developed for use in implementing the steps in the decision making process described in Chapter 5. They are organized here in the same order as they are used in the decision process.

1. Sample Task Force Work Plan
2. Issues for the Task Force's Attention
3. Sample Newsletter Piece
4. Sample Advance Flier
5. Guidelines and Sample Materials for Conducting an Employee Needs Survey
   a. Conducting a Survey
   b. How to Use the Sample Survey
   c. Sample Survey—Part 1
   d. Sample Survey—Part 2
   e. Notes on the Sample Survey
   f. Sample Data Summary Worksheet—Part 1
   g. Sample Data Summary Worksheet—Part 2
   h. Notes on using the Sample Data Summary Worksheet
   i. Sample Cover Letter for Survey
   j. Sample Response Verification Card
   k. Sample Follow-up Fliers
6. Guidelines and Sample Materials for Conducting Focus Groups on Employee Needs
   a. Conducting Focus Groups

b. Sample Warm-up talk for Focus Group
c. Sample Focus Group Discussion Questions
7. Guidelines and Sample Materials for Using Referral Record Data on Employee Needs
a. Using Referral Record Data
b. Note on Sample Referral Forms
c. Sample Referral Forms
8. Guidelines for Writing the Task Force Report
9. Sample Task Force Report Outline

1. SAMPLE TASK FORCE WORKPLAN

This workplan is an example which can be adapted to suit the Child Care task force's own data collection methods and decision making process.

Task No.	*Step. No.*	*Description*	*Assigned to*	*Estimated Person Days*	*Scheduled Dates Start-Complete*
		PRELIMINARIES			
		Clarify company goals attainable through child care service. See Chapter 1, Part I.			
		Review possible child care options. See Part IV.			
		ASSESSMENT			
		Research future recruitment needs.			
		Research estimation of child care needs in future labor pool.			
		Plan collection of data on employee needs and effects on company: –logistics: handout at meeting; return by company mail. –method: survey. –analysis: computer.			
		Adapt sample survey and cover letter; review with Human Resources.			
		Plan advance communication: –letter from CEO (draft). –departmental meetings (plan agenda). –newsletter article (write).			
		Distribute CEO's letter.			
		Hold departmental meetings.			

Task No.	*Step. No.*	*Description*	*Assigned to*	*Estimated Person Days*	*Scheduled Dates Start-Complete*
		Publish newsletter article.			
		Distribute survey.			
		Accumulate survey results; clean, code, keypunch data.			
		Analyze results.			
		Draw profile of employee needs.			
		Research and prepare inventory of community services. –family day care homes. –child care centers, nursery schools. –after-school care and summer programs. –care for sick children. –referral services. –financial assistance. –parent information.			
		Compare employee needs with community services to identify gaps in service.			
		ANALYSIS AND DECISION			
		Describe options that match employees' unmet needs, including how these options address company goals; develop rough budget for each.			
		Draft report for decision makers.			
		Present report to senior management and obtain commitment.			
		Develop detailed plans and budget for child care services.			

2. ISSUES FOR THE TASK FORCE'S ATTENTION

The following issues may be first discussed among the task force. Members may then want to meet with small groups in the work force for example, supervisors, union leaders, shopstewards, heads of departments, and departmental employees) to explain these points. A company newsletter article or series covering this information could be a useful advance communication technique.

1. Why the company is interested in the concept of employer-supported child care and the level of management support for exploring the issue.
   a. Changes in the work force (for example, increases in female employ-

ment, two-income couples, single-parent families) which make child care one of the "tools" of the workplace.

b. Concern with turnover, recruitment, absenteeism, or other work behaviors related to child care needs.

c. Management philosophy which relates productivity to employee morale, work satisfaction, and other factors (compatibility of quality of life with productivity).

d. Interest in social issues, public relations, or community well-being.

2. Clarify "child care" so that term is clearly understood. It is used here to mean any kind of caring for children by someone other than the parent—for example, in nursery schools, play groups, day care centers, preschools, Head Start, child care centers, or family day care homes or by babysitters, neighbors, or relatives. It refers to all children from birth through age 11 (or older children who need an adult to check in with), including infants and preschool and school-age children before and after school. It applies to all care needed while parents are working, which may include evenings, weekends, school vacations, and summers.

3. A range of ways that a company can help meet child care needs:

   a. Arrange with child care providers that employees currently use for improved services to parents (for example, longer hours or reduced costs).

   b. Help parents locate child care through a referral service or written information (in-house or outside agency).

   c. Allow more flexibility in work schedules so that employees can better coordinate child care with their spouses or with other available care.

   d. Help new programs get started so parents have a wider choice of services (for example, care for infants and before- and after-school care of school-age children).

   e. Help to reduce the cost of child care to parents.

4. How both the company and the employees (both parents and nonparents) stand to benefit from employees' having access to adequate child care services:

   a. Examples of other companies' publicity, improved morale, and reduced absenteeism after helping with child care needs.

   b. Case histories from within the company of how child care difficulties affected both the employee and the company (for example someone who had received training and then had to quit due to lack of child care). Care should be taken to protect the privacy of employees.

5. How the company is trying to determine whether and how to become involved in child care:

   a. Who comprises the task force; who will make the final decision.

   b. Data collection on employees' needs, effects on company, and existing supply of care in the community.

      (1) Purpose: complete and accurate information provides sound basis for decisions regarding whether and how to become involved in child care.

(2) What data collection methods will be used.
(3) How methods will be used; which employees will participate.
(4) Find out if supervisors need any support from management or the company to make the upcoming survey, group discussions, and other procedures easier on them.
(5) Give names of people (for example, task force members and consultants) whom employees can contact with questions about the collection of information on employee needs.
(6) How data on community services will be gathered.

c. Feedback: when and how employees will learn the results of decision process.

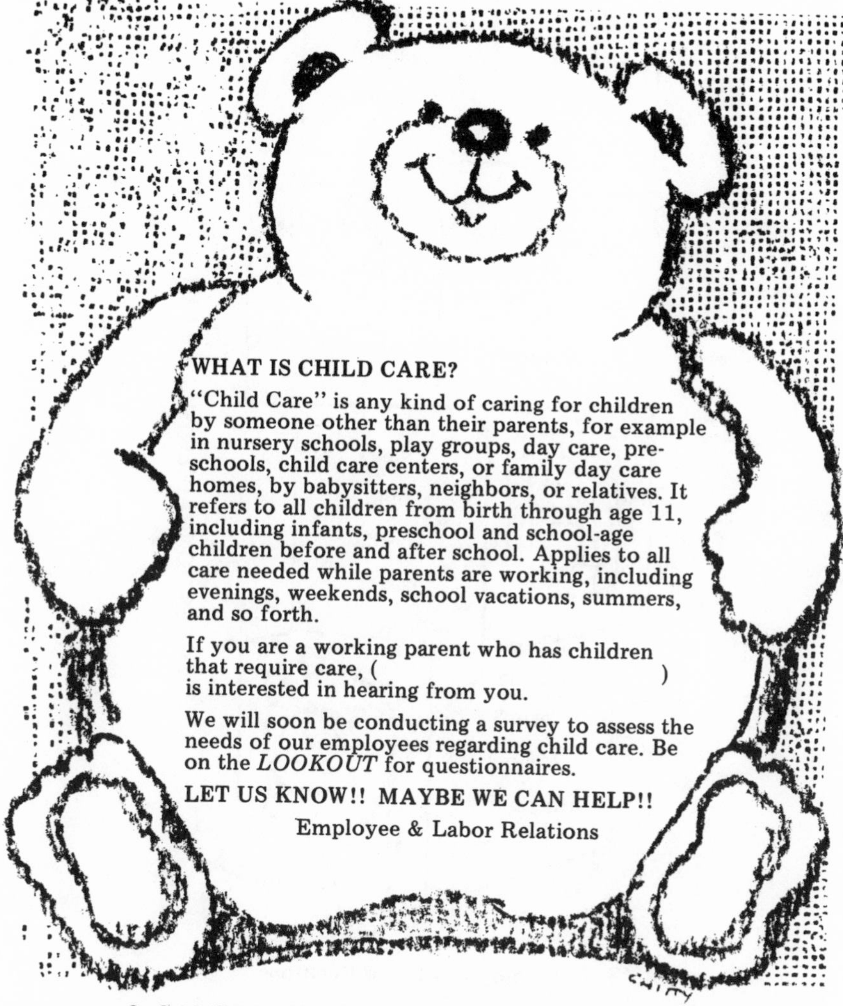

WHAT IS CHILD CARE?

"Child Care" is any kind of caring for children by someone other than their parents, for example in nursery schools, play groups, day care, preschools, child care centers, or family day care homes, by babysitters, neighbors, or relatives. It refers to all children from birth through age 11, including infants, preschool and school-age children before and after school. Applies to all care needed while parents are working, including evenings, weekends, school vacations, summers, and so forth.

If you are a working parent who has children that require care, (   ) is interested in hearing from you.

We will soon be conducting a survey to assess the needs of our employees regarding child care. Be on the *LOOKOUT* for questionnaires.

LET US KNOW!! MAYBE WE CAN HELP!!

Employee & Labor Relations

3. SAMPLE NEWSLETTER ANNOUNCEMENT

d. Clear up any final doubts about the worth of employer-supported child care, the equity issue for employees without children, and problems with the data collection process. Get reservations, and objections, and psychological barriers out in the open.

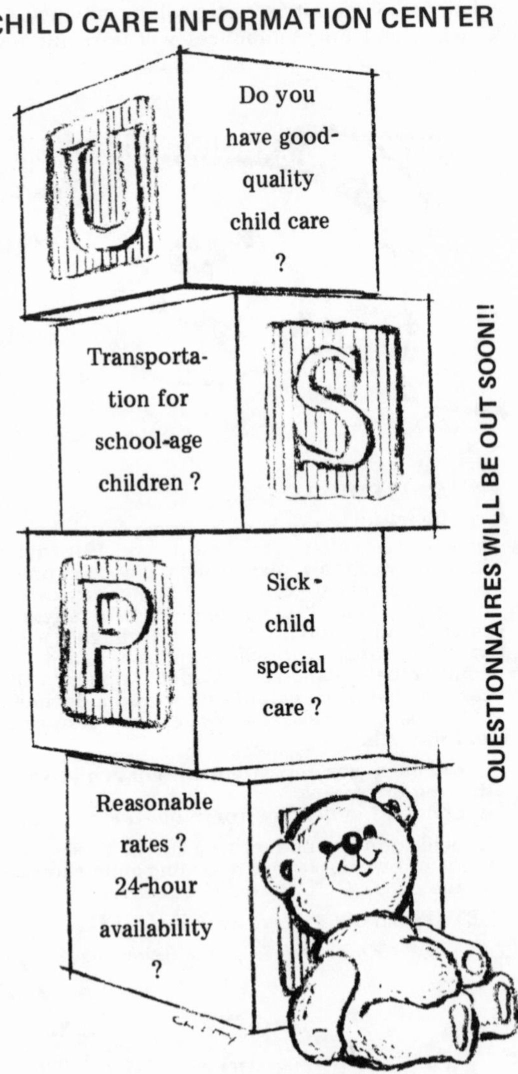

CHILD CARE INFORMATION CENTER
U
Do you have good-quality child care ?
Transportation for school-age children ?
S
P
Sick-child special care ?
Reasonable rates ? 24-hour availability ?
QUESTIONNAIRES WILL BE OUT SOON!!
Employee & Labor Relations

4. SAMPLE ADVANCE FLIER

5. GUIDELINES AND SAMPLE MATERIALS FOR CONDUCTING A SURVEY

5(a) Conducting a Survey

1. Participants

It is possible to survey all employees, certain groups (for example, one department, site, or union), or a random sample of employees. The advantage of sampling is economy. Keep these points in mind when considering sampling with a survey:

- A sample may not be cost-effective unless there are enough employees. A suggested rule of thumb is to use sampling with no fewer than 1000 employees.
- A random sample or stratified random sample ensures that data will reflect the total population and not just the people in the sample.
- Probably not all employees have children, and the return rate may be less than 50%, so survey enough people to get a *reasonable* number of respondents.
- Include both women and men, since child care is a concern of both parents.
- Oversample any very small groups in your population whose needs are important to detect (for example, women managers).
- If all employees are to have the opportunity to voice their opinions it may be better to survey everyone rather than a sample.

2. Distribution

a. Methods:

- Fill out at department meetings.
- Send in paycheck.
- Send in company mail.
- Send via U.S. mail to home (with return address and stamped envelope included).
- Give as personal handout by task force or supervisors. For non-English speakers or non-readers, survey can be administered in groups, with translator reading questions and aides helping employees fill it out; but anonymity should be maintained. College student can be recruited to translate.

b. Timing: Avoid major holidays, vacation times, and off-seasons when people are likely to be away from work. Avoid peak work periods when people are too busy to complete the survey.

c. Duration: Allow 1–2 weeks for return of surveys. (People forget if given longer.) Or make the survey "due" at the end of the meeting called to fill it out, or at the end of the work day.

d. Cover letter: It is very important to let people know who is conducting the survey (including the name and phone number of at least 1 contact person) and the purpose of the survey. Avoid raising unrealistic expectations by underscoring that the survey is an exploration and not a promise that a program will be established (see sample cover letter).

3. Return:
   a. Methods:
      - On-the-spot return of survey.
      - Enclosed stamped envelope.
      - Return box in convenient area(s).

   b. To maximize return rate:
      - Make return as easy as possible.
      - Follow-up those who do not return it soon.
      - Give prizes for return (for example via raffle tickets given to individuals when survey is returned or to department with high return rate).
      - Have plenty of extra surveys available.
      - Maintain respondents' anonymity: avoid putting collection box on supervisors' desks, letting others look over returned surveys, or putting mailing labels directly on surveys.

4. Follow-up Methods:
   - Set up network of supportive employees in each department to remind and encourage on a one-to-one basis during lunch and breaks and on the phone.
   - Task force members call department heads to remind employees.
   - Use response verification card with survey to yield list of people to be contacted.
   - Send follow-up reminder notices or use posters, newletters, and so forth.

5. Tabulating the Data:

Usually the data is tallied by recording the number of responses to each possible answer either directly on a copy of the survey or on a data worksheet. Some companies also like to figure the percentage of respondents who select each answer. Percentages make comparison across questions easier; however, sometimes raw numbers are more persuasive and less deceptive than percentages.

6. Computer vs. Hand Analysis

The amount of data and type of analysis to be done will help determine whether to process the data by hand or computer. Of course the computer makes it a much easier task if:

   a. One is available that can handle the proposed analysis. If the appropriate software is not on hand, it probably would not be cost-efficient to develop it just for this task.
   b. The survey format is designed to facilitate data processing. Otherwise, it may take a major effort just to code the raw data so that it can be entered into the computer. The company data processing department will probably be able to offer advice on how to design a survey to match the company's data processing capabilities. Alternatively, external consultants could be hired to completely handle all the data processing and analysis.

7. Summarizing the Data

Decision makers are usually interested in the general picture, and a useful way of providing it is to develop a summary or profile of parents and children who have child care needs and who might use a company-supported program. The Data Summary, Part 1 provides a relatively short profile containing the basic information gathered via Sample Survey-Part 1. The Data Summary, Part 2 includes additional details to be considered in selecting and developing a specific service.

5(b) How to Use the Sample Survey

The sample survey has been designed in two parts to help companies efficiently collect the needed data. Part 1 will help to answer these questions:

- Do employees have unmet child care needs?
- How are these needs distributed throughout the company?
- What needs do employees have?
- How do these needs affect the company?

Part 2 of the survey, along with Part 1, is to be used when a company is also interested in gathering detailed information to help select and design a program.

The sample survey is just that—a sample that may be adapted to suit a company's own decision needs. The "notes" on using the items and the data summary may be of help in adapting the survey. Pilot testing any survey before giving it to an entire population is advised. Ten to twenty employees should be enough to point up any problems with the distribution, the language of the survey, or the data analysis plans.

The sample survey has been field-tested with over a thousand employees in five companies of various sizes and types. The format has been designed for easy adaptation to computerized analysis. Since each company differs in its data processing capabilities, the company's own data processing department should be consulted for specific guidelines before finalizing the survey format.

Why aren't these questions on the survey? The following questions have not been included on this questionnaire:

- How satisfied are you with your current child care arrangements?
- What is the most you can afford to pay?
- Would you leave your present arrangements if a new center were built at your work site?

Some companies would like to have this information. However, research and experience have shown that such general questions do a poor job of describing complex situations and that it is not feasible to predict behavior that is influenced by so many variables.

Can't companies just ask questions about the program or service in which they are interested? When conducting a needs assessment, it is useful to consider all possible types of services until the data is collected. Employees may need or prefer a service that the company did not anticipate initially. Programs which closely match identified needs are better utilized and are generally more economical and beneficial to the company.

5(c) Sample Survey—Part 1

(Use to determine if employees have child care needs, who they are, and how the company is affected.)

WE WOULD APPRECIATE HEARING FROM *ALL* OF YOU, EVEN IF YOU DO NOT HAVE CHILDREN OR DO NOT HAVE A NEED FOR CHILD CARE. THE INFORMATION YOU PROVIDE WILL BE VERY HELPFUL.

( ) If you DON'T have children under 12 years living with you, check this box; then answer questions 1-3 and return the survey.

( ) If you DO have children under 12 living with you, check this box; answer all the questions below, except #2, and then return the survey in the enclosed envelope.

1. Please tell us about your job:
   a. ( ) exempt ( ) non-exempt
   b. department:__________________
   c. ( ) part-time ( ) full-time
   d. regular work hours: ____________
   e. regular work days:
   ( ) Mon.-Fri. ( ) Other: ________________________________
2. Do you plan to have children within the next 5 years?
   ( ) yes ( ) no ( ) haven't decided
3. During the past year has your work been more difficult or inconvenient when other employees had child care problems? (For example, has your work been held up when they had to stay home with their children?)
   ( ) not applicable or unaware of problems
   ( ) no effect
   ( ) minor difficulty
   ( ) moderate difficulty
   ( ) major difficulty

[If you DON'T HAVE CHILDREN UNDER 12, stop here. Thank you for your help. Please feel free to add comments and then return the survey. If you DO have children 12 or under, please continue.]

4. Please list the birthdates of your children under 12 living with you:
   child #1____________ #2 ____________#3____________ #4____________
   mo/day/yr
5. Here are some common problem areas for working parents who need or use child care. Have you had problems in any of these areas in the past year? (CIRCLE THE NUMBER)

	No Problem	*Minor Problem*	*Moderate Problem*	*Major Problem*
cost of care	1	2	3	4
convenience of location	1	2	3	4
transportation	1	2	3	4
schedule to match work and school	1	2	3	4
quality of care	1	2	3	4
dependability of care	1	2	3	4
finding care for sick child	1	2	3	4
finding temporary/emergency care	1	2	3	4
finding care for child under 2	1	2	3	4
finding care for 2-5 year old	1	2	3	4
finding care for 6-11 year old	1	2	3	4
finding care for special needs	1	2	3	4
Other (describe):____________________				

6. Sometimes child care arrangements affect parents at work. During the past year, have you had difficulties related to child care in any of these areas? (CIRCLE THE NUMBER)

	No Problem	*Minor Problem*	*Moderate Problem*	*Major Problem*
traveling on the job	1	2	3	4
taking training for job	1	2	3	4
scheduling vacation time	1	2	3	4
working desired schedule or overtime	1	2	3	4
returning to work after child birth	1	2	3	4
ability to do job well; concentration	1	2	3	4
level of stress	1	2	3	4
other (describe) ____________________				

7. Approximately how many days have you been absent in the past 6 months because of child care difficulties or because your child was ill?

____

8. Approximately how many days in the past 6 months have you missed *part* of a day (e.g., arrived late, left early, had significant interruption) due to child care difficulties?________________
9. Have you ever considered quitting your job at this company because of child care difficulties? ( ) yes ( ) no

THANK YOU VERY MUCH FOR TAKING THE TIME TO ANSWER THESE QUESTIONS. PLEASE FEEL FREE TO ADD ADDITIONAL COMMENTS; THEN RETURN YOUR SURVEY.

5(d) Sample Survey—Part 2

(Use in conjunction with Part 1 to gather specific information to help with program selection and design.)

10. What is the average total amount you pay per month for child care for *all* your children while you work? (Include care during school vacations and summer, overtime, emergencies. etc.)
( ) under $100
( ) $100–149
( ) $150–199
( ) $200–249
( ) $250–299
( ) $300 or more

For questions 11–14, your answers for Child #1 should refer to the same child whose birthdate you gave for Child #1 in question No. 4. Follow the same procedure for Child #2 and so forth.

11. What type of care do you *now use* for your children? If any child is usually cared for in more than one arrangement, mark the one used for the most hours.

Child #1	Child #2	Child #3	Child #4	
( )	( )	( )	( )	relative in your home or theirs
( )	( )	( )	( )	unrelated person in your home
( )	( )	( )	( )	unrelated person in his or her home (family day care provider)
( )	( )	( )	( )	center based care (including preschools, Head Start)
( )	( )	( )	( )	other (describe)________

12. What type of child care would you *prefer* to have for you children if *different* from your answers to #11 above?

Child #1	Child #2	Child #3	Child #4	
( )	( )	( )	( )	relative in your home or theirs
( )	( )	( )	( )	unrelated person in your home
( )	( )	( )	( )	unrelated person in their home or family day care provider
( )	( )	( )	( )	center, preschool, before or after-school program

13. Where do you *prefer* your children's care be located?

Child #1	Child #2	Child #3	Child #4	
( )	( )	( )	( )	at or near work
( )	( )	( )	( )	at or near home
( )	( )	( )	( )	at or near school:________ (which school?)
( )	( )	( )	( )	other (describe)________
( )	( )	( )	( )	no preference

14. When do you usually need child care? Check all that apply.

Child #1	Child #2	Child #3	Child #4	
				WEEKDAYS:
( )	( )	( )	( )	before 7 a.m.
( )	( )	( )	( )	all or part of 7 a.m.–6 p.m.
( )	( )	( )	( )	all or part of 6–11 p.m.
( )	( )	( )	( )	after 11 p.m.
( )	( )	( )	( )	WEEKENDS

15. If you could get the kind of child care you want at a reasonable cost, would you choose to work:
    a different shift? ( ) no ( ) yes (describe)__________
    a different dept./location? ( ) no ( ) yes (describe)__________
    overtime? ( ) no ( ) yes
    full-time instead of part-time? ( ) no ( ) yes
    part-time instead of full-time? ( ) no ( ) yes
    other:____________________
16. Would you consider or prefer a child care center near the work site as opposed to your regular arrangements?
    ( ) yes, consider ( ) yes, prefer ( ) no
17. Would you like to have an in-house child care referral service to help you find the care you want?
    ( ) yes ( ) no ( ) unsure
18. When do you need care for your school age children? Check all that apply.
    ( ) before school ( ) after school ( )holidays ( ) summer
19. Would you need transportation for your child to attend a before and/or after-school program?
    ( ) yes ( ) no
20. How many times have you had to change your child care arrangements over the past 2 years?
    ( ) none
    ( ) once
    ( ) twice
    ( ) three times
    ( ) more than three times
21. How far do you commute to work (one-way)? ___ (miles) or ___hours
22. How do you usually commute to work?
    ( ) private car, alone
    ( ) carpool
    ( ) public transportation

Optional demographic items:

Use only necessary questions; avoid asking superfluous ones that may discourage employees from responding.

Family income and number of people supported gives some indication, together with what people currently pay (item #10), of what employees can be expected to afford. Adapt categories as necessary for your workforce.

Is your job: ( ) management ( ) non-management
Is your job: ( ) union ( ) non-union
Is your job: ( ) classified ( ) non-classified

What is your job title? ______________________________
How long have you been employed at this company? ____(yrs.)
ZIP code at home __________
( ) age ( ) female ( ) male
Are you single, separated, widowed or divorced? ( ) yes ( ) no
If separated or divorced, how much time do your children usually live in your home?

( ) always or nearly always
( ) more than half the time
( ) about half the time
( ) weekends or holidays only
( ) summer only
( ) almost none of the time

If married, is your spouse . . .
( ) employed full time ( ) employed part-time ( ) not employed
Total family income per year *before* taxes:

( ) under $15,000
( ) $15,000-$19,999
( ) $20,000-$24,999
( ) $25,000-$29,999
( ) $30,000-$39,999
( ) $40,000-$49,999
( ) $50,000-or more

Number of people supported by this income: ________

5(e) Notes on the Sample Survey

Directions to survey respondents: Add how, where, and when to return the survey.

Item 1. Use whatever demographic information is needed. For example, if exempt/non-exempt are not the categories your company uses, you may want to use union/non-union, management/non-management, or other categories.

You may be more interested in categorizing responses by work site rather than department if you have several sites that you plan to survey at the same time. Printing each site's survey on different colored paper may be helpful, too.

If you have several well-defined shifts, you may prefer to list them rather than have employees fill in the blank for work hours.

If you use additional demographic items, you may want to insert them here—or at the end of the survey if questions are very personal.

Item 2. The period of five years is somewhat arbitrary. You may wish to forecast some other number of years (for example, 2 years).

Item 4. Birthdates will help you predict how many children will need what type of care and when, which is especially useful if the program will not be implemented for a year or more. The company can inquire about children over 11 where appropriate.

Item 7 & 8. Time period may be adjusted to suit company needs. A year is a long time to remember absences reliably; however, since child care problems may be seasonal, absences for a short time period (1-3 months) may not be representative of the usual situation.

Item 10. What people currently pay gives an idea of what they can afford or are willing to pay—particularly when considered along with gross family income.

Item 14. Adapt question to include hours that are relevant to company shifts.

Item 15. Indicates ways child care service might affect the work place. Adapt question to ask about schedules the company is particularly interested in.

Items 16-20. Optional items for considering specific programs.

Item 16. Use a description of the specific program options being considered (for example, supervised family day care homes, preschool center, after-school activities program, or summer camp for school-age children.) This infant care center question is just an example.

Item 17. Use description of specific auxiliary program (option(s) being considered (for example, care for mildly ill children, referral service, voucher plan.)

Item 21 & 22. Use with home ZIP code demographic item to help determine whether employees are likely to commute with children to care arrangements at or near work vs. using care near home. If many use public transportation, they may not wish to commute with children, so care arrangements near work may not be fully utilized.

5(f) Sample Data Summary Worksheet—Part 1

RESPONDENTS:
(Item 2)
Who was surveyed: ______________________________
Total number of surveys distributed: ________
Who responded: total number responded: ________
response rate: ________
No. of employees w/children under 12: ________
% of total respondents: ________%
No. of employees w/no children under 12: ________
% of total respondents: ________%
No. planning children in 5 years: ________
% of total respondents: ________%

DEMOGRAPHICS:
(Item 1)

	Parents	*Non-Parents*
exempt	______	______
non-exempt	______	______
depts: 1	______	______
2	______	______
3	______	______
4	______	______
part-time	______	______
full-time	______	______
hours: 8-5	______	______
other	______	______
days: M-F	______	______
other	______	______

CHILDREN:
(Item 4)

Total under 12	______		
Under 12 months	______	6-6 yr. 11 mos.	______
12-23 months	______	7-7 yr. 11 mos.	______
24-35 months	______	8-8 yr. 11 mos.	______
3-3 yr. 11 mos.	______	9-9 yr. 11 mos.	______
4-4 yr. 11 mos.	______	10-10 yr. 11 mos.	______
5-5 yr. 11 mos.	______	11-11 yr. 11 mos.	______

PROBLEMS WITH CHILD CARE:
(Item 5)

	No Problem	*Minor Problem*	*Moderate Problem*	*Major Problem*
cost	______	______	______	______
convenience of location	______	______	______	______
transportation	______	______	______	______
schedule to match work and school	______	______	______	______
quality	______	______	______	______
dependability	______	______	______	______
care for sick child	______	______	______	______
temporary/emergency care	______	______	______	______
care for under 2	______	______	______	______
care for 2-5	______	______	______	______
care for 6-11	______	______	______	______
care for special needs	______	______	______	______
others	______	______	______	______

EFFECTS ON COMPANY:

(Item 3)

Work made more difficult by other employees' child care problems?

_______ not apply or unaware of problems
_______ no effect
_______ minor difficulty
_______ moderate difficulty
_______ major difficulty

(Item 6)

Work areas affected by parents' child care difficulties:

	No Problem	*Minor Problem*	*Moderate Problem*	*Major Problem*
traveling	_______	_______	_______	_______
training	_______	_______	_______	_______
scheduling vacation	_______	_______	_______	_______
working schedule, overtime	_______	_______	_______	_______
return to work after baby	_______	_______	_______	_______
ability to do job well	_______	_______	_______	_______
level of stress	_______	_______	_______	_______

others: __________
____

(Item 7)

Days absent in past 6 months due to child care:

_______ total days lost
__ to __ range
_______ average number days lost

(Item 8)

Partial days lost:

total: _______
range: _______
avg: _______

(Item 9)

Ever considered quitting due to child care difficulties?

_______ yes
_______ no

5(g) Sample Data Summary Worksheet—Part 2

COST FACTORS:

(Item 10)

Average total amount paid per month for all children in family:

$100	$100–149	$150–199	$200–249	$250–299	$300 & over
_____	_____	_____	_____	_____	_____

(Demog.)

Total family income before taxes:

under $15,000______	$30–39,999 ______
$15–19,999 ______	$40–49,999 ______
$25–29,999 ______	50,000 or over______

(Demog.)

Number of people supported: range:________ to ________

average number: ___________

median:______

TYPE OF CARE ARRANGEMENTS:

(Item 11) Current Use:

For All Children	*Children Under 2*	*2–5 Year-Olds*	*6–8 Year-Olds*	*9–11 Year-Olds*	
______	______	______	______	______	relatives in your home or theirs
______	______	______	______	______	unrelated person in your home
______	______	______	______	______	unrelated person in their home
______	______	______	______	______	child care center, preschool; after school program
______	______	______	______	______	other

(Item 12) Preference:

For All Children	*Children Under 2*	*2–5 Year-Olds*	*6–8 Year-Olds*	*9–11 Year-Olds*	
______	______	______	______	______	relatives in your home or theirs
______	______	______	______	______	unrelated person in your home
______	______	______	______	______	unrelated person in their home
______	______	______	______	______	child care center, preschool; after-school program
______	______	______	______	______	other

(Item 16)

Consider or prefer infant care center as opposed to regular arrangements?

yes, consider	yes, prefer	no
_____	_____	_____

NEED FOR REFERRAL SERVICE:

(Item 17)

Like to have referral service? yes _____ no _____ unsure _____

(Item 20)

How often changed child care arrangements in past 2 years?

_____ none
_____ once
_____ twice
_____ three times
_____ more than 3 times

WHEN CARE NEEDED:

(Item 14)

All Children	*Under 2*	*2-5*	*6-8*	*9-11*	
_____	_____	_____	_____	_____	weekdays—before 7 a.m.
_____	_____	_____	_____	_____	all or part of 7 a.m.-6 p.m.
_____	_____	_____	_____	_____	6-11 p.m.
_____	_____	_____	_____	_____	after 11 p.m.
_____	_____	_____	_____	_____	weekends

(Item 18)

When school-age care needed:

before school only _____
after school only _____
both _____
summer _____
holidays _____

LOCATION/TRANSPORTATION:

(Item 13)

Preferred location: (by age group)

All Children	*Under 2*	*2-5*	*6-8*	*9-11*	
_____	_____	_____	_____	_____	at, near work
_____	_____	_____	_____	_____	at, near home
_____	_____	_____	_____	_____	at, near school
_____	_____	_____	_____	_____	other

Schools listed: (frequency of response)

1. __________ ( ) 4. __________ ( )
2. __________ ( ) 5. __________ ( )
3. __________ ( ) 6. __________ ( )

(Item 19)

Need transportation for school-age program?

yes _____
no _____

(Item 21)

How far commute to work? Range: _____ to _____ (miles)

Avg.: __________

Median: __________

(Demog.)
Home ZIP Codes (with frequency for each): ______

(Item 22)
How Commute: private car, alone ______
carpool ______
public transportation ______

ADDITIONAL DEMOGRAPHICS ON EMPLOYEES

Job type: management ______ union ______ classified ______
non-mgmt. ______ non-union ______ non-classified ______

Job titles (with frequency for each): ______

How long employed at company? range: ______ to ______
avg: ______

Age: range: ______ to ______ Parents: avg. ______
avg: ______ Non-parents: avg. ______
median: ______

Gender: male ______ Parents: M ____ F ____
female ______ Non-parents: M ____ F ____

		All:	*Parents:*	*Non-Parents:*
Spouse employed:	full-time	______	______	______
	part-time	______	______	______
	not employed	______	______	______

	Parents:	*Non-Parents:*
Divorced, single, widowed, separated?	yes ______	yes ______
	no ______	no ______

If yes, how much time do children live with you?

______ always
______ more than half
______ half
______ weekends, holidays only
______ summer only
______ other

5(h) Notes on Using the Sample Data Summary Worksheet

1. Enter frequency of response for each category. If desired, also enter percent of total which that frequency represents.
2. For items answered by both parents and non-parents, frequencies and percents may be reported for parents and non-parents separately as well as for the total population responding.
3. Children's birthdates may be converted to current ages. Alternatively, the birthyears may be listed with associated frequencies, such as:

Number of children born in 1981 ______
1982 ______
1983 ______

Or approximate cut-off dates for entering school may be used:

Number of children born between 12/79–11/80 ______

12/80–11/81 ______

12/82–11/83 ______

4. For items 11, 12, 13, and 14, give frequency (and percent) for each answer (A) for all children combined and then (B) for each age range of children. Assign children to appropriate age range by using birthdates given in item 4.
5. Adapt DATA SUMMARY to match version of survey used. If items are omitted or changed, same changes should be made on DATA SUMMARY.

5(i) Sample Cover Letter for Survey

(Use Company Letter Lead or Logo)

Dear Employee,

We would like your help in gathering information on employees' child care arrangements and needs. We know that both employees and employers benefit when working parents can find reliable, good quality child care at reasonable cost. At this time we are only exploring the need and cannot promise any specific program. But the information we are collecting will help us make plans and recommendations for ways that our company can help employees with child care.

We would appreciate your completing the enclosed survey, *whether or not you need child care services.* We need to find out how many employees need or use child care and how many do not. It will only take a few minutes of your time, and we want to obtain an accurate picture of our entire work force.

Your answers to the questions will be strictly confidential and will be analyzed only as part of a group of employees. *Please return the enclosed card separately* so that we will know that you have returned the survey and will not need to contact you again. Feel free to write down any additional comments that you think might help us understand your situation and experiences better.

Thank you very much for your cooperation. We will be sharing the results with you as soon as they are available. If you have any questions, please feel free to contact ______(who, where)______ .

____

(to be signed by head of Task Force and/or well-known and liked person in upper management.)

Child Care Task Force Members: (list names)

5(j) Sample Response Verification Card

1. Enclose with survey to facilitate follow-up.
2. Questions at the bottom are optional.

I have returned my Employee Child Care Needs Assessment Survey.

(Please print name) ______________________

Submission deadline: (date) ______________________

Thank you for your help. The information you provided is very important. Your opinions count!

Would you be interested in attending brown bag lunch programs on child care issues?

yes ___ no ___

Would you be interested in helping to plan a child care service that *might* be considered by the company as a result of this survey?

yes ___ no ___

5(k) Sample Follow-Up Fliers

6(a) *Conducting Focus Groups**

1. *Participants:*
   10–15 people per group.
   1–2 experienced leaders per group.
   Companies who use this method recommend the use of "pure groups":
   - supervisors and subordinates separately.
   - men and women separately.
   - hourly and salaried separately.
   - parents and non-parents separately.

   Sample 5–10% of population (less if groups are supplement to survey or referral records.)
   Selecting participants by random sample ensures representativeness of data.
   Participation is invited, not required.
   Participants may be paid the usual rate for other focus groups (e.g., $15–25).

*Approved adaptation of a fundamental small group technique developed at TRW by Harrison Johnson.

Hold groups during work time if possible. If held at night or on weekends, participants will need child care.

Interview setting should be casual; sit in circle, first-name-only name tags; coffee and snack.

2. *Timing:* Avoid times people are likely to be off work (e.g., holidays) and peak work periods when people are too busy to want to participate.
3. *Duration:* Conduct all groups within 1-3 day period, if possible, each group session lasting 1-2 hours.
4. *Data Collection:* Warm-up talk by leader to get group ready and focus discussion. Leader is there to evoke discussion, not to answer employees' questions. Leader talks only to guide, probe, and keep discussion on target. Use open-ended questions to elicit full range of attitudes and experiences without biasing response climate.
5. *Recording Information:* During the group sessions, comments should be recorded by hand, audio tape, or both. If done by hand, record actual words of participants on easel so group can see and respond to them. Include non-verbal data where relevant.
6. *Summarizing the Results:* Analysis of information from focus groups is less formalized than with a survey because the information is more qualitative than quantitative. Summary should generally include three sections:
   - Identification and definition of major problems or issues, with some indication of intensity, frequency, ranked by importance.
   - Samples of comments for each problem or issue.
   - General mood, tone, feeling of the groups.

   A particularly effective way of using focus groups is to supplement survey data. Ten minutes or so of the most salient and expressive comments from the written record or audio tapes could be part of the final presentation of results to decision makers. Comments can be selected which best illustrate the quantitative findings of the survey.

6(b) Sample Warm-Up Talk for Focus Group

1. Who we are.
2. Important to find out what's going on and what people think about the way things are (for example, balancing their responsibilities and concerns as a parent and an employee).
3. Why we are here: to find out your child care needs and problems and how they affect your life (career, home) and the company.
4. During the next several days we will be asking for this help from different groups just like this one. We will be meeting with production people, office people, supervisors and managers, parents and non-parents.
5. Management makes two commitments:
   - Feedback on the major concerns you and the other groups identify in these meetings (and on survey, if given).
   - Action on what can be done—now and after study; feedback on what cannot be done at all and why.

6. How focus group participants were selected (for example, every 20th name on a master list); results made public. No "stacking"—that is, (all shades of opinions represented.
7. Anonymity: We have no interest in *who* says it, only in *what* is said!
8. Every comment made in this group will be written down on the easel (or tape-recorded) if o.k. with group, for two reasons: group ownership and accuracy check.
9. Some guidelines: (a) leader and recorder are here to listen and record, not to answer questions or suggest ideas; (2) best to hold specific questions until after meeting.
10. This entire process is dependent upon your help. We can't possibly recommend solutions if we do not know what the real needs are.
11. "It's your meeting . . . ."

6(c) Sample Focus Group Discussion Questions

What is it like to balance work responsibilities with the responsibility to see that your children are cared for while you work?

How are you affected? How are your children affected? How is your work affected? Are others you work with affected? What are their reactions?

What child care arrangements do you use? What do you like about these arrangements? What don't you like about them? What changes/improvements would help you?

If you could get the kind of child care you want, what would it be? Describe: type, hours, location, program emphasis, auxiliary services and so forth.

How many children do you have? How old are they? Are you single, divorced, widowed, or separated? How much of the time do the children live with you? Are any of you grandparents, aunts, uncles, with child care responsibilities for your relatives? Do you plan to have any children (first child or additional child) in the next five years?

What do you do about child care when your children are sick? When sitter or provider is not available?

What are the problems in balancing work and family life? What would make it easier?

7. GUIDELINES AND SAMPLE MATERIALS FOR USING REFERRAL RECORD DATA ON EMPLOYEE NEEDS

7(a) Using Referral Record Data

1. *Timing and Duration:* Data should be collected for a sufficient period of time—for example, 9–12 months—to cover the different types of needs and problems that are likely to occur. Spring and summer are usually the heaviest referral periods because they coincide with the ending and starting of school and the need for child care in the summers. A milder peak is often observed in January, which seems to be another time parents are likely or willing to change care arrangements.

2. *Follow-up:* A ten-minute phone survey usually obtains significantly higher response rate than a written survey. See sample referral forms for contents.

3. *Tabulating the Data:* Data on employee needs from referral records may be tabulated (frequencies and percents) in the same way as survey data (for example, number of employees seeking referrals per month, demographics on them, number and ages of children, type, hours, cost, location of day care sought and eventually found, and referral requests for which no services could be found).

4. *Summarizing the Data:* Both brief and expanded summaries may be drawn as with survey data. The data summary worksheet for the sample survey may be used as a guide for what referral information is pertinent (documenting the need and effects on the company, and selecting and designing a specific service).

For the task force report, quantitative data is best supplemented with illustrative comments from telephone or personal interviews with employees seeking referrals.

7(b) Note on Sample Referral Forms

The following forms have been included as an example of the records one company supported referral program has developed, the Steelcase Child Care Referral Service in Grand Rapids, Michigan. The list of employer-supported programs in the United States in Appendix E includes other companies with referral services which may be able to offer additional examples or other assistance.

7(c) Sample Referral Forms

Steelcase Child Care Service — Date__________
Employee Referral Sheet — Referred by__________

Name__________ Phone__________
Address __________ Zip Code__________
Major Cross Streets__________ School __________
Work Location/Department __________ Work Phone__________
Work Hours__________
Family Status: Single Parent _____ Two Parents _____ Other _____
Minority: no_____ yes _____ Salaried: no_____ yes _____
Other Adults Living in Family:
Name__________ Work Location__________ Hours__________
Children in Family:

Name	*Date of Birth*	*Sex*	*Description*

Preferred Type of Care: In Home _____ FHP_____ Center _____ Other_____
Present Type of Care and Child Care History:

Why Looking for Care:

Hours Needed for Care: ______________ Starting Date ______________
Payment ______________ Location ______________
Referred to:

1.

2.

3.

4.

Steelcase Child Care Service User Follow-Up Survey

Client Number ______________ Male ______ Female ______
Minority yes ______ no ______ Salaried yes ______ no ______
Two Parents ______________ Single Parent ______________
Work Location/Function ______________ Hours ______
Home Location SE ______ SW ______ NE ______ NW ______
Years at Steelcase ______________
How Referred to the Child Care Service ______________
Birthdate and Sex of Child(ren):
Child 1 *Child 2* *Child 3*

Hello, I am ______________ from the Child Care Service. I'm doing a follow-up survey of people who have used the Service in the last six months. Is it convenient for us to talk for about 5–10 minutes now, or is there a better time?

You called in ______________ looking for child care. I would like to ask you some questions about both your search for child care and the Child Care Service as a resource.

1. Why were you looking for child care? (NOTE: If parent responds s/he was not satisfied with old child care arrangement, probe for reasons.)

2. What type of child care arrangement were you looking for?

2(a). What type of child care arrangement did you find?

	Child 1	*Child 2*	*Child 3*
In child's home			
Unregulated care*			
Family day care			
Center care			
Other			

*Unregulated care is care by relative, friend, neighbor who is not registered with the Department of Social Services.

3. Were you successful in finding child care?

	Child 1	*Child 2*	*Child 3*
Yes			
No (see 3C)			

3(a). To what extent are you satisfied with the child care you are now using?

	Child 1	*Child 2*	*Child 3*
Very satisfied			
Satisfied			
Not satisfied			
Unsure			

3(b). Why did you select the child care you are now using? How many caregivers did you interview before you found care?

3.(c). The following is a list of problems you may have experienced in selecting a child care arrangement. Did you experience a problem with the following:

No opening ________
Available openings too expensive ________
Nothing available in desired location ________
Nothing available for hours needed ________
Your child is too young or too old ________
Transportation difficulties ________
Not satisfied with available child care ________
Other reasons you were not able to locate or arrange child care:

4. How many caregivers has your child had in the past six months?________

4(a). Reasons for changes?

5. Where is the care you are using located?

In your home ________ Near your home ________
Near work ________ Between home and work ________
Near child's school ________ Other: ________

6. How much are you paying for child care per week for each child?

	Child 1	*Child 2*	*Child 3*
$0			
$1–25			
$26–50			
$51–75			
$76–100			
$101–125			

Total amount ____________

7. Time of day needed for child care?

	Child 1	*Child 2*	*Child 3*
Permanent full day			
Permanent full night			
Part time			
Temporary			

8. How did you find out about the care you are using?
   Friend/relative/neighbor________ Co-worker ________
   Newspaper ________ Other:______________
   Steelcase Child Care Service ________

9. Please respond to the following statements in regard to your search for child care:

	Yes	*To Some Extent*	*No*	*Unsure*
a. I felt that talking with the Child Care Coordinator was helpful in knowing what to look for in choosing care for my child.	( )	( )	( )	( )
b. As a result of using the Child Care Service and finding child care, I feel more relaxed at work.	( )	( )	( )	( )
c. As a result of finding child care, the number of times I have been late for work has been reduced.	( )	( )	( )	( )
d. I would recommend the Child Care Service to a co-worker who was having child care problems or use it again myself.	( )	( )	( )	( )

10. Do you have any questions or comments about the Child Care Service?

Thank you very much for your time. If we can help you in the future, please call.

STEELCASE CHILD CARE RESOURCE AND REFERRAL SERVICE ACTIVITY REPORT FOR ____________

Child Care Needs by Age of Child and Time of Day

	Permanent Full Day	*Permanent Full Night*	*Part Time*	*This Month*	*Year to Date*
0–1					
1–2					
2–3					
3–4					
4–5					
5–6					
6–7					
7 Up					
Total					

Referral Information

	This Month	*Year to Date Since 1/82*
Cases carried forward		XXXXXXXXXXXXXX
Cases opened		
Reapplications		XXXXXXXXXXXXXX
Cases closed		
Current caseload		XXXXXXXXXXXXXX

Type of Child Care Used

	This Month	*Year to Date*
Type of child care		
In child's home		
Unregulated Care		
Family day care		
Center care		

*Cases Opened by Location/Function**

Work Location/Function	*This Month*	*Year to Date*
Research/Dev.		
Finance		
Marketing		
Operations		
Admin. Services		
Human Resources		
File		
Shipping		
Desk		
Chair		
Panel		
Systems		
Other		
Total		

*Work location/function of *both* husband and wife sometimes noted.

Geographic Location of Referrals

	This Month	*Year to Date*
(Grand Rapids)		
Southeast		
Southwest		
Northwest		
Northeast		
(Outside Grand Rapids)		
Jenison		
ADA		
Other		

Cases Opened by Groups

	This Month	*Year to Date*
Minority		
Salaried		
Female		
Male		
2nd/3rd Shift		
Two-parent families		
One parent families		

8. GUIDELINES FOR WRITING THE TASK FORCE REPORT

Writing up committee recommendations is a critical step for the task force. Decision makers may fail to act positively despite demonstrated need if the results of the investigation and the proposals of the task force are not presented effectively.

Of course there is no blueprint for the ideal report, because the precise purpose, form, content, and intended audience will vary from one company to another. Effective reports, however, are usually concise, clear, and comprehensive. The following outline offers an adaptable model. The body of the report might be 10–15 pages, preceded by a one- or two-page executive summary and followed by appendices that give all the facts and details necessary to further support or explain the body of the report. The bibliography in Appendix F of this book cites several companies' reports that can serve as additional examples.

9. SAMPLE TASK FORCE REPORT OUTLINE

I. One-page executive summary.
II. Body of the report.
   A. Introduction (who comprised task force, what they did, and why).
   B. Relevance of child care to company goals:
      1. Review company goals, priorities, or problems which can be positively affected by the child care services to be proposed later in the report.
      2. Review factors that may be having an impact on the company's ability to reach its goals and that are related to the child care services to be proposed (for example, local shortage of necessary personnel such as secretaries, nurses, and geologists; greater percentage of employees of child-bearing age; and increase in workers from single-parent or dual-career families).
      3. Describe how providing an employer-supported child care service can help the company achieve its goals by addressing the factors mentioned above:
         a. Cost-benefit information on existing programs to demonstrate that other companies have found these employer-supported child care solutions to have real, positive effects (see Chapter 1).
         b. Supporting data from company's needs assessment showing the type and extent of child care difficulties that affect the company. (Give detail about specific difficulties—for example, child care arrangements are unreliable, causing absenteeism; child care is expensive, causing high turnover; child care worries distract employees from their work, decreasing productivity.)
   C. Recommendations
      1. Describe and prioritize the employer-supported child care options the task force feels would best meet the employee's needs and preferences, taking community resources into consideration. (See Part IV of this book.)

2. Identify the specific child care needs and preferences reported by employees in the needs assessment, leading the task force to its recommendation (for example, inadequate hours of care available, insufficient care, excessive expense, trouble finding care, lack of infant care, and lack of after school care).
3. Describe the gap between employee needs and community resources that support the task force's recommendations. (If employees report they need infant care but there is actually plenty of good infant care available, then what may be needed is not more care but help in locating it.)
4. Provide cost and benefit information on each proposed service, projecting the net cost after estimated benefits are quantified (see Chapter 3).
5. Identify issues to be addressed before implementing the service and offer recommendations where appropriate (for example, equity, insurance, tax considerations, and licensing).

III. Appendices:
  A. Description of needs assessment method and participants.
  B. Full summary of needs assessment data.
  C. List of illustrative comments from employees on their child care needs and preferences and on the ways child care problems affect the company.
  D. Copy of surveys, referral forms, or interview questions used.
  E. Summary of child care services in the area including information on type of care (such as day care homes or centers), hours, ages, location, cost and capacity.
  F. Benefit and cost projections and methods used to arrive at them.
  G. List of other companies (for example, competing companies or those in the same area) that have employer-supported child care programs, possibly with some details on type and age of program, program capacity, and statistics company has on how child care services have affected their recruitment capabilities, turnover rate, and so forth.
  H. List of task force members and other helpers.

Appendix E

EMPLOYER-SUPPORTED CHILD CARE PROGRAMS IN THE U.S. (1981–1982)

KEY TO TERMS

LIST FORMAT:

- *Program Name* (If designated)
  * = programs designed primarily for community use rather than employees' children
- *Program Address*
- *Company Name*
- *Type of Company* (If *not* indicated in company name)
- *Program Description* (Including when established)
- *Hours* (Indicated only if *other than* M-F days)
- *Capacity and Age* (Maximum number of children the program may serve at any one time and eligible ages)
- *Startup Support* (company assistance to program)
- *Ongoing Support* (company assistance to program)

PROGRAM OWNERSHIP AND MANAGEMENT

- CO/CM = *C*ompany *O*wns and *C*ompany *M*anages Program
- CO/XM = *C*ompany *O*wns Program but it is Externally *M*anaged by for-profit or non-profit organization
- XO/XM = *Ex*ternally *O*wned and *Ex*ternally *M*anaged Program by for-profit or non-profit organization
- LS = Program affiliated with Company but set up as a *L*egally *S*eparate Entity

[H] = Health Care Organization
[I] = Industry or Business
[U] = Union
[G] = Government Agency

CHILDREN'S AGE DESCRIPTION

- *Infants* = up to 2 years (earliest entry age is 4 weeks)
- *Preschoolers* = 2 years to 6 years
- *Schoolage children* = over 6 years

- *Intergenerational component* = Interaction between children in a child care program and elderly residents of a nursing home or retirement facility.

STARTUP SUPPORT AND ONGOING SUPPORT CATEGORIES

- *NOT INDICATED* = Information *not* indicated in study
- *NO* = *NO* assistance provided by company to program
- *YES* = Assistance was/is provided by company to program but specific type of assistance *NOT* indicated in study

- Subsidy
- Contribution
- Budgeted Funds
- Space
- Space Renovation
- Utilities
- In-Kind Services
- In-Kind Donations

} = Specific type of assistance indicated in study

TYPES OF ASSISTANCE

- *Subsidy* = financial assistance from company to company owned program
- *Contribution* = financial assistance from company to program owned and managed by External for-profit or non-profit organization
- *Budgeted Funds* = company funds designated for child care services as a line item of a department's operating budget (i.e.personnel, employee assistance, counseling services, etc.)
- *Space* = All or part of the land and/or building used for progam
- *Space Renovation* = Renovation of building used by program
- *In-Kind Services* = Donated services which may include accounting, administration, maintenance food service, laundry, transportation, fund-raising, publicity, medical exams, etc.
- *In-Kind Donations* = Donated materials or goods which may include office equipment, toys, furniture, etc.
- *Utilities* = payment of past or all of utilities used by program

---

This list represents companies participating in the National Employer Supported Child Care Project, with the exception of those wishing to remain anonymous. It includes virtually the entire population of employer-supported child care programs in existence at the time of the study. It was prepared by Kay Clarke.

Alabama

EMPE ROR CLOCK COMPANY DAY CARE CENTER
329 S. Greeno Road
Fairhope, AL 36532
Emperor Clock Company [I]
Manufacturer of Furniture Kits & Clock Kits
Description: CO/CM On-site center established in 1972
Capacity: 15 Infants, Preschoolers & Schoolage children
Startup support: Entire cost
Ongoing support: Subsidy, space & in-kind services

HUNTSVILLE HOSPITAL CHILD CARE CENTER
314 1/2 Lowell Drive
Huntsville, AL 35801
Huntsville Hospital [H]
Description: CO/CM Center established in 1966.
Hours: M-F days plus weekends
Capacity: 45 Infants & Preschoolers
Startup support: Not indicated
Ongoing support: Space, utilities & in-kind services

KINDER-CARE LEARNING CENTER
C/O Kinder-Care Learning Centers, Inc.
P.O. Box 2151
Montgomery, AL 36103
Springhill Memorial Hospital [H] (Mobile, AL)
Description: Support of XO/XM center in exchange for reduced tuition
Startup support: No
Ongoing support: Guaranteed payment for specified # of spaces

OPP AND MICHOLAS MILLS KINGERGARTEN
1035 Douglas Avenue
Opp, AL 36467
Opp Cotton Mills [I]
Apparel/Textiles
Description: CO/CM Off-site center, estabished in 1930's
Capacity: 37 Preschoolers
Startup support: Entire cost
Ongoing support: Entire cost

Arizona

KIDDIE KORRAL
4500 S. 40th Street
Phoenix, AZ 85036
Circle K Corporation [I]
Retail Food
Description: CO/CM On-site center established in 1982
Hours: M-F days plus Sat.
Capacity: 65 Preschoolers
Startup support: Subsidy
Ongoing support: Subsidy

Arkansas

BAPTIST MEDICAL CHILD CARE CENTER
9600 W. Kanis
Little Rock, AR 72201
Baptist Medical Center [H]
Description: CO/CM On-site infant center and off-site preschool center established in 1974
Hours: M-F days plus evening shift & weekends
Capacity: 117 Infants, Preschoolers & School-age children
Startup support: Entire cost
Ongoing support: Space, utilities & in-kind services

CENTRAL BAPTIST CHILD CARE CENTER
129 Marshall
Little Rock, AR 72201
Central Baptist Hospital [H]
Description: CO/CM On-site center established in 1972
Capacity: 30 Infants & Preschoolers
Startup support: Not indicated
Ongoing support: Space, utilities & in-kind services

ST. MARY'S HOSPITAL INFANT CENTER & PRESCHOOL CENTER
12th and Walnut
Rogers, AR 72756
St. Mary's Hospital [H]
Description: Two CO/CM centers established in 1981
Capacity: 49 Infants, Preschoolers & School-age children
Startup support: Subsidy & space
Ongoing support: Subsidy, space, utilities & in-kind services

ST. VINCENT'S INFIRMARY CHILD CARE CENTER
5812 W. Markham
Little Rock, AR 72201
St. Vincent's Infirmary [H]
Description: CO/CM On-site center established in 1969. CO/CM information & referral service for children under 6 months
Hours: M-F days plus evening shift & weekends
Capacity: 93 Infants, Preschoolers & Schoolage children
Startup support: Not indicated
Ongoing support: Subsidy, space, utilities & in-kind services

California

Bailey Corporation [I]
702 S. Bridge
Visalia, CA 93277
Apparel/Textiles
Description: XO/XM Off-site center established in 1977
Capacity: 25 Preschoolers
Startup support: Rent subsidy
Ongoing support: Rent subsidy

BURBANK COMMUNITY HOSPITAL CHILD CARE CENTER
466 E. Olive
Burbank, CA 91501
Burbank Community Hospital [H]
Description: CO/CM Off-site center established in 1981
Capacity: 23 Preschoolers
Startup support: Subsidy, space & in-kind services
Ongoing support: Space, utilities & in-kind services

CHILD CARE INFORMATION SERVICE [I]
363 E. Villa
Pasadena, CA 91101
Private, non-profit agency
Description: Monthly flat rate reimbursement for licensed child care (optional alternative to health insurance) established in 1981
Startup support: In-kind services
Ongoing support: In-kind services

CHILD EDUCATIONAL CENTERS
140 Foothill Blvd. (Center One)
La Canada, CA 91011
293 S. Chester Ave. (Center Two)
Pasadena, CA 91106
Jet Propulsion Laboratory/Caltech [I]
Aerospace
Description: Two XO/XM Centers established in 1970 & 1979
Capacity: 149 Infants & Preschoolers
Startup support: Subsidy, loan & space
Ongoing support: Subsidy & in-kind donations

THE CHILDREN'S CENTER
133 E. Roseburg
Modesto, CA 95350
National Medical Enterprises [H]
Hospital
Description: XO/XM Off-site center established in 1982; transportation provided to off-site summer schoolage care
Hours: M–F days plus evening shift, night shift (on-call) & weekends
Capacity: 120 Preschoolers & Schoolage children
Startup support: Space
Ongoing support: Subsidy

COTTAGE HOSPITAL CHILDREN'S CENTER
422 W. Pueblo
Santa Barbara, CA 93105
Cottage Hospital [H]
Description: CO/CM On-site center established in 1981
Capacity: 23 Preschoolers
Startup support: Space
Ongoing support: Space

CROSS CULTURAL FAMILY CENTER
1830 Sutter Street
San Francisco, CA 94115
Pacific Medical Center [H]
Mt. Zion Hospital [H]
French Hospital [H]
Description: Support of XO/XM center and family day care home network in exchange for priority admission
Startup support: No
Ongoing support: Contributions

DMV CHILD CARE CENTER
2415 1st Avenue
Sacramento, CA 95818
California Department of Motor Vehicles [G]
State Government Agency
Description: XO/XM On-site center established in 1975
Capacity: 54 Preschoolers
Startup support: Space
Ongoing support: Space

EVERHEALTH CHILD CARE CENTER
8036 Ocean View
Whittier, CA 90631
Everhealth Foundation [H]
Health Care
Description: XO/XM Center established in 1980
Capacity: 72 Infants & Preschoolers
Startup support: Contribution & in-kind services
Ongoing support: No

EXPANDED CHILD CARE REFERRAL
1838 El Camino Real
Suite 214
Burlingame, CA 94010
Peninsula Hospital and Medical Center [H]
Mills Memorial Hospital [H]
Sequoia Hospital [H]
Description: XO/XM On-site information and referral service
Startup support: No
Ongoing support: Payment for services

FAMILY DAY CARE NETWORK
Children's Home Society
3200 Telegraph Avenue
Oakland, CA 94609
Children's Hospital [H]
Merritt Hospital [H]
Providence Hospital [H]
Peralta Hospital [H]
Description: Support of XO/XM family day care home network in exchange for access to services
Startup support: No
Ongoing support: Monthly administrative fee

FEMINIST WOMEN'S HEALTH CENTER CHILD CARE PROGRAM
330 Flume Street
Chico, CA 95922
Feminist Women's Health Center [H]
Description: CO/CM On-site child care program established in 1975
Hours: M–F days plus evening shift & Sat.
Capacity: 15 Infants, Preschoolers & Schoolage children
Startup support: In-kind services
Ongoing support: Subsidy

GERBER CHILDREN'S CENTER
501 E. 27th Street
Long Beach, CA 90801
Long Beach Memorial Hospital [H]
Description: CO/XM On-site center established in 1981
Hours: M–F days plus evening shift, night shift & weekends
Startup support: Space
Ongoing support: Subsidy

HAYDON CHILD CARE CENTER
1210 Royal Oaks Drive
Monrovia, CA 91010-0267
Santa Teresita Hospital [H]
Description: CO/CM center established in 1967
Capacity: 40 Peschoolers & Schoolage children
Startup support: Not indicated
Ongoing support: Space, utilities & in-kind services

HEMET VALLEY HOSPITAL CHILD CARE CENTER
1116 E. Latham Avenue
Hemet, CA 92343
Hemet Valley Hospital [H]
Description: CO/CM On-site center & information & referral service established in 1981
Capacity: 24 Preschoolers
Startup support: Entire cost
Ongoing support: Subsidy, space, utilities & in-kind services

HOLLYWOOD PRESBYTERIAN MEDICAL CENTER CHILD CARE CENTER
1300 N. Vermont Avenue
Los Angeles, CA 90027
Hollywood Presbyterian Medical Center [H]
Description: CO/CM On-site center established in 1979
Capacity: 32 Preschoolers
Startup support: Space & in-kind services
Ongoing support: Subsidy, space, utilities & in-kind services

THE HOSPITAL OF THE GOOD SAMARITAN CHILD CARE CENTER
632 Lucas Avenue
Los Angeles, CA 90017
The Hospital of the Good Samaritan [H]
Description: CO/CM On-site center established in 1980
Capacity: 45 Infants & Preschoolers
Startup support: Subsidy
Ongoing support: Subsidy

HUNTINGTON MEMORIAL HOSPITAL CHILD CARE CENTER
100 Congress Street
Pasadena, CA 91105
Huntington Memorial Hospital [H]
Description: CO/CM On-site center, information and referral service & support of XO/XM family day care homes established in 1981, 1980 & 1980
Hours: M–F days plus evening shift & weekends
Capacity: 33 Infants & Preschoolers (Center)
Startup support: Subsidy, space & in-kind services
Ongoing support: Subsidy & in-kind services

KAISER PERMANENTE [H]
Personnel Administration
2nd Floor
4747 Sunset Boulevard
Los Anglees, CA 90027
Health Care
Description: CO/CM On-site information and referral service & parenting seminars established in 1982
Startup support: Not indicated
Ongoing support: Not indicated

KATHY KREDEL NURSERY SHCOOL
300 W. Huntington Drive
Arcadia, CA 91006
Methodist Hospital of Southern California [H]
Description: CO/CM On-site center established in 1958
Capacity: 96 Preschoolers
Startup support: Subsidy, space & in-kind services
Ongoing support: Subsidy

KIDDIE CARE NURSERY
2020 N. Weber
Fresno, CA 93705
Terrace Care Convalescent Hospital [H]
Description: CO/CM On-site center established in 1979
Hours: M–F days plus weekends
Capacity: 29 Infants, Preschoolers & Schoolage children
Startup support: Not indicated
Ongoing support: Space, utilities, in-kind services & in-kind donations

KPFA Radio [I]
2207 Shattuck
Berkeley, CA 94704
Radio Station
Description: Montly flat rate reimbursement for child care established in 1980
Startup support: Subsidy
Ongoing support: Subsidy

LITTLE PEOPLE'S CENTER
207 W. Legion Road
Brawley, CA 92227
Pioneers Memorial Hospital [H]
Description: CO/CM Center established in 1978
Capacity: 32 Infants & Preschoolers
Startup support: Not indicated
Ongoing support: Space & in-kind services

NATIONAL SEMICONDUCTOR [I]
Employee Assistance Program
M/S 16257
2900 Semiconductor Drive
Santa Clara, CA 95051
Electronics/Computers
Description: CO/CM On-site information and referral service established in 1980
Startup support: Not indicated
Ongoing support: Not indicated

NIGHT CHILD CARE CENTER
4650 Sunset Boulevard
Box 54700
Los Angeles, CA 90027
Children's Hospital [H]
Description: CO/CM On-site center established in 1979
Hours: M–F night shift plus weekends
Capacity: 6 Infants, Preschoolers & Schoolage children
Startup support: Not indicated
Ongoing support: Entire cost

PALM HARBOR GENERAL HOSPITAL [H]
12601 Garden Grove Boulevard
Garden Grove, CA 92643
Description: Monthly flat rate reimbursement for child care established in 1981
Startup support: Not indicated
Ongoing support: Not indicated

PALO ALTO COMMUNITY CHILD CARE
3990 Ventura Court
Palo Alto, CA 94306
Raychem Corporation Foundation [I]
Envirotech Corporation Foundation [I]
Syntex Corporation Foundation [I]
Hewlett-Packard Foundation [I]
charitable Institutions (All above companies)
Description: Support of XO/XM center established in 1973
Startup support: No
Ongoing support: Annual contributions

GOOD SAMARITAN SMALL WORLD
15344 National Avenue
San Jose, CA 95030
Good Samaritan Hospital [H]
Description: Refers employees to XO/XM center in exchange for reduced tuition
Startup support: No
Ongoing support: Referrals

PARKVIEW PRE-SCHOOL
329 N. Real Road
Bakersfield, CA 93309
Parkview Real Convalescent Hospital [H]
Parkview Julian Convalescent Hospital [H]
Description: CO/CM On-site center with intergenerational component & information and referral service for children under 2 years established in 1981
Capacity: 35 Preschoolers & Schoolage children (center)
Startup support: Not indicated
Ongoing support: Not indicated

REDLANDS COMMUNITY DAY CARE CENTER [H]
P.O. Box 391
Redlands, CA 92373
Redlands Community Hospital [H]
Description: CO/CM On-site center established in 1981
Capacity: 32 Infants & Preschoolers
Startup support: Subsidy, space & in-kind services
Ongoing support: Subsidy, space, utilities & in-kind services

SAN JUAN BATISTA CHILD DEVELOPMENT CENTER
1945 Terilyn Avenue
San Jose, CA 95122
Levi Strauss Foundation [I]
Charitable Institution
Hewlett-Packard Foundation [I]
Charitable Institution
Description: Support of XO/XM program for care of sick children in exchange for reduced tuition
Capacity: 10 Infants & Preschoolers
Startup support: One-time contribution
Ongoing support: No

SUNNYVALE CHILD CARE SERVICE CENTER
1500 Partridge Avenue
Sunnyvale, CA 94087
TRW Vidar [I]
Aerospace
TRW DSSG [I]
Aerospace
ESL, Inc. [I]
Aerospace
Aertech Industries [I]
Aerospace
Hewlett-Packard [I]
Computers
Description: Support of XO/XM center; some contribution in exchange for tuition discount or priority admission
Startup support: Not indicated
Ongoing support: Annual contributions

TIMESAVERS [I]
1296 Lawrence Station Road
Sunnyvale, CA 94086
Temporary Employment Service
Description: % reimbursement for licensed child care; support of XO/XM center
Startup support: Not indicated
Ongoing support: Contributions (center)

YWCA NIGHT AND DAY CARE CENTER
118 Second Street
Watsonville, CA 95076
The Pillsbury Company Foundation [I]
Charitable Institution
Description: Support of XO/XM center in exchange for access to program established in 1981
Hours: M–F days plus evening shift
Capacity: 35 Preschoolers & Schoolage children
Startup support: One-time contribution
Ongoing support: No

Colorado

BOULDER JUNIOR ACADEMY DAY CARE CENTER
2641 4th Street
Boulder, CO 80302
Boulder Memorial Hospital [H]
Description: Support of XO/XM off-site center established in 1981
Capacity: Preschoolers & Schoolage children
Startup support: Contribution & in-kind services
Ongoing support: Contributions

CHILDREN'S WORLD
1805 S. Bellaire Street
Suite 550
Denver, CO 80222
Current, Inc. [I]
Direct Marketing of Stationery & Gifts
Description: Support of XO/XM center in exchange for reduced tuition
Startup support: No
Ongoing support: Guaranteed payment for specified # of spaces

MAHLON D. THATCHER CHILD CARE CENTER
511 W. 14th Street
Pueblo, CO 81003
Parkview Episcopal Hospital [H]
Description: CO/CM center established in 1969
Capacity: 45 Preschoolers & Schoolage children
Startup support: Subsidy, space & in-kind services
Ongoing support: Space & in-kind services

MOUNTAIN BELL TELEPHONE COMPANY [I]
1005 17th Street
Room 440
Denver, CO 80202
Utility
Description: CO/CM On-site information and referral service and parenting seminars
Startup support: Subsidy for staff salary
Ongoing support: Subsidy for staff salary

TITLE DATA, INC. [I]
3540 S. Poplar
Denver, CO 80237
Data Entry/Keypunch
Description: % reimbursement for licensed child care for children under 12 years established in 1978
Startup support: Not indicated
Ongoing support: Not indicated

Connecticut

BURGER KING [I]
70 Airport Road
Hartford, CT 06114
Fast Food Franchise
Description: Total reimbursement for child care expenses established in 1980
Startup support: Not indicated
Ongoing support: Not indicated

CHARLIE MILLS PRESCHOOL
61 Burban Drive
Branford, CT 06405
Connecticut, Hospital [H]
Health Facility
Description: XO/XM On-site center established in 1981
Capacity: 14 Preschoolers
Startup support: Space
Ongoing support: Contribution & space

CHILD CARE CENTER
129 Woodland Street
Hartford, CT 06105
St. Francis Hospital and Medical Center [H]
Description: CO/CM On-site center established in 1981
Capacity: 30 Preschoolers
Startup support: Subsidy, in-kind services & in-kind donations
Ongoing support: Space, utilities & in-kind services

HARTFORD HOSPITAL PRESCHOOL EDUCATION CENTER
80 Seymour Street
Hartford, CT 06115
Hartford Hospital [H]

Description: CO/CM On-site center established in 1982
Capacity: 22 Preschoolers
Startup support: Space & in-kind services
Ongoing support: Subsidy, space, utilities & in-kind services

KINDER-CARE LEARNING CENTER
1312 Hall Boulevard
Bloomfield, CT 06002
Connecticut General Life Insurance Company [I]
Description: CO/CM On-site center established in 1975
Capacity: 70 Infants, Preschoolers & School-age children
Startup support: Space renovation
Ongoing support: Not indicated
Stamford Hospital [H]
Shelburn and West Broad
STAMFORD HOSPITAL [H]
Description: Support of XO/XM center in exchange for reserved spaces.
Startup support: One-time contribution
Ongoing support: No

Florida

BAPTIST HOSPITAL DAY CARE CENTER
8900 N. Kendall Drive
Miami, FL 33176
Baptist Hospital of Miami [H]
Description: CO/CM On-site center established in 1962
Hours: M–F days plus evening shift & weekends
Capacity: 70 Infants & Preschoolers
Startup support: Entire cost
Ongoing support: Not indicated

COMMUNITY COORDINATED CHILD CARE FOR CENTRAL FLORIDA, INC.
816 Broadway
Orlando, FL 32803
3 Companies (confidential) [I]
Description: XO/XM Information & referral service plus social services and financial assistance for income eligible employees
Startup support: No
Ongoing support: Payment for services

*HARLEM DAY CARE CENTER
P.O. Drawer 1207
Clewiston, FL 33440
U.S. Sugar Company Charitable Trust [I]
Charitable Institution
Description: Support of XO/XM center serving low income community residents
Startup support: Not indicated
Ongoing support: Contributions

HIALEAH HOSPITAL DAY CARE CENTER
691 E. 26th Street
Hialeah, FL 33013
Hialeah Hospital [H]
Description: CO/CM On-site center established in 1981
Hours: M–F days plus evening shift & weekends
Capacity: 72 Infants, Preschoolers & Schoolage children
Startup support: Not indicated
Ongoing support: Subsidy

KINDER-CARE LEARNING CENTER
c/o Kinder-Care Learning Centers, Inc.
P.O. Box 2151
Montgomery, AL 36103
Florida Medical Center (Ft. Lauderdale, FL) [H]
Description: Support of XO/XM center in exchange for reduced tuition
Startup support: No
Ongoing support: Guaranteed payment for specified # of spaces

KINDER-CARE LEARNING CENTER
c/o Kinder-Care Learning Centers, Inc.
P.O. Box 2151
Montgomery, AL 36103
Walt Disney World (Buena Vista, FL) [I]
Outdoor Entertainment
Description: CO/XM On-site center
Startup support: Space
Ongoing support: Not indicated

NORTH SHORE CHILD CARE CENTER
1100 N. W. 95th Street
Miami, FL 33150
North Shore Medical Center
Description: CO/CM On-site center established in 1974
Hours: M–F days plus evening shift & weekends
Capacity: 75 Infants, Preschoolers & School-age children
Startup support: Subsidy, space & in-kind services
Ongoing support: Space, utilities & in-kind services

PALMETTO HOSPITAL [H]
P.O. Box 4810
Hialeah, FL 33014
Description: % reimbursement for child care at approved centers.
Startup support: Not indicated
Ongoing support: Not indicated

RAINBOW'S END CENTER
500 Cleveland Street
Clearwater, FL 33516

Church of Scientology [I]
Religious Organization
Description: CO/CM On-site center established in 1975
Hours: M–F days plus evening shift & weekends
Capacity: 97 Infants, Preschoolers & Schoolage children
Startup support: Not indicated
Ongoing support: Entire cost

Georgia

DEKALB GENERAL HOSPITAL CHILD CARE CENTER
460 Winn Way
Decatur, GA 30033
Dekalb General Hospital [H]
Description: CO/CM center established in 1969
Hours: M–F days plus evening shift & weekends
Capacity: 44 Infants & Preschoolers
Startup support: Space & in-kind donation
Ongoing support: Subsidy, space, utilities & in-kind services

GEORGIA BAPTIST MEDICAL CENTER DAY CARE CENTER
285 Boulevard N.E.
Atlanta, GA 30312
Georgia Baptist Medical Center [H]
Description: CO/CM On-site center established in 1965
Hours: M–F days plus evening shift
Capacity: 48 Infants & Preschoolers
Startup support: Not indicated
Ongoing support: Subsidy, space, utilities & in-kind services

KENNESTONE HOSPITAL CHILD CARE CENTER
115 Cherry Street
Marietta, GA 30060
Kennestone Hospital [H]
Description: CO/CM Off-site center
Hours: M–F days plus evening shift & weekends
Capacity: 80 Infants, Preschoolers & Schoolage children
Startup support: Space
Ongoing support: Subsidy & in-kind services

KINDER-CARE LEARNING CENTER
c/o Kinder-Care Learning Centers, Inc.
P.O. Box 2151
Montgomery, AL 36103
Equitable Life Insurance Company [I] (Atlanta, GA)
Description: Support of XO/XM center in exchange for reduced tuition
Startup support: No
Ongoing support: Guaranteed payment for specified # of spaces

SHERRI LYNN DAY CARE
P.O. Box 406
Zebulon, GA 30295
Sherri Lynn, Inc. [I]
Manufacturer of Apparel/Textiles
Description: CO/CM On-site center established in 1979
Hours: M–F days plus Sat.
Capacity: 45 Infants & Preschoolers (Schoolage children summer only)
Startup support: Not indicated
Ongoing support: Not indicated

UNIVERSITY HOSPITAL CHILD CARE CENTER
1350 Walton Way
Augusta, GA 30910
University Hospital [H]
Description: CO/CM On-site center established in 1979
Hours: M–F days plus evening shift & weekends
Capacity: 115 Infants, Preschoolers & Schoolage children
Startup support; Not indicated
Ongoing support: Space, utilities & in-kind services

Hawaii

MAUI PINE CHILDREN'S CENTER
P.O. Box 187
Kahului, Maui, Hawaii 96732
Maui Pineapple Company Ltd. [I]
Canned Fruit Processing
Description: CO/CM On-site center established in 1981
Hours: M–F days plus Sat. (occasionally)
Capacity: 50 Preschoolers
Startup support: Subsidy & space
Ongoing support: Subsidy & space

Idaho

BOISE VALLEY SUNSET EMPLOYEE DAY CARE CENTER
3115 Sycamore
Boise, ID 83703
Boise Valley Sunset Nursing Home [H]
Description: CO/CM On-site center established in 1978 with intergenerational component
Capacity: 15 Preschoolers & Schoolage children
Startup support: Space & in-kind services
Ongoing support: Subsidy, space, utilities & in-kind services

YMCA INFANT/TODDLER PRESCHOOL CHILD CARE CENTER
1050 W. State Street
Boise, ID 83702
1 Company (confidential) [I]

Description: Support of XO/XM center in exchange for access to program
Capacity: 60 Infants & Preschoolers
Startup support: One-time contribution
Ongoing support: No

Illinois

AMALGAMATED CHILD DAY CARE & HEALTH CENTER
323 S. Ashland Avenue
Chicago, IL 60607
Amalgamated Clothing & Textile Workers Union [U]
Description: Center established in 1970 for union members
Capacity: 60 Preschoolers
Startup support: Not indicated
Ongoing support: Not indicated

BLESSING HOSPITAL CHILD CARE CENTER
Channel 5 Broadway
Quincy, IL 62301
Blessing Hospital [H]
Description: CO/CM center established in 1975
Hours: M–F days plus evening shift & weekends
Capacity: 117 Infants, Preschoolers & School-age children
Startup support: Subsidy
Ongoing support: Subsidy

EDGEWATER HOSPITAL PLAYROOM
5700 N. Ashland Avenue
Chicago, IL 60660
Edgewater Hospital [H]
Description: CO/CM center established in 1972
Capacity: 21 Preschoolers
Startup support: Not indicated
Ongoing support: Space, utilities & in-kind services

LAKEVIEW CHILD CARE CENTER
900 W. Oakdale
Chicago, IL 60657
Illinois Masonic Medical Center [H]
Description: CO/CM On-site center established in 1976 & support of XO/XM family day care home network
Capacity: 35 Preschoolers (Center); 14 Infants (Family day care)
Startup support: Subsidy, space & in-kind services
Ongoing support: Budgeted funds

LAURANCE ARMOUR DAY SCHOOL
630 S. Ashland
Chicago, IL 60625
Rush-Presbyterian-St. Luke's Medical Center [H]
Description: CO/CM On-site center established in 1970
Capacity: 100 Infants & Preschoolers
Startup support: Not indicated
Ongoing support: Subsidy, space, utilities & in-kind services

LUTHERAN GENERAL HOSPITAL DAY CARE CENTER
1775 Dempster
Park Ridge, IL 60068
Lutheran General Hospital [H]
Description: CO/CM Off-site center established in 1979
Capacity: 100 Infants & Preschoolers
Startup support: Subsidy, space & in-kind services
Ongoing support: Subsidy & in-kind services

THE NEXT GENERATION
802 E. Emerson
Bloomington, IL 61701
Brokaw Hospital [H]
Mennonite Hospital [H]
St. Joseph's Hospital [H]
Description: Support of XO/XM off-site center in exchange for reserved spaces
Capacity: 100 Infants, Preschoolers & School-age children
Startup support: No
Ongoing support: Monthly contributions

OFFICIAL AIRLINE GUIDES DAY CARE CENTER
2000 Clearwater Drive
Oakbrook, IL 60521
Official Airline Guides [I]
Publishing
Description: CO/CM On-site center established in 1981
Capacity: 66 Infants & Preschoolers
Startup support: Subsidy, space renovation & in-kind services
Ongoing support: Space, utilities & in-kind services

PAUL K. KENNEDY CHILD CARE CENTER
Building 50 V.A.M.C.
North Chicago, IL 60064
Veterans Administration Medical Center [H]
Description: XO/XM On-site center established in 1977
Capacity: 80 Infants & Preschoolers (Schoolage children summer only)
Startup support: Not indicated
Ongoing support: Space

STEP BY STEP LEARNING CENTER INC.
621 E. Mason Street
Springfield, IL 62702
St. John's Hospital [H]
Description: XO/XM On-site center established in 1981

Hours: M-F days plus evening shift, night shift & weekends
Capacity: 160 Infants, Preschoolers & Schoolage children
Startup support: Space renovation & in-kind donation
Ongoing support: Utilities & in-kind services

TRIPLE R SUMMER CAMP
7450 N. McCormick Boulevard
Skokie, IL 60076
Fel-Pro, Inc. [I]
Manufacturer of Auto Replacement Parts
Description: CO/CM Summer camp for schoolage children established in 1973
Capacity: 300 Schoolage children
Startup support: Subsidy & space
Ongoing support: Subsidy & space

Indiana

DAY NURSERY ASSOCIATION OF INDIANAPOLIS
Medical Center Branch
1001 W. 10th Street
Indianapolis, IN 46202
Wishard Memorial Hospital [H]
Description: CO/CM On-site center established in 1980
Capacity: 126 Preschoolers
Startup support. Not indicated
Ongoing support: Low rent space, utilities & in-kind services

LUTHERAN HOSPITAL CHILD CARE CENTER
3024 Fairfield Avenue
Fort Wayne, IN 46807
The Lutheran Hospital of Fort Wayne, Inc. [H]
Description: CO/CM On-site center established in 1979
Hours: M-F days plus evening shift, night shift & weekends
Capacity: 65 Infants & Preschoolers
Startup support: Not indicated
Ongoing support: Subsidy

NYLONCRAFT CHILD CARE CENTER
P.O. Box 6336
Mishawaka, IN 46660
Nyloncraft [I]
Injection Molding
Description: CO/CM Center established in 1981
Hours: M-F days plus evening shift & night shift
Capacity: 120 Infants, Preschoolers & Schoolage children
Startup support: Subsidy, space & in-kind services
Ongoing support: Subsidy, space & in-kind services

ST. FRANCIS HOSPITAL CENTER
52 S. 16th Street
Beech Grove, IN 46107
St. Francis Hospital [H]
Description: CO/CM Off-site center established in 1967
Capacity: 30 Preschoolers & Schoolage children
Startup support: Subsidy, space & in-kind services
Ongoing support: Subsidy, space, utilities & in-kind services

Iowa

IOWA LUTHERAN HOSPITAL DAY CARE
University at Penn
Des Moines, IA 50316
Iowa Lutheran Hospital [H]
Description: CO/CM On-site center established in 1977
Hours: M-F days plus evening shift & every other weekend
Capacity: 133 Infants, Preschoolers & Schoolage children
Startup support: Not indicated
Ongoing support: Subsidy

IOWA METHODIST MEDICAL CENTER DAY CARE CENTER
1200 Pleasant
Des Moines, IA 50309
Iowa Methodist Medical Center [H]
Description: CO/CM On-site center established in 1966
Hours: M-F days plus weekends
Capacity: 90 Infants & Preschoolers
Startup support: Space renovation & in-kind services
Ongoing support: Subsidy, space & in-kind services

MERCY HEALTH CENTER CHILD CARE CENTER
Mercy Drive
Dubuque, IA 52001
Mercy Health Center [H]
Description: CO/CM Center established in 1975
Capacity: 90 Infants, Preschoolers & Schoolage children
Startup support: Not indicated
Ongoing support: Subsidy, space, utilities & in-kind services

WEE CARE CENTER
704 8th Street S.E.
Cedar Rapids, IA 52403
Mercy Hospital [H]
Description: CO/CM On-site center established in 1976
Capacity: 46 Infants, Preschoolers & Schoolage children

Startup support: Space & in-kind services
Ongoing support: Space, utilities & in-kind services

Kansas

SHAWNEE MISSION MEDICAL CENTER CHILD CARE CENTER
74th and Grandview
Shawnee Mission, KS 66201
Shawnee Mission Medical Center [H]
Description: CO/CM On-site center established in 1979
Hours: M--F days plus evening shift
Capacity: 100 Infants, Preschoolers & School-age children
Startup support: Space & in-kind services
Ongoing support: Subsidy & space

WESLEY CHILDREN'S CENTER
2225 E. Central
Wichita, KS 67214
Wesley Medical Center [H]
Description: Support of XO/XM center in exchange for reserved spaces
Hours: M–F days plus evening shift
Capacity: 53 Infants & Preschoolers
Startup support: In-kind services
Ongoing support: Contribution & in-kind services

Kentucky

CAMPBELL CHILD DEVELOPMENT CENTER
4400 Churchman Avenue
Louisville, KY 40215
SS. Mary and Elizabeth Hospital [H]
Description: CO/CM On-site center established in 1981
Hours: M–F days plus evening shift & weekends
Capacity: 60 Infants & Preschoolers
Startup support: Subsidy, space & in-kind services
Ongoing support: Subsidy, space, utilities & in-kind services

KIDS CORNER
224 E. Broadway
Suite 175
Louisville, KY 40202
Norton Children's Hospital [H]
Jewish Hospital, Inc. [H]
Description: CO/CM (Norton Hosp.) Off-site center established in 1980
Hours: M–F days plus evening shift & weekends
Capacity: 100 Infants & Preschoolers
Startup support: Space renovation & in-kind donation
Ongoing support: Space, utilities & in-kind services

ST. ANTHONY CHILD DEVELOPMENT CENTER
1313 St. Anthony Place
Louisville, KY 40204
St. Anthony Hospital [H]
Description: CO/CM On-site center established in 1971
Hours: M–F days plus evening shift & weekends
Capacity: 100 Infants & Preschoolers
Startup support: Not indicated
Ongoing support: Subsidy, space, utilities & in-kind services

ST. JOSEPH CHILDREN'S CENTER
One St.Joseph Drive
Lexington, KY 40504
St. Joseph Hospital [H]
Description: CO/CM On-site center established in 1980
Hours: M–F days plus evening shift & weekends
Capacity: 39 Infants & Preschoolers
Startup support: Space & in-kind services
Ongoing support: Space, utilities & in-kind services

Louisiana

BATON ROUGE GENERAL HOSPITAL DAY CARE CENTER
3662 North Boulevard
Baton Rouge, LA 70821
Baton Rouge General Hospital [H]
Description: CO/CM On-site center established in 1968
Hours: M–F days plus evening shift, night shift & weekends
Capacity: 95 Preschoolers & Schoolage children
Startup support: Subsidy & space
Ongoing support: Subsidy

DOCTOR'S HOSPITAL DAY CARE CENTER
P.O. Box 1526
Shreveport, LA 71165
Doctor's Hospital [H]
Description: CO/CM On-site center established in 1967
Hours: M–F days plus evening shift, night shift & weekends
Capacity: 32 Infants & Preschoolers
Startup support: Not indicated
Ongoing support: Not indicated

OUR LADY OF LOURDES CHILD CARE CENTER
807 W. St. Mary
Lafayette, LA 70502
Our Lady of Lourdes Hospital [H]
Description: CO/CM On-site center established in 1981
Hours: M–F days plus evening shift

Capacity: 32 Infants & Preschoolers
Startup support: Not indicated
Ongoing support: Not indicated

SEVENTH WARD GENERAL HOSPITAL DAY CARE CENTER
P.O. Box 2668
Hammond, LA 70404
Seventh Ward General Hospital [H]
Description: CO/CM On-site center established in 1968
Hours: M–F days plus evening shift, night shift & weekends
Capacity: 26 Infants, Preschoolers & Schoolage children
Startup support: Not indicated
Ongoing support: Subsidy

SOUTHERN BAPTIST HOSPITAL DAY NURSERY
4545 Magnolia
New Orleans, LA 70115
Southern Baptist Hospital [H]
Description: CO/CM Center established in 1957
Hours: M–F days plus evening shift & weekends
Capacity: 42 Infants & Preschoolers
Startup support: Not indicated
Ongoing support: Subsidy & space

TOURO INFIRMARY CHILD CARE PROGRAM
3450 Chestnut Street
New Orleans, LA 70115
Touro Informary [H]
Description: CO/CM Center established in 1968
Hours: M–F days plus evening shift, night shift & weekends
Capacity: 21 Infants, Preschoolers & Schoolage children
Startup support. Not indicated
Ongoing support: Subsidy, space, utilities, & in-kind services

Maine

KINDER-CARE LEARNING CENTER
2195 Congress Street
Portland, ME 04107
Union Mutual Insurance Company [I]
Description: CO/XM Off-site center established in 1978
Capacity: 90 Infants & Preschoolers (Schoolage children summer only)
Startup support: Space
Ongoing support: No

Maryland

BARC CHILD CARE CENTER
Beltsville Agricultural Research Center
Building 003, Room 219
Beltsville, MD 20705
U.S. Department of Agriculture [G]
Federal Government Agency
Description; XO/XM Center established in 1967
Capacity: 19 Preschoolers
Startup support: Subsidy & space
Ongoing support: Space, utilities & in-kind services

GODDARD CHILD DEVELOPMENT CENTER
GSFC/NASA
Code 200.3 Building 86
Greenbelt, MD 20771
Goddard Space Flight Center [G]
Federal Government Agency
Description: XO/XM On-site center established in 1973
Capacity: 45 Preschoolers
Startup support: Space
Ongoing support: Space & utilities

HYMAN BLUMBERG CHILD DAY CARE CENTER
600 W. North Avenue
Baltimore, MD 21217
Amalgamated Clothing & Textile Workers Union [U]
Description: Center established in 1969
Capacity: 300 Preschoolers
Startup support: Subsidy
Ongoing support: Subsidy

NIH PRESCHOOL
Building 35 Room 1B05
National Institute of Health
Bethesda, MD 20205
National Institute of Heatlh [G]
Federal Government Agency
Description: XO/XM On-site center established in 1973
Capacity: 57 Preschoolers
Startup support: Space
Ongoing support: Subsidy & space

PRINCE GEORGE'S GENERAL HOSPITAL CHILD CARE CENTER
Cheverly, MD 20785
Prince George's General Hospital [H]
Description: CO/CM On-site center established in 1975
Hours: M–F days plus evening shift
Capacity: 84 Infants, Preschoolers & Schoolage children
Startup support: Not indicated
Ongoing support: Subsidy

Massachusetts

CHILD CARE RESOURCE CENTER
187 Hampshire Street
Cambridge, MA 02139
First National Bank of Boston [I]
Federal Reserve Bank of Boston [I]
John Hancock Mutual Life Insurance Company [I]

Gillette Company [I]
Manufacturer of grooming aids & small appliances
Description: XO/XM information & refererral service
Startup support: No
Ongoing support: Annual fees based on # of employees

COLE HARRINGTON CHILDREN'S CENTER
3 Randolph Street
Canton, MA 02021
Massachusetts Hospital School/Enable, Inc. [H]
Description: CO/CM On-site center established in 1978
Capacity: 24 Preschoolers
Startup support: Space
Ongoing support: Space, utilities, & in-kind services

FRANKLIN SQUARE HOUSE DAY CARE CENTER
1575 Tremont Street
Boston, MA 02120
Brigham and Women's Hospital [H]
Description: XO/XM Off-site center established in 1970
Capacity: 42 Infants & Preschoolers
Startup support: Space
Ongoing support: In-kind services

GOVERNMENT CENTER CHILD CARE CORPORATION
JFK Federal Building Room G54
Boston, MA 02129
Four Federal Agencies (confidential) [G]
Description: XO/XM On-site center established in 1978
Capacity: 30 Infants & Preschoolers
Startup support: Space
Ongoing support: No

MIDDLESEX COUNTY HOSPITAL DAY CARE CENTER
775 Trapelo Road
Waltham, MA 02154
Middlesex County Hospital [H]
Description: CO/CM On-site center
Capacity: 38 Infants & Preschoolers
Startup support: Not indicated
Ongoing support: Yes

NEW ENGLAND MERCHANTS NATIONAL BANK [I]
One Washington Mall
Boston, MA 02108
Description: Parenting seminars
Startup support: Not indicated
Ongoing support: Not indicated

NEWTON-WELLESLEY CHILDREN'S CORNER, INC.
2014 Washington Street
Newton, MA 02162
Newton-Wellesley Hospital [H]
Description: XO/XM On-site center established in 1978
Capacity: 40 Infants & Preschoolers
Startup support: Subsidy, loan & space
Ongoing support: Space, utilities & in-kind services

POLAROID CHILD CARE SUBSIDY PROGRAM
575 Technology Square
Cambridge, MA 01239
Polaroid Corporation [I]
Manufacturer of cameras & film
Description: Nation-wide sliding scale reimbursement for income eligible employees' child care established in 1971
Startup support: Not indicated
Ongoing support: Not indicated

PRIME COMPUTER [I]
Human Resources Department
Prime Park
Natick, MA 01760
Computers/Electronics
Description: Information & referral through distribution of company child care handbook
Startup support: Not indicated
Ongoing support: Publishing costs.

RODGERS AND RUDMAN, INC.
93 Abbottsford Road
Brookline, MA 02146
Joslin Diabetes Clinic [H]
Sydney Farber Cancer Institute [H]
Children's Hospital & Medical Center [H]
New England Deaconess Hospital [H]
Beth Israel Hospital [H]
Harvard Community Health Plan [H]
Harvard University Medical School & School of Public Health [H]
Description: XO/XM Information and referral service established in 1981
Startup support: Contributions
Ongoing support: Contributions based on # of employees

STRAWBERRY MILL DAY CARE CENTER
5 Woodland Road
Stoneham, MA 02180
New England Memorial Hospital [H]
Description: CO/CM On-site center established in 1965
Capacity: 25 Preschoolers
Startup support: Subsidy, space & in-kind services
Ongoing support: Subsidy, space, utilities & in-kind services

STRIDE RITE CHILDREN'S CENTER
960 Harrison Avenue
Boston, MA 02118
Stride Rite Corporation [I]
Manufacturer of Shoes
Description: LS On-site center established 1971
Capacity: 55 Preschoolers
Startup support: Subsidy & in-kind services
Ongoing support: Not indicated

UNIVERSITY OF MASSACHUSETTS MEDICAL CENTER DAY CARE CENTER
55 Lake Avenue, North
Worcester, MA 01605
University of Massachusetts Medical Center [H]
Description: CO/CM On-site center established in 1978
Capacity: 37 Infants & Preschoolers
Startup support: Subsidy, space, utilities & in-kind services
Ongoing support: Subsidy, space, utilities & in-kind services

WANG LABORATORIES CHILD CARE CENTER, INC.
84 Billerica Road
Chelmsford, MA 01824
Wang Laboratories, Inc. [I]
Computers
Description: LS Off-site center established in 1980
Capacity: 150 Infants & Preschoolers
Startup support: Contribution, space & in-kind services
Ongoing support: Contributions, space, utilities & in-kind services

Michigan

CHELSEA COMMUNITY HOSPITAL CHILD CARE CENTER
775 S. Main
Chelsea, MI 48118
Chelsea Community Hospital [H]
Description: CO/CM Center established in 1977
Capacity: 30 Preschoolers (Schoolage children summer only)
Startup support: Subsidy & in-kind services
Ongoing support: In-kind services

CORNER COTTAGE CHILD CARE CENTER, INC.
2215 Fuller Road
Ann Arbor, MI 48105
Ann Arbor Veterans Administration Medical Center [H]
Description: XO/XM On-site center established in 1980
Capacity: 30 Infants & Preschoolers
Startup support: Space
Ongoing support: Space

STEELCASE CHILD CARE RESOURCE AND REFERRAL SERVICE
P.O. Box 1967
Grand Rapids, MI 49501
Steelcase, Inc. [I]
Manufacturer of Office Furniture
Description: CO/CM On-site information and referral service and parenting seminars
Startup support: Subsidy, space & in-kind services
Ongoing support: Subsidy, space & in-kind services

Minnesota

ARMS DAY CARE CENTER
4050 Coon Rapids Boulevard
Coon Rapids, MN 55433
Mercy Medical Center [H]
Description: CO/CM On-site center
Capacity: 50 Infants, Preschoolers & School-age children
Startup: Space
Ongoing support: Yes

BUSY BEE LEARNING CENTER
4100 Hamline Avenue
Arden Hills, MN 55113
Cardiac Pacemakers [I]
Manufacturer of pacemakers
Description: CO/CM On-site center established in 1981
Capacity: 45 Infants, Preschoolers & Schoolage children
Startup support: Space
Ongoing support: No

C.H.I.L.D.
2511 E. Franklin Avenue
Minneapolis, MN 55454
Fairview Hospital [H]
Fairview Deaconess Hospital [H]
Description: CO/CM Off-site center established in 1977
Capacity: 50 Preschoolers
Startup support: Loan
Ongoing support: Subsidy

CHILD CARE SERVICES, INC.
400 E. Lake Street
Minneapolis, MN 55408
First Minneapolis Bank [I]
Northern States Power Company [I]
Utility
Tennant Company [I]
Manufacturer of Industrial Sweepers & Scrubbers
Description: Support of XO/XM program providing in-home care for sick children
Startup support: No
Ongoing support: Contributions

CHILD CARE INFORMATION NETWORK
111 E. Franklin
Minneapolis, MN 55404
Williams Steel & Hardware [I]
Distribution
Northwestern National Life Insurance Company [I]
11 Additional Companies (confidential)
Description: Support of XO/XM computerized information and referral service established in 1981
Startup support: Contributions & in-kind services
Ongoing support: Contributions & in-kind services

CHILDREN'S HOSPITAL [H]
345 N. Smith
St. Paul, MN 55102
Description: % reimbursement for licensed child care established in 1980
Startup support: Not indicated
Ongoing support: Not indicated

GENERATIONS DAY CARE [H]
200 Park Lane
Buffalo, MN 55313
Retirement Center of Wright County
Description: XO/XM On-site center with intergenerational component established in 1979
Capacity: 31 Infants & Preschoolers
Startup support: Space & in-kind services
Ongoing support: Space, utilities & in-kind services

GOLDEN HEART CHILD CARE CENTER
1825 Commerce Drive
P.O. Box 8700
N. Mankato, MN 56002-8700
Carlson Craft [I]
Printing Company
Description: LS On-site center established in 1980
Hours: M–F days plus Sat.
Capacity: 100 Preschoolers (Schoolage children summer only)
Startup support: Space & in-kind donations
Ongoing support: Subsidy & in-kind services

HONEYWELL, INC. [I]
Corporate and Community Responsibility Department
Honeywell Plaza
Minneapolis, MN 55408
Electronics/Computers
Description: CO/CM On-site information and referral service and parenting seminars established in 1981; support of XO/XM child care programs
Startup support: Not indicated
Ongoing support: Not indicated

MT. SINAI CHILD CARE CENTERS
2414 Chicago Avenue, S.
Minneapolis, MN 55404
Mt. Sinai Hospital [H]
Description: Three XO/XM Off-site centers established in 1981
Hours: M–F days plus evening shift & weekends
Capacity: 60 Infants, Preschoolers & Schoolage children
Startup support: Subsidy, space & in-kind services
Ongoing support: Subsidy, space & utilities

NEW HORIZON CHILD CARE CENTER
2733 Park Avenue, S.
Minneapolis, MN 55407
Abbot-Northwestern Hospital [H]
Description: Support of XO/XM center in exchange for reduced tuition
Capacity: 21 Infants, Preschoolers & Schoolage children
Startup support: Not indicated
Ongoing support: Guaranteed payment for specified # of spaces

NORTHERN STATES POWER COMPANY [I]
414 Nicollet Mall
Minneapolis, MN 55401
Utility
Description: CO/CM On-site information and referral service established in 1980
Startup support: Not indicated
Ongoing support: Budgeted funds

NORTHSIDE CHILD DEVELOPMENT CENTER
1011 14th Avenue N.
Minneapolis, MN 55411
Control Data and 3 other companies (confidential) [I]
Description: XO/XM center established in 1971 (originally)
Startup support: Yes (Control Data)
Ongoing support: Board membership

*NORTHWESTERN NATIONAL BANK OF MINNEAPOLIS [I]
7th and Marquette
Minneapolis, MN 55479
Description: Support of XO/XM schoolage care program established in 1976
Startup support: Grant & in-kind services
Ongoing support: Contributions

ST. ANSGAR DAY CARE CENTER
715 11th Street, N.
Moorhead, MN 56560
St. Ansgar Hospital [H]
Description: CO/CM Off-site center established in 1980
Capacity: 42 Infants & Preschoolers

Startup support: Subsidy, space renovation, rent, utilities & in-kind services
Ongoing support: Subsidy, space & utilities

TOYS 'N THINGS
906 N. Dale Street
St. Paul, MN 55101
Alexandria Bank & Trust Company [I]
Citizens State Bank [I]
American State Bank [I]
Bank of Wilmard Trust Company [I]
Farmers & Merchants State Bank [I]
State Bank of Shelly [I]
International State Bank [I]
Pako Corporation [I]
Film Developer
Liberty State Bank [I]
Group Health Plan [I]
Insurance Company
Drovers State Bank [I]
First American National Bank [I]
State Bank of Redwood Falls [I]
Western Bank and Trust [I]
First National Bank [I]
Detroit State Bank [I]
Minnesota Department of Employee Relations [G]
State government agency
Description: XO/XM Noon hour parenting seminar series
Startup support: No
Ongoing support: Payment for services

UNITED HOSPITAL [H]
333 N. Smith
St. Paul, MN 55102
Description: % reimbursement for licensed child care established in 1980
Startup support: Not indicated
Ongoing support: Not indicated

Mississippi

DOMINI-CARE LEARNING CENTER
969 Lakeland Drive
Jackson, MS 39216
St. Dominic-Jackson Memorial Hospital [H]
Description: CO/CM On-site center established in 1980
Hours: M–F days plus evening shift & weekends
Capacity: 105 Infants & Preschoolers
Startup support: Entire cost
Ongoing support: Yes

Missouri

CHILD DAY CARE ASSOCIATION OF ST. LOUIS
915 Olive Street
St. Louis, MO 63101
4 Companies (confidential)
Description: XO/XM Information and referral service established in 1981
Startup support: Not indicated
Ongoing support: Payment of fees based on # of employees

CLAYTON CHILD CENTER
7501 Maryland
Clayton, MO 63105
Apex Oil [I]
Petroleum
Metro Life Insurance Company [I]
General Dynamics [I]
Aerospace/Defense
Brown Shoe Company [I]
Manufacturer of shoes
Clayton Times [I]
Newspaper
Chamber of Commerce [I]
5 Banks [I]
Description: Support of XO/XM center in exchange for access to program established in 1980
Capacity: 110 Infants & Preschoolers
Startup support: Loans (banks)
Ongoing support: Contributions & in-kind donations

DOWNTOWN DAY CARE CENTER
1210 Locust Street
St. Louis, MO 63103
15 Companies (confidential) [I]
Description: Support of XO/XM center in business district established in 1978
Capacity: 60 Preschoolers
Startup support: Subsidy, space & in-kind services
Ongoing support: Subsidy & in-kind services

INDEPENDENCE SANITARIUM AND HOSPITAL DAY CARE
1509 W. Truman Road
Independence, MO 64050
Independence Sanitarium and Hospital [H]
Description: CO/CM On-site center established in 1966
Hours: M–F days plus evening shift & Sat.
Capacity: 30 Preschoolers & Schoolage children
Startup support: Not indicated
Ongoing support: Space, in-kind services & in-kind donations

NORTH KANSAS CITY MEMORIAL DAY CARE CENTER
2800 Hospital Drive
N. Kansas City, MO 64116
North Kansas City Memorial Hospital [H]
Description' CO/CM On-site center established in 1975
Hours: M–F days plus evening shift & weekends

Capacity: 40 Infants, Preschoolers & Schoolage children
Startup support: Space renovation & in-kind services
Ongoing support: Subsidy, space, utilities & in-kind services

ST. JOSEPH EDUCATIONAL CHILD CARE CENTER
535 Couch Avenue
Kirkwood, MO 63122
St. Joseph Hospital [H]
Description: CO/CM Off-site center established in 1981
Capacity: 34 Preschoolers
Startup support: Subsidy
Ongoing support: Yes

Montana

THE GARDEN CITY DOWNTOWN DAY CARE CENTER
236 E. Spruce
Missoula, MT 59802
City of Missoula [G]
Bankers Clearing House [I]
Finance
The Missoulian [I]
Newspaper
Montana Power Company [I]
Utility
First Federal Savings & Loan [I]
Champion Products [I]
Manufacturer of Athletic Apparel and Accessories
Description: Support of XO/XM center in business district established in 1978
Capacity: 38 Preschoolers
Startup support: One-time contributions
Ongoing support: No

Nebraska

BRYAN HOSPITAL EMPLOYEE DAY CARE
4848 Sumner
Lincoln, NE 68506
Bryan Memorial Hospital [H]
Description: CO/CM On-site center established in 1961
Capacity: 35 Infants, Preschoolers & Schoolage children
Startup support: Not indicated
Ongoing support: Yes

THE CHILDREN'S ARK
921 East F Street
Hastings, NE 68901
Good Samaritan Village [H]
Health Care
Description: CO/CM On-site center with intergenerational component established in 1981
Hours: M–F days plus evening shift & weekends
Capacity: 100 Infants, Preschoolers & School-age children
Startup support: In-kind services
Ongoing support: Space, utilities & in-kind services

IMMANUEL EMPLOYEE DAY CARE CENTER
6901 N. 72nd Street
Omaha, NE 68122
Immanuel Medical Center [H]
Description: CO/CM On-site center established in 1981
Capacity: 60 Infants, Preschoolers & Schoolage children
Startup support: Not indicted
Ongoing support: Not indicated

SRI/ST. ELIZABETH CHILD DEVELOPMENT CENTER
301 S. 68th Street
Lincoln, NE 68510
Selection Research, Inc. [I]
Human Services Consulting Firm
St. Elizabeth Hospital [H]
Description: LS Center on-site at SRI established in 1982
Hours: M–F days plus evening shift & weekends
Capacity: 30 Infants & Preschoolers
Startup support: Contributions & space
Ongoing support: Contributions & in-kind services

Nevada

SUNRISE HOSPITAL MEDICAL CENTER [H]
3186 Maryland Parkway
Las Vegas, NV 89109
Description: Flat hourly rate reimbursement for child care in approved facilities established in 1981
Startup support: Not indicated
Ongoing support: Not indicated

New Jersey

CHILDREN IN GENERAL
925 E. Jersey Street
Elizabeth, NJ 07201
Elizabeth General Medical Center [H]
Description: CO/CM center established in 1981
Capacity: 100 Infants, Preschoolers & School-age children
Startup support: Subsidy, space & in-kind services
Ongoing support: Subsidy, space, utilities & in-kind services

THE EMPLOYEE'S CENTER FOR YOUNG CHILDREN, INC.
P.O. Box 2000
Rahway, NJ 07065

Merck Company, Inc. [I]
Manufacturer of Pharmaceuticals & Health Care Products
Description: XO/XM Off-site center established in 1980
Capacity: 58 Infants & Preschoolers
Startup support: Space renovation
Ongoing support: In-kind donations

MERCER CHILDREN'S CENTER
446 Bellevue Avenue
Trenton, NJ 08607
Mercer Medical Center [H]
Description: CO/CM On-site center established in 1979
Capacity: 120 Infants & Preschoolers
Startup support: Not indicated
Ongoing support: Space

MOUNTAINSIDE HOSPITAL DAY CARE CENTER
Bay & Highland Avenues
Montclair, NJ 07042
Mountainside Hospital [H]
Description: CO/CM On-site center established in 1981
Capacity: 46 Infants & Preschoolers
Startup support: Subsidy & space
Ongoing support: Space & in-kind services

NEWTON MEMORIAL HOSPITAL CHILD CARE PROGRAM
175 High Street
Newton, NJ 07860
Newton Memorial Hospital [H]
Description: CO/CM On-site program
Hours: M–F afternoons
Startup support: Not indicated
Ongoing support: Entire cost

ROCHE CHILD CARE
500 Kingsland Street
Nutley, NJ 07110
Hoffmann-LaRoche, Inc. [I]
Pharmaceutical Company
Description: CO/CM On-site center and information & referral service established in 1977
Capacity: 46 Preschoolers & Schoolage children (center)
Startup support: Not indicated
Ongoing support: Not indicated

SANDYHOOK CHILD CARE CENTER
P.O. Box 13
Fort Hancock, NJ 07732
U.S. Department of Commerce [G]
Federal Government Agency
Description: XO/XM On-site center established in 1980
Capacity: 15 Infants, Preschoolers & Schoolage children
Startup support: Space & utilities
Ongoing support: Space & utilities

New Mexico

DIGITAL EQUIPMENT CORPORATION [I]
Personnel Office
5600 Kircher Boulevard, N.E.
P.O. Box 82
Albuquerque, NM 87103
Manufacturer of Computers
Description: Information & referral through distribution of company child care handbook
Startup support: Publishing costs & in-kind services
Ongoing support: Not indicated

KINDER-CARE LEARNING CENTER
c/o Kinder-Care Learning Centers, Inc.
P.O. Box 2151
Montgomery, AL 36103
Equitable Life Insurance Company [I] (Albuquerque, NM)
Description: Support of XO/XM center in exchange for reduced tuition
Startup support: No
Ongoing support: Guaranteed payment for specified # of spaces

New York

THE CHILDREN'S COMMUNITY
The Community Programs Center of Long Island, Inc.
645 Half Hollow Road
Dix Hills, NY 11789
AIL Division Eaton Corporation [I]
Aerospace
Automatic Data Processing [I]
Data Processing Service
Chemical Bank [I]
Fairchild Republic [I]
Aerospace
Gould Simulation Systems Division [I]
Electrical Equipment
Hazeltine [I]
Manufacturer of Electronics & Computer Equipment
I.W. Industries [I]
Manufacturer of Machine Products Parts
Long Island Lighting Company [I]
Utility
Mergenthaler-Linotype [I]
Manufacturer of Typesetting and Composing Equipment
Newsday [I]
Newspaper
Venus Scientific [I]
Manufacturer of High Power Voltage Supplies
Chase Manhattan Bank [I]
Citibank [I]
Suffolk County Federal Savings & Loan [I]
Description: Support of XO/XM center
Capacity: 130 Infants, Preschoolers & Schoolage children

Startup support: Contributions
Ongoing support: Contributions

CITIBANK, N.A. [I]
111 Wall Street
New York, NY 10043
Description: CO/CM On-site information and referral service and parenting seminars
Startup support: Not indicated
Ongoing support: Not indicated

CORNING CHILDREN'S CENTER
Box 11
Corning, NY 14830
Corning Glass Works [I]
Manufacturer of Glass Products
Description: XO/XM Off-site center and information & referral service established in 1981
Capacity: 50 Preschoolers (center)
Startup support: Contributions & in-kind services
Ongoing support: Contributions & in-kind services

EMPIRE HANGER DAY CARE CENTER
Oneida County Airport
Oriskany, NY 13424
Empire Airlines [I]
Description: CO/CM center established in 1980
Capacity: 35 Infants & Preschoolers
Startup support: Space, utilities & in-kind services
Ongoing support: Subsidy, space, utilities & in-kind services

EMPIRE STATE DAY CARE, INC.
Empire State Plaza
Agency Building 2 13th Floor
Albany, NY 12223
New York State Government [G]
Description: Network of centers throughout state
Startup support: Seed $ for space
Ongoing support: Space & utilities

FORD FOUNDATION [I]
320 E. 43rd
New York, NY 10017
Charitable Institution
Description: % reimbursement for income eligible employees' child care for children under 12 years established in 1972
Startup support: Not indicated
Ongoing support: Not indicated

GENESSEE HOSPITAL CHILD CARE CENTER
224 Alexander Street
Rochester, NY 14607
Genessee Hospital [H]
Description: CO/CM Off-site center established in 1967
Capacity: 75 Infants & Preschoolers
Startup support: In-kind services & in-kind donations
Ongoing support: Space & in-kind services

HARBOR DAY CARE, INC.
93 Central Avenue
Sea Cliff, NY 11579
Pall Corporation [I]
Manufacture of Filters & Fluid Clarification Equipment
Description: Support of XO/XM infant day care home network in exchange for access to program
Capacity: 14 Infants
Startup support: One-time contribution
Ongoing support: No

PLYMOUTH INFANT CENTER
340 Montgomery Street
Syracuse, NY 13202
2 Companies (confidential) [I]
Description: Support of XO/XM infant care program in business district in exchange for preferential admission established in 1981
Capacity: 30 Infants
Startup support: Contributions
Ongoing support: No

UPSTATE DAY CARE CENTER
175 Elizabeth Blockwell Street
Syracuse, NY 13202
Upstate Medical Center [H]
Description: XO/XM On-site center established in 1972
Capacity: 22 Preschoolers
Startup support: Not indicated
Ongoing support: Space, utilities & in-kind services

North Carolina

DUKE MEDICAL CENTER [H]
Child Care Referral Service
Box 3017
Durham, NC 27710
Description: CO/CM On-site information & referral service established in 1980
Startup support: Not indicated
Ongoing support: Space & in-kind services

FORSYTH MEMORIAL HOSPITAL CHILD CARE CENTER
3333 Silas Creek Parkway
Winston-Salem, NC 27103
Forsyth Memorial Hospital [H]
Description: CO/CM On-site center established in 1974
Hours: M–F days plus evening shift & weekends
Capacity: 130 Infants, Preschoolers & School-age children
Startup support: Space
Ongoing support: Space, utilities, & in-kind services

GILFORD-WESLEYAN DAY CARE CENTER
4902 W. Market Street
Greensboro, NC 27407
Gilford Mills, Inc. [I]
Manufacturer of Apparel/Textiles
Description: Support of XO/XM center in exchange for access to progam established in 1980
Startup support: One-time contribution
Ongoing support: No

PCA CHILD DEVELOPMENT CENTER
801 Crestdale Avenue
Matthews, NC 28105
PCA International, Inc. [I]
Photography Development
Description: CO/CM On-site center established in 1972
Hours: M–F days plus evening shift
Capacity: 175 Infants, Preschoolers & School-age children
Startup support: Not indicated
Ongoing support: Not indicated

PLAY WORLD CHILD DEVELOPMENT CENTER, INC.
P.O. Box 286
Hildebran, NC 28637
Neuville-Mobil Sox, Inc. [I]
(Performance Hosiery Mills)
Manufacturer of Apparel/Textiles
Description: CO/CM On-site center established in 1979
Capacity: 35 Infants, Preschoolers & Schoolage children
Startup support: Subsidy, space & in-kind services
Ongoing support: Subsidy, space, utilities & in-kind services

PRESBYTERIAN HOSPITAL CHILD DEVELOPMENT CENTER
P.O. Box 33549
Charlotte, NC 28233
Presbyterian Hospital [H]
Description: CO/CM center established in 1980
Hours: M-F days plus evening shift & weekends
Capacity: 110 Infants & Preschoolers
Startup support: Subsidy & space
Ongoing support: Subsidy, space, utilities & in-kind services

REX HOSPITAL DAY CARE UNIT
4420 Lake Boone Trail
Raleigh, NC 27607
Rex Hospital [H]
Description: CO/CM On-site center established in 1969
Capacity: 43 Infants & Preschoolers
Startup support: Space
Ongoing support: Yes

SAS CARE
Box 8000
Carey, NC 27511
SAS Institute, Inc. [I]
Computer Software
Description: CO/CM On-site center established in 1981
Capacity: 25 Infants & Preschoolers
Startup support: Not indicated
Ongoing support: Entire cost

North Dakota

HILLTOP DAY CARE CENTER
Box 476
Jamestown, ND 58401
North Dakota State Hospital [H]
Description: XO/XM Center esbalished in 1966
Capacity: 25 Infants & Preschoolers
Startup support: Not indicated
Ongoing support: Space, utilities & in-kind services

RAINBOW DAY CARE
702 First Street, S.W.
Crosby, ND 58730
St. Lukes Hospital [H]
Description: CO/CM On-site center established in 1981
Hours: M–F days plus evening shift & Sat.
Capacity: 18 Infants, Preschoolers & School-age children
Startup support: Space, utilities & in-kind services
Ongoing support: Space, utilities & in-kind services

RESIDENT COUNCIL OF VILLA MARIA DAY CARE CENTER
3102 South University Drive
Fargo, ND 58103
Villa Maria Nursing Home [H]
Description: XO/XM On-site center established in 1980
Capacity: 10 Infants & Preschoolers
Startup support: Not indicated
Ongoing support: Space, utilities & in-kind services

Ohio

CENTER FOR HUMAN RESOURCES
3030 Euclid Avenue
Cleveland, OH 44115
St. Vincent Charity Hospital [H]
Society National Bank [I]
University Hospital of Cleveland [H]
Ameri Trust Bank [I]
Description: XO/XM On-site information & referral service and/or parenting seminars
Startup support: No
Ongoing support: Payment for services

CHILDREN'S WORLD, INC.
345 Wyoming Street
Dayton, OH 45432
Miami Valley Hospital [H]
Description: Support of XO/XM center in exchange for expanded hours of service
Hours: M–F days plus evening shift & Sat.
Capacity: 65 Infants, Preschoolers & School-age children
Startup support: No
Ongoing support: Contributions

KINDER-CARE LEARNING CENTER
c/o Kinder-Care Learning Centers, Inc.
P.O. Box 2151
Montgomery, AL 36103
Equitable Life Insurance Company [I] (Columbus, OH)
Description: Support of XO/XM center in exchange for reduced tuition
Startup support: No
Ongoing support: Guaranteed payment for specified # of spaces

MERCY MEDICAL CENTER DAY NURSERY
1343 Fountain Boulevard
Springfield, OH 45501
Mercy Medical Center [H]
Description: CO/CM Off-site center established in 1951
Hours: M–F days plus weekends
Capacity: 68 Infants, Preschoolers & School-age children
Startup support: Not indicated
Ongoing support: Subsidy & in-kind services

*PARK VILLAGE DAY CARE CENTER
9221 Hough Avenue
Cleveland, OH 44106
Service, Hospital, Nursing Home, & Public Employees Union [U]
International Food & Commercial Workers Union [U]
Description: Support of XO/XM center serving low income children established in 1978
Startup support: Contribution, space, in-kind donations & in-kind services
Ongoing support: In-kind services

RIVERSIDE HOSPITAL DAY CARE CENTER
1600 Superior Street
Toledo, OH 43604
Riverside Hospital [H]
Description: CO/CM On-site center established in 1947
Hours: M–F days plus weekends
Capacity: 140 Infants, Preschoolers & School-age children
Startup support: Not indicated
Ongoing support: Space, utilities & in-kind services

ST. CHARLES CHILD DEVELOPMENT CENTER
2600 Navarre Avenue
Oregon, OH 43616
St. Charles Hospital [H]
Description: CO/CM On-site center established in 1954
Capacity: 70 Infants & Preschoolers
Startup support: Space
Ongoing support: Space, utilities & in-kind services

Oklahoma

AVE MARIA HOUSE
6161 S. Yale
Tulsa, OK 74117
St. Francis Hospital [H]
Description: CO/CM On-site center established in 1969
Hours: M–F days plus evening shift & weekends
Capacity: 178 Infants & Preschoolers (50 schoolage children summer only)
Startup support: Subsidy & in-kind services
Ongoing support: Subsidy & in-kind services

CHILDREN'S WORLD
5500 N. Independence
Oklahoma City, OK 73112
Baptist Medical Center [H]
Description: CO/CM Off-site center established in 1964
Capacity: 184 Infants, Preschoolers & School-age children
Startup support: Not indicated
Ongoing support: Not indicated

COMMUNITY CONNECTION
1001 S.W. 44th
Oklahoma City, OK 73109
South Community Hospital [H]
Description: CO/CM On-site information & referral service established in 1981
Startup support: Subsidy & in-kind services
Ongoing support: No

HILLCREST MEDICAL CENTER CHILD DEVELOPMENT CENTER
1120 S. Utica Street
Tulsa, OK 74104
Hillcrest Medical Center [H]
Description: CO/CM center established in 1957
Hours: M–F days plus evening shift & weekends
Capacity: 120 Infants & Preschoolers
Startup support: Space & in-kind services
Ongoing support: Subsidy, space, utilities & in-kind services

Oregon

HOLLADAY PARK HOSPITAL CHILD CARE CENTER
1225 N.E. 2nd Avenue
Portland, OR 97232

Holladay Park Hospital [H]
Description: CO/CM On-site center
Hours: M–F days plus evening shift, night shift & weekends
Capacity: 37 Infants, Preschoolers & School-age children
Startup support: Space
Ongoing support: Subsidy

MULTNOMAH COUNTY DAY CARE, INC.
1624 N.E. Hancock
Portland, OR 97212
Multnomah County Government [G]
Description: Support of XO/XM center established in 1981 in exchange for reduced tuition
Capacity: 35 Infants & Preschoolers
Startup support: One-time contribution
Ongoing support: No

Pennsylvania

CHAMBERSBURG DAY CARE CENTER
871 Stanley Avenue
Chambersburg, PA 17201
Amalgamated Clothing and Textile Workers Union [U]
Description: Center established in 1970
Capacity: 300 Preschoolers and Schoolage children
Startup support: Subsidy
Ongoing support: Subsidy

CHILDREN'S CIRCLE
1000 Wood Circle
Philadelphia, PA 19151
Lankenau Hospital [H]
Description: CO/CM Center and information and referral service established in 1982
Capacity: 34 Infants & Preschoolers
Startup support: Subsidy, space & in-kind services
Ongoing support: Subsidy, space, utilities, & in-kind services

CHILDREN'S VILLAGE
8th and Arch
Philadelphia, PA 19107
Flash Trimming Company [I]
Apparel/Textiles
Other companies (confidential)
Council of Labor and Industry [U]
Description: Support of XO/XM center established in 1976
Capacity: 125 Preschoolers
Startup support: Contributions
Ongoing support: Contributions (Flash Trimming Co. & Others)

CREATIVE BEGINNINGS
700 Cedar Road
Philadelphia, PA 19111
Fox Chase Cancer Center (complex):
Institute for Cancer Research [H]
American Oncological Hospital [H]
Description: Center established in 1981
Capacity: 50 Infants & Preschoolers
Startup support: Subsidy
Ongoing support: Space, utilities & in-kind services

FAIR ACRES GERIATRIC CENTER DAY CARE
352 Old Forge Road
Lima, PA 19037
Fair Acres Geriatric Center [H]
Description: CO/CM center established in 1979
Capacity: 25 Infants & Preschoolers
Startup support: Subsidy
Ongoing support: Not indicated

GRAND VIEW HOSPITAL CHILDREN'S CENTER
826 Lawn Avenue
Sellersville, PA 18960
Grand View Hospital [H]
Description: CO/CM On-site center established in 1981
Capacity: 30 Infants & Preschoolers
Startup support: Space & in-kind services
Ongoing support: Subsidy, space, utilities & in-kind services

HORSHAM HOSPITAL [H]
Welsh Road and Butler Pike
Ambler, PA 19002
Description: % reimbursement for licensed child care established in 1981
Startup support: Not indicated
Ongoing support: Not indicated

LEARNING CENTER OF MEDICAL COLLEGE OF PENNSYLVANIA
3217 West Clearfield Street
Philadelphia, PA 19132
Medical College of Pennsylvania [H]
Description: CO/CM Off-site center established in 1972
Capacity: 70 Infants & Preschoolers
Startup support: Space renovation
Ongoing support: Subsidy & in-kind services

McNEIL CONSUMER PRODUCTS [I]
Camp Hill Road
Ft. Washington, PA 19034
Pharmaceutical Company
Description: Support of XO/XM off-site center in exchange for reduced tuition established in 1981
Startup support: Contribution
Ongoing support: Contributions

RED ROPE LEARNING CENTER
Wood Avenue and Cherry Street
Bristol, PA 19007
Red Rope Industries [I]
Manufacturer of Paper Products

Description: CO/CM On-site center established in 1972
Capacity: 35 Preschoolers
Startup support: Yes
Ongoing support: Entire cost

RENAISSANCE II CHILD CARE CENTER
Smithfield Congregational Church
620 Smithfield Street
Pittsburgh, PA 15222
Alcoa Foundation [I]
Charitable Institution
Koppers Foundation [I]
Charitable Institution
Pittsburgh Plate Glass Foundation [I]
Charitable Institution
Heinz Foundation [I]
Charitable Institution
Bell Telephone [I]
Utility
Description: Support of XO/XM center in exchange for access to program established in 1981
Startup support: Contributions
Ongoing support: Contributions

UNION FIDELITY CHILD DEVELOPMENT CENTER
4850 Street Road
Trevose, PA 19047
Union Fidelity Life Insurance Company [I]
Description: CO/CM On-site center established in 1980
Capacity: 44 Infants & Preschoolers
Startup support: Subsidy, space & in-kind services
Ongoing support: Subsidy, space, utilities & in-kind services

South Carolina

SPARTANBURG GENERAL HOSPITAL CHILD DEVELOPMENT CENTER
101 E. Wood Street
Spartanburg, SC 29303
Spartanburg General Hospital [H]
Description: CO/CM Center established in 1974
Hours: M–F days plus evening shift & weekends
Capacity: 153 Infants, Preschoolers & School-age children
Startup support: Subsidy & space
Ongoing support: Subsidy

South Dakota

SIOUX VALLEY HOSPITAL CHILD CARE CENTER
1100 S. Euclid Street
Sioux Falls, SD 57117-5039
Sioux Valley Hospital [H]
Description: CO/CM On-site center established in 1980
Hours: M–F days plus evening shift & weekends
Capacity: 135 Infants, Preschoolers & School-age children
Startup support: Not indicated
Ongoing support: Subsidy

Tennessee

BAPTIST MEMORIAL EMPLOYEES' NURSERY
1025 Crump Street
Memphis, TN 38103
Baptist Memorial Hospital [H]
Description: CO/CM Center established in 1955 for registered nurses
Hours: M–F days plus evening shift, night shift & weekends
Capacity: 100 Infants & Preschoolers
Startup support: Space & in-kind services
Ongoing support: Space, utilities & in-kind services

*CHILDREN'S CENTER OF KNOXVILLE, INC.
2829 Kingston Pike
Knoxville, TN 37919
Tennessee Valley Authority [G]
Government Agency
Description: Support of XO/XM center serving community residents established in 1976
Capacity: 88 Infants & Preschoolers
Startup support: Legislated funds
Ongoing support: No

COMMERCE UNION BANK [I]
One Commerce Place
Nashville, TN 37219
Description: Support of XO/XM center in exchange for reduced tuition established in 1981
Startup support: No
Ongoing support: Guaranteed payment for specified # of spaces

KINDER-CARE LEARNING CENTER
1380 Gunbarrel Road
Chattanooga, TN 37421
Parkridge Hospital [H]
Description: Support of XO/XM center in exchange for reduced tuition
Startup support: No
Ongoing support: Contributions

MEMORIAL HOSPITAL CHILD CARE CENTER
602 Wyndot Street
Chattanooga, TN 37404
Memorial Hospital [H]
Description: CO/CM On-site center established in 1980
Hours: M–F days plus evening shift & weekends
Capacity: 32 Infants & Preschoolers
Startup support: Space & in-kind services
Ongoing support: Space, utilities & in-kind services

PARKVIEW HOSPITAL CHILD CARE CENTER
230 25th Avenue , N.
Nashville, TN 37203
Parkview Hospital [H]
Description: CO/CM On-site center established in 1967
Hours: M–F days plus weekends
Capacity: 60 Infants & Preschoolers
Startup support: Yes
Ongoing support: Yes

ST. MARY'S DAY CARE CENTER
Emerald Avenue
Knoxville, TN 37917
St. Mary's Medical Center [H]
Description: CO/CM On-site center established in 1967
Capacity: 60 Infants & Preschoolers
Startup support: Subsidy
Ongoing support: Yes

Texas

ALL SAINTS HOSPITAL CHILD CARE FACILITY
1400 Eighth Avenue
Forth Worth, TX 76101
All Saints Episcopal Hospital [H]
Description: CO/CM Center established in 1960
Hours: M–F days plus evening shift, night shift & weekends
Capacity: 263 Infants &Preschoolers
Startup support: Space & in-kind services
Ongoing support: Space, utulities & in-kind services

A.P. BEUTEL II DAY CARE CENTER
1912 Victoria Street
Freeport, TX 77541
Intermedics, Inc. [I]
Manufacturer of Pacemakers
Description: CO/CM Off-site center established in 1979
Capacity: 260 Infants & Preschoolers
Startup support: Subsidy, space & in-kind services
Ongoing support: Subsidy, space & in-kind services

HOUSTON GENERAL INSURANCE COMPANY [I]
4100 Equitable Drive Tower II
P.O. Box 2932
Fort Worth, TX 76113-2932
Description: Employees' schoolage children may attend XO/XM summer camp program
Startup support: No
Ongoing support: Company refers employees to summer camp program & allows the program to park its vans on company property in exchange for free transportation for employees' children to the summer camp

MARY GRACE HUTCHESON CHILD DEVELOPMENT CENTER
3405 Wiley Post Road
Carrollton, TX 75006
Forney Engineering Company [I]
Electronics/Computers
Description: CO/CM On-site center established in 1973
Capacity: 70 Preschoolers
Startup support: Entire Cost
Ongoing support: Yes

PRESBYTERIAN HOSPITAL OF DALLAS CHILDREN'S DAY CARE CENTER
8200 Walnut Hill Lane
Dallas, TX 75231
Presbyterian Hospital of Dallas [H]
Description: CO/CM Center established in 1968
Hours: M–F days plus evening shift & weekends
Capacity: 88 Infants & Preschoolers
Startup support: Yes
Ongoing support: Subsidy, space, utilities & in-kind services

RENILDA HILKEMEYER CHILD CARE CENTER
5614 HMC Street
Houston, TX 77021
Texas Medical Center (complex):
Ben Taub General Hospital [H]
Methodist Hospital [H]
Texas Children's Hospital [H]
Texas Institute for Research & Rehabilitation [H]
Hermann Hospital [H]
M.D. Anderson Hospital [H]
St. Lukes Hospital [H]
Description: CO/CM Off-site center established in 1968
Hours: M–F days plus evening shift, night shift & weekends
Capacity: 323 Infants & Preschoolers
Startup support: Not Indicated
Ongoing support: Shared subsidy; amount based on useage

ROSEWOOD GENERAL HOSPITAL [H]
9200 Westheimer
Houston, TX 77063
Desciption: Flat hourly rate child care reimbursement for nurses and pharmacy personnel on evening shift
Startup support: Not indicated
Ongoing support: Not indicated

SANTA ROSA CHILD CARE CENTER
414 N. San Saba
San Antonio, TX 78285
Santa Rosa Medical Center [H]
Description: CO/CM On-site center established in 1973
Hours: M–F days plus evening shift

Capacity: 43 Infants, Preschoolers & School-age children
Startup support: Not indicated
Ongoing support: In-kind services

SOUTHEAST BAPTIST HOSPITAL DAY CARE CENTER
4214 E. Southcross Blvd.
San Antonio, TX 78286
Southeast Baptist Hospital [H]
Description: CO/CM On-site center established in 1970
Hours: M–F days plus evening shift & weekends
Capacity: 43 Infants, Preschoolers & Schoolage children
Startup support: Yes
Ongoing support: Subsidy, space, utilities & in-kind services

TEXAS INSTITUTE FOR FAMILIES
11311 Richmond #L107
Houston, TX 77082
Texas Commerce Bank [I]
Exxon [I]
United Gas Pipe Line [I]
Prudential Life Insurance Company [I]
Description: XO/XM Working parent seminar series
Startup support: No
Ongoing support: Payment for services

TOTS VILLA CHILD DEVELOPMENT CENTER
215 E. 3rd Avenue
Amarillo, TX 79163
Pioneer Corporation [I]
Petroleum
Description: XO/XM off-site center established in 1981
Capacity: 74 Infants & Preschoolers
Startup support: Subsidy, space renovation & in-kind services
Ongoing support: Space & in-kind services

*URBAN AFFAIRS CORPORATION
2815 Reid
Houston, TX 77026
15 Companies (confidential) [I]
Description: Support of XO/XM center for low income community children
Startup support: Contributions to match Title XX funds
Ongoing support: Not indicated

ZALES CORPORATION CHILD CARE CENTER
2979 Irving Blvd.
Dallas, TX 75247
Zale Diamond Corporation [I]
Retail Jewelry
Description: CO/CM On-site center established in 1979
Capacity: 70 Infants & Preschoolers
Startup support: Subsidy
Ongoing support: Not indicated

Vermont

JEANNE C. SIMON VISITING NURSE ASSOCIATION CHILD CARE CENTER
260 College Street
Burlington, VT 05401
Visiting Nurse Association, Inc. [H]
Health Care
Description: CO/CM center established in 1975
Capacity: 35 Infants & Preschoolers
Startup support: Space & in-kind services
Ongoing support: Not indicated

Virginia

COMMUNITY HOSPITAL CHILD CARE CENTER
P.O. Box 12946
Roanoke, VA 24029
Community Hospital of Roanoke Valley [H]
Description: CO/CM On-site center established in 1981
Hours: M–F days plus evening shift & weekends
Capacity: 40 Infants, Preschoolers & School-age children
Startup support: Not indicated
Ongoing support: Not indicated

MT. VERNON HOSPITAL CHILD CARE CENTER
2501 Parker's Lane
Alexandria, VA 22306
Mt. Vernon Hospital [H]
Description: CO/CM On-site center established in 1982
Capacity: 180 Infants, Preschoolers & School-age children
Startup support: Subsidy
Ongoing support: Subsidy

NORFOLK COMMUNITY HOSPITAL CHILD CARE PROGRAM
2639 Corprew Avenue
Norfolk, VA 23504
Norfolk Community Hospital [H]
Description: CO/CM center established in 1968 for nurses
Hours: M–F days plus evening shift & weekends
Capacity: 10 Infants, Preschoolers & School-age children
Startup support: Subsidy & in-kind services
Ongoing support: Subsidy, space & in-kind services

VERONA CHILD DAY CARE CENTER
Box 976
Verona, VA 24482
Amalgamated Clothing and Textile Workers Union [U]

Description: Center established in 1968
Capacity: 240 Preschoolers
Startup support: Yes
Ongoing support: Yes

Washington

BEGINNINGS CHILDCARE CENTER
1821 15th Ave.
Seattle, WA 98122
Group Health Cooperative of Puget Sound [H]
Health Care
Description: XO/XM on-site center established in 1978
Capacity: 24 Infants & Preschoolers
Startup support: Loan & space
Ongoing support: In-kind services

CONSOLIDATED HOSPITALS DAY CARE CENTER
P.O. Box 5277
Tacoma, WA 98405
Consolidated Hospitals [H]
Description: CO/CM On-site center established in 1960
Capacity: 49 Preschoolers & Schoolage children
Startup support: Not indicated
Ongoing support: Subsidy

PUGET CONSUMER COOPERATIVE [I]
6518 Fremont Avenue, N.
Seattle, WA 98103
Retail Food
Description: Flat hourly rate childcare partial reimbursement for children under 18
Startup support: Subsidy
Ongoing support: Subsidy

VIRGINIA MASON MEDICAL CENTER CHILDREN'S CENTER
925 Seneca Street
P.O. Box 1930
Seattle, WA 98111
Virginia Mason Hospital [H]
Description: CO/CM On-site center established in 1974
Capacity: 39 Infants & Preschoolers
Startup support: Subsidy
Ongoing support: Subsidy

Washington D.C.

BROADCASTERS CHILD DEVELOPMENT CENTER
3920 Alton Place, N.W.
Washington, D.C. 20016
National Academy of Television Arts and Sciences [I]
WJLA [I]
WDVM [I]
WRC/NBC T.V. [I]
WMAI RADIO [I]
WTTG [I]
Description: XO/XM center established in 1980
Startup support: NATAS contribution
Ongoing support: In-kind services

DEPARTMENT OF LABOR DAY CARE CENTER, INC.
200 Constitution Avenue, N.W.
Room N1453
Washington, D.C. 20210
U.S. Department of Labor [G]
Federal Government Agency
Description: Center
Capacity: 100 Infants & Preschoolers
Startup support: Space
Ongoing support: Space

HUD CHILD CARE CENTER
451 7th Street S.W. B278
Washington, D.C. 20410
U.S. Department of Housing and Urban Development [G]
Federal Government Agency
Description: XO/XM off-site center established in 1978
Capacity: 60 Preschoolers (Schoolage children summer only)
Startup support: Loan & space
Ongoing support: Space, utilities & in-kind services

MAENYLIE REED LEARNING CENTER
(Formerly: Federal Employees Cooperative Learning Center, Inc.)
400 Maryland Avenue, S.W.
Washington, D.C. 20202
U.S. Department of Education [G]
Federal Government Agency
Description: Center
Capacity: 40 Preschoolers & Schoolage Children
Startup support: Space
Ongoing support: Space, utilities & in-kind services

PENTHOUSE NURSERY, INC.
200 Independence Avenue, S.W.
Room 100F
Washington, D.C. 20201
U.S. Department of Health and Human Services [G]
Federal Government Agency
Description: XO/XM center
Capacity: 60 Infants & Preschoolers
Startup support: Space
Ongoing support: Space, utilities & in-kind services

West Virginia

CAMC CHILD CARE CENTER
P.O. Box 1547
Charleston, WV 25326

Charleston Area Medical Center [H]
Description: CO/CM On-site center established in 1981
Hours: M–F days plus evening shift, night shift & weekends
Capacity: 50 Infants & Preschoolers
Startup support: Not indicated
Ongoing support: Not indicated

Wisconsin

CAROUSEL DAY CARE CENTER
Route 2
Rinelander, WI 54501
The Friendly Village [H]
Health Care
Description: CO/CM Off-site center established in 1980
Capacity: 35 Infants & Preschoolers
Startup support: Not indicated
Ongoing support: Not indicated

CHILDREN'S PLAYROOM
Highway 50
Lake Geneva, WI 53147
Playboy Resort and Country Club [I]
Recreation/Entertainment
Description: On-site center established in 1975
Hours: M–F days plus weekends
Capacity: 12 Preschoolers
Startup support: Not indicated
Ongoing support: Not indicated

FAMILY HOSPITAL CHILD CARE PROGRAM
2711 West Wells Street
Milwaukee, WI 53208
Family Hospital [H]
Description: CO/CM Off-site center established in 1969
Capacity: 47 Infants, Preschoolers & Schoolage children
Startup support: Not indicated
Ongoing support: Not indicated

FRANCISCAN VILLA CHILD CARE CENTER
3501 S. Chicago Avenue
South Milwaukee, WI 53172
Franciscan Villa Nursing Home [H]
Description: CO/CM On-site center with intergenerational component established in 1981
Capacity: 22 Infants & Preschoolers
Startup support: Space
Ongoing support: Subsidy

LUTHER HOSPITAL CHILD CARE CENTER
310 Chestnut Street
Eau Claire, WI 54701
Luther Hospital [H]
Description: CO/CM center established in 1970
Capacity: 65 Infants & Preschoolers (Schoolage children summer only)
Startup support: Subsidy
Ongoing support: Subsidy & in-kind services

NORTHWOODS HOSPITAL DAY CARE CENTER
Phelps, WI 54554
Northwoods Hospital Association [H]
Description: CO/CM On-site center established in 1980
Capacity: 20 Infants, Preschoolers & Schoolage children
Startup support: Subsidy & in-kind services
Ongoing support: Subsidy & in-kind services

ROSALIE INFANT CENTER
Elmbrook Family Counseling Center
19305 North Avenue
Brookfield, WI 53005
Elmbrook Memorial Hospital [H]
Description: XO/XM center established in 1980
Capacity: 20 Infants & Preschoolers
Startup support: Not indicated
Ongoing support: Subsidy

ST. JOSEPH'S CHILD CARE CENTER
9244 29th Avenue
Kenosah, WI 53140
St. Joseph's Home for the Aged [H]
Description: CO/CM On-site center with intergenerational component established in 1981
Capacity: 26 Preschoolers
Startup support: Space & in-kind services
Ongoing support: Subsidy, space, utilities & in-kind services

ST. JOSEPH'S HOSPITAL DAY CARE CENTER
611 St. Joseph Avenue
Marshfield, WI 54449
St. Joseph's Hospital [H]
Description: CO/CM center established in 1981
Capacity: 60 Infants & Preschoolers
Startup support: Subsidy
Ongoing support: Subsidy

ST. MARY'S CHILDREN'S SCHOOL
2323 N. Lake Drive
Milwaukee, WI 53201
St. Mary's Hospital [H]
Description: Center established in 1981
Capacity: 51 Infants & Preschoolers
Startup support: Yes
Ongoing support: Subsidy

ST. NICHOLAS HOSPITAL CHILD CARE CENTER
1601 N. Taylor Drive
Sheboygan, WI 53081
St. Nicholas Hospital [H]

Description: CO/CM On-site center established in 1976
Capacity: 85 Preschoolers and Schoolage children
Startup support: Subsidy & in-kind services
Ongoing support: Subsidy & in-kind services

ST. VINCENT HOSPITAL CHILD CARE CENTER
1825 Riverside Drive
Green Bay, WI 54305
St. Vincent Hospital [H]
Description: CO/CM Off-site center established in 1979
Capacity: 60 Infants & Preschoolers (Schoolage children summer only)
Startup support: Yes
Ongoing support: Subsidy, space, utilities & in-kind services

WEE CARE DAY CARE NURSERY
9035 Watertown Plank Road
Milwaukee, WI 53226
Milwaukee Regional Medical Center [H]
Description: XO/XM On-site center established in 1980
Capacity: 48 Peschoolers, & Schoolage children
Startup support: Space renovation
Ongoing support: In-kind services

Wyoming

EATON DAY CARE
Technical Park
Riverton, Wyoming 82501
Eaton Printer Products [I]
Manufacturer of Printer Components
Description: CO/CM On-site center established in 1978 and information & referral services for infants & evening employees
Capacity: 42 Preschoolers & Schoolage children
Startup support: Subsidy
Ongoing support: Space, utilities & in-kind services

SELECTED BIBLIOGRAPHY

Baden, Clifford, and Dana E. Friedman, eds. *New Management Initiatives for Working Parents.* Boston, Mass.: Wheelock College, 1981. (Available from the Office of Continuing Education, Wheelock College, 200 The Riverway, Boston, MA 02215.)

Baden, Ruth K., Andrea Genser, James A. Levine, and Michelle S. Seltzer. *School-Age Child Care: An Action Manual.* Boston, Mass.: Auburn House, 1982.

Bane, Mary Jo, Laura Lein, Lydia O'Donnell, Ann C. Stueve, and Barbara Wells. "Childcare Arrangements of Working Parents." *Monthly Labor Review* 102 (1979), pp. 50–56.

Burud, Sandra. "For the Company Suggestion Box: Tactful Notes on Child Care." *Working Mother* 5 (October 1982), p. 38.

Burud, Sandra. "So You Want to Enlist Employer Support for Child Care." *Day Care Journal* 1 (Fall 1982).

Cawsey, Thomas and William Wedley. "Labor Turnover Costs: Measurement and Control." *Personnel Journal.* February 1979, pp. 90–92.

The Child Care Law Center. *Legal Aspects of Child Care as an Employee Benefit.* (Available from Child Care Law Center, 625 Market Street, Suite 816, San Francisco, CA 94105.)

The Child Care Law Center. *Liability Insurance.* (Available from Child Care Law Center, 625 Market Street, Suite 816, San Francisco, CA 94105.)

The Child Care Law Center. *Property and Vehicle Insurance.* (Available from Child Care Law Center, 625 Market Street, Suite 816, San Francisco, CA (94105.)

The Child Care Law Center. *The Child Care Tax Credit–A Booklet for Parents.* (Available from Child Care Law Center, 625 Market Street, Suite 816, San Francisco, CA 94105.)

The Child Care Law Center. *Protection from Liability for Child Care Resource and Referral Agencies.* (Available from Child Care Law Center, 625 Market Street, Suite 816, San Francisco, CA 94105.)

Children's Defense Fund. *The Child Care Handbook: Needs, Programs, and Possibilities.* Washington, D.C.: Children's Defense Fund, 1982. (Available from the Children's Defense Fund, 1520 New Hampshire Avenue, N.W., Washington, D.C. 20036.)

Children's Defense Fund. *Employed Parents and Their Children: A Data Book.* Washington, D.C.: Children's Defense Fund, 1982.

Collins, Natalie M., ed. *Business and Child Care Handbook.* Minneapolis, Minn.: Greater Minneapolis Day Care Association, 1982.

Commerce Clearinghouse, Inc. *Tax Incentives for Employer-Sponsored Day Care Programs.* Chicago: Commerce Clearinghouse, Inc., 1980.

Day Care Council of America, Inc. *How to Start a Day Care Center.* Washington, D.C.: Day Care Council of America, Inc., 1981. (Available from the Day Care Council of America, Inc., 1602 17th Street, N.W., Washington, DC 20009.)

Department of Labor, Department of Labor Statistics. *Marital and Family Characteristics of the Labor Force.* March 1979, Special Labor Force Report 237. Washington, D.C.: Department of Labor, January 1981.

Empire State Day Care Services, Inc. *On-Site Day Care: State of the Art and Models Development.* Albany, N.Y.: Empire State Day Care Services, Inc., 1980. (Available from Empire State Day Care Services, Agency Building #2, Empire State Plaza, Albany, NY 12223.)

Fong, Pauline L., and Karen S. Marsh. *The Child Care Job and Economic Development Project, A Model for Job Creation in Small Business Child Care Service Enterprise.* 4 Vols. Summary Report. San Francisco: Asian, Inc.

Friedman, Dana, E. *Encouraging Employer Support to Working Parents: Community Strategies for Change.* New York: Carnegie Corporation, 1983.

Friedman, Dana E. *State and Local Strategies Promoting Employer Supported Child Care.* New York, N.Y.: Center for Public Advocacy Research, 1983.

Governor's Advisory Committee on Child Development Programs. *Employer-Sponsored Child Care.* Sacramento, Calif., Governor's Advisory Committee on Child Development Programs, 1980.

Hall, Thomas. "How to Estimate Employee Turnover Costs." *Personnel Journal.* July–August 1981, pp. 43–52.

Hayghe, Howard. "Marital and Family Patterns of Workers: An Update." *Monthly Labor Review.* May 1982, pp. 53–6.

Hewitt Associates. "Child Care Assistance: Issues for Employer Consideration." Lincolnshire, Illinois: Hewitt Associates, 1982. (Available from Hewitt Associates, General Offices, 100 Half Day Road, Lincolnshire, IL 60015.)

Hofferth, Sandra. "Day Care Demand for Tomorrow: A Look at the Trends." *Day Care Journal* 1 (Fall 1982).

Hofferth, Sandra L. *Day Care in the Next Decade: 1980–1990.* Washington, D.C.: Urban Institute Press, 1979. (Available from the Urban Institute, Publications Office, 2100 M. St., N.W. Washington, DC 20037).

Human Resources and Community Development Division. *Demographic and Social Trends: Implications for Federal Support of Dependent-Care Services for Children and the Elderly.* Washington, D.C.: Congressional Budget Office, 1983.

Johnson, Beverly, and Elizabeth Waldman. "Marital and Family Patterns of the Labor Force." *Monthly Labor Review.* October 1981, pp. 36–8.

Kamerman, Sheila B. *Parenting in an Unresponsive Society: Managing Work and Family.* New York: The Free Press, 1980.

Kamerman, Sheila B. *Maternity and Parental Leaves and Benefits.* Impact on Policy Series Monograph 1. New York: Columbia University, Fall 1980.

Kuzmits, Frank. "How Much is Absenteeism Costing Your Organization?" *Personnel Administrator.* June 1979, pp. 29–33.

Lane, Nancy M., Rex H. Todd, Janet Roberts, and Gregory Miller. *Study of Employer Cost Benefit.* Raleigh, N.C.: Work Place Options, August 1983.

Louis Harris and Associates. *Families At Work: Strengths and Strains.* The General Mills American Family Report, 1980-81. Minneapolis, Minn.: General Mills, 1981.

McCroskey, Jacquelyn. "Work and Families: What is the Employer's Responsibility?" *Personnel Journal.* January 1982, pp. 30-38.

Milkovich, George T., and Luis R. Gomez. "Day Care and Selected Employee Work Behaviors." *Academy of Management Journal* 19 (1976), pp. 111-115.

Morgan, Gwen. *Caring About Children in Massachusetts, Feasible Day Care Policy for the Eighties.* (Available from Child Care Resource Center, 24 Thorndike Street, Cambridge, MA 02141.)

New Ways to Work; A Selected Bibliography on Work Time Options. San Francisco, Calif., N.W.T.W., 1983. (Available from N.W.T.W., 149 Ninth Street, San Francisco, CA 94103, $4.50.)

Olmsted, Barney, and Suzanne Smith. *The Job Sharing Handbook.* New York: Penguin Books, 1983.

Perry, Kathryn Senn. "Survey and Analysis of Employer Supported Day Care in the United States." Doctoral Dissertation, University of Wisconsin, 1980. (Available from University Microfilms, 300 N. Zeeb Road, Ann Arbor, MI 48106.)

Rodgers and Rudman, Inc. *Child Care Options for High Technology Companies: A Decision-Making Guide.* Boston, Mass.: High Tech Council, 1982. (Available from the Massachusetts High Tech Council, 60 State Street, Boston, MA 02109.)

Soloway, Ronald. *The Inequities of Salary Reduction As National Child Care Policy: Where Do We Go From Here?* Center for Public Advocacy Research, New York, July 1983.

Squibb, Betsy. *Family Day Care: How to Provide It in Your Home.* Harvard, Mass.: Harvard Common Press, 1976.

Toys 'N Things Training and Resource Center, Inc. *Parents in the Workplace Series.* St. Paul: Toy's n Things Press, 1982.

U.S. Department of Health and Human Services, Office of Human Development Services, Administration for Children, Youth, and Families. *A Parent's Guide to Day Care,* DHHS (OHDS) 80-30254. Washington, D.C.: U.S. Government Printing Office, 1980. (Available from the Superintendent of Documents, U.S. Government Printing Office, Washington, DC 20402.)

U.S. Department of Labor, Office of the Secretary, Women's Bureau. *Employers and Child Care: Establishing Services Through the Workplace.* Washington, D.C.: U.S. Government Printing Office, 1982. (Available from the U.S. Department of Labor, Office of the Secretary, Women's Bureau, Washington, DC 20210.)

Whitebook, M., C. Howes, P. Darrah, and J. Friedman. "Who's Minding the Child Care Workers? A Look at Staff Burnout." *Children Today.* January-February 1982.

Zigler, Edward F., and Edmund W. Gordon, eds. *Day Care: Scientific and Social Policy Issues.* Boston, Mass.: Auburn House, 1982.

RESOURCES: AGENCIES AND ORGANIZATIONS VISITED

Appalachian Regional Commission
1666 Connecticut
Washington, DC 20009

Arthur Anderson and Company
101 Eisenhower Parkway
Roseland, NJ 08618

Bank Street College of Education
610 W. 112th Street
New York, NY 10025

Boulder Child Care Support Center
P.O. Box 791
Boulder, CO 80306

Catalyst
14 East 60th Street
New York, NY 10022

Center for Public Advocacy Research
12 West 37th Street
New York, NY 10018

Child Care Resource Center
24 Thorndike Street
Cambridge, MA 02141

Children at Work
569 Lexington Avenue
New York, NY 10022

City of Baltimore
400 City Hall
100 North Holliday Street
Baltimore, MD 21202

Colorado Commission on Children
and Their Families
1550 Lincoln, Room 103
Denver, CO 80203

Columbia University School of
Social Work
622 West 113th Street
New York, NY 10025

Conference Board
845 Third Avenue
New York, NY 10022

Contemporary Ventures in Child Care
8101 North Central #6
Pheonix, AZ 85020

Corporate Policies Project
Children's Defense Fund
122 C Street NW
Washington, DC 20036

Alan Cranston's Office
Room SH 112
United States Senate Building
Washington, DC 20510

Creative Partnerships for Child Care
330 South Oak Knoll, Room 26
Pasadena, CA 91101

Day Care and Child Development
Council of America
1602 17th Street NW
Washington, DC 20009

Department of Administration
Division of Policy
116 West Jones Street
Raleigh, NC 27611

Employee Benefits Research Institute
2121 K Street NW, Suite 860
Washington, DC 20037

Family and Work Project
American Association of University Women
2401 Virginia Avenue, 7th Floor
Washington, DC 20037

Greater Minneapolis Day Care Association
111 E. Franklin
Minneapolis, MN 55404

Maryland Committee for Child Care
608 Water Street
Baltimore, MD 21202

Carlos Moorehead's Office
2346 Rayburn Building
Washington, DC 20515

National Medical Enterprises
11620 Wilshire Boulevard
Los Angeles, CA 90025

New York City Chamber of Commerce
200 Madison Avenue
New York, NY 10016

Parents in the Workplace
906 N. Dale Street
St. Paul, MN 55103

Preschool Association of the West Side
610 W. 112th Street
New York, NY 10025

Quality Child Care, Inc.
74 Main Street
Marlboro, MA 01752

School of Family Studies
San Diego State University
San Diego, CA 92182

U.S. Chamber of Commerce
1615 H Street NW
Washington, DC 20062

University Research Corporation
5530 Wisconsin Avenue
Washington, DC 20015

Urban Institute
2100 M. Street
Washington, DC 20037

Wellesley College Center for Research on Women
Wellesley, MA 02181

Wheelock College
180 River Way
Boston, MA 02215

Women's Bureau
200 Constitution Avenue NW
Department of Labor
Washington, DC 20001

INDEX

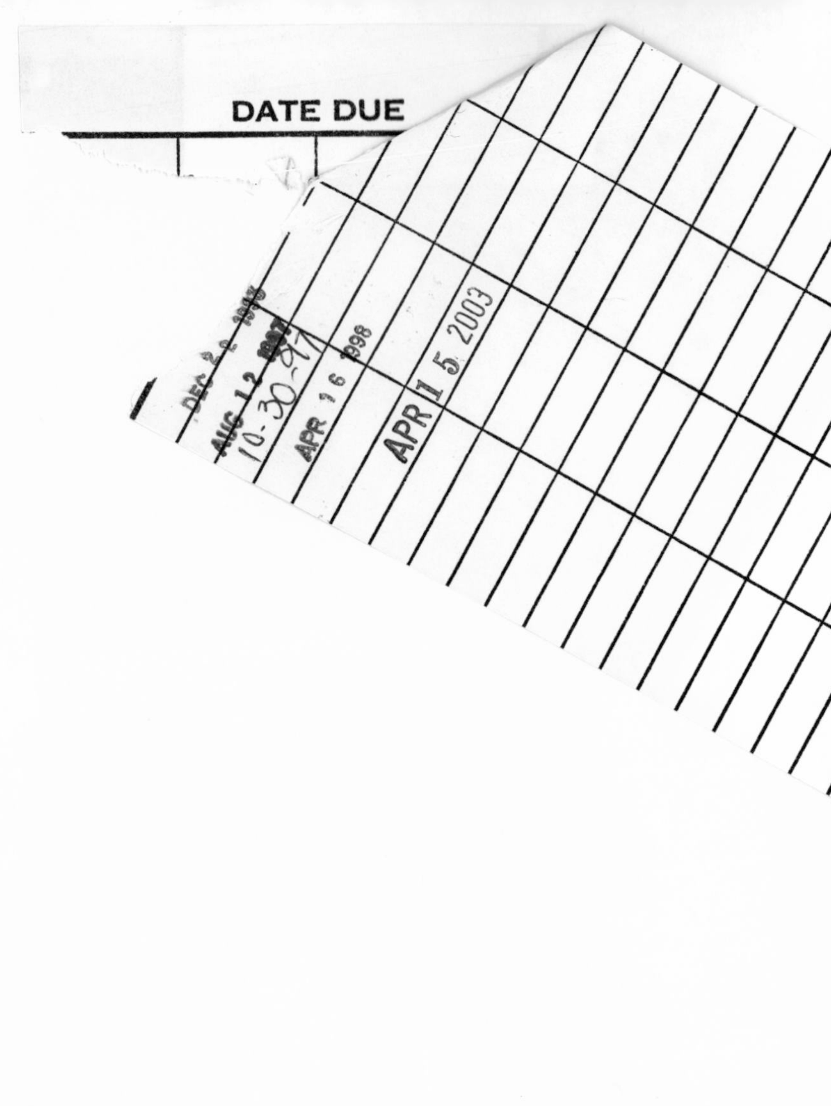